# LEVEL I SCHWESER'S SECRET SAUCE®

SCHWESER'S SECRET SAUCE®: 2011 CFA LEVEL I

©2011 Kaplan, Inc. All rights reserved.

Published in 2011 by Kaplan Schweser.

Printed in the United States of America.

ISBN: 978-1-4277-2750-3 / 1-4277-2750-3

PPN: 3200-0254

# FOREWORD

This book will be a valuable addition to the study tools of any CFA exam candidate. It offers a very concise and very readable explanation of the major parts of the Level I CFA curriculum. Here is the disclaimer: this book does not cover every Learning Outcome Statement (LOS) and, as you are aware, any LOS is "fair game" for the exam. We have tried to include those LOS that are key concepts in finance and accounting, have application to other LOS, are complex and difficult for candidates, require memorization of characteristics or relationships, or are a prelude to LOS at Levels II and III.

We suggest you use this book as a companion to your other, more comprehensive study materials. It is easier to carry with you and will allow you to study these key concepts, definitions, and techniques over and over, which is an important part of mastering the material. When you get to topics where the coverage here appears too brief or raises questions in your mind, this is your clue to go back to your SchweserNotes™ or the textbooks to fill in the gaps in your understanding. For the great majority of you, there is no shortcut to learning the very broad array of subjects covered by the Level I curriculum, but this volume should be a very valuable tool for learning and reviewing the material as you progress in your studies over the months leading up to exam day.

Pass rates have recently been between 35% and 45%, and returning Level I candidates make comments such as, "I was surprised at how difficult the exam was." You should not despair because of this, but you should definitely not underestimate the task at hand. Our study materials, practice exams, question bank, videos, seminars, and *Secret Sauce* are all designed to help you study as efficiently as possible, help you to grasp and retain the material, and apply it with confidence come exam day.

Best regards,

*Doug Van Eaton*                                    *Craig S. Prochaska*

Dr. Doug Van Eaton, CFA                    Craig S. Prochaska, CFA
Head of CFA Education                        Content Specialist

Kaplan Schweser

# ETHICAL AND PROFESSIONAL STANDARDS

| Weight on Exam | 15% |
|---|---|
| SchweserNotes™ Reference | Book 1, Pages 1–96 |

Ethics is 15% of the Level I examination and is extremely important to your overall success (remember, you can fail a topic area and still pass the exam, but we wouldn't recommend failing Ethics). Ethics can be tricky, and small details can be important on some ethics questions. Be prepared.

In addition to starting early, study the ethics material more than once. Ethics is one of the keys to passing the exam.

## STANDARDS OF PRACTICE HANDBOOK
Cross-Reference to CFA Institute Assigned Readings #1 & 2

We recommend you read the original *Standards of Practice Handbook*. Although we are very proud of our reviews of the ethics material, there are *two* reasons we recommend you read the original *Standards of Practice Handbook* (*10th Ed., 2010*). (1) You are a CFA® candidate. As such, you have pledged to abide by the CFA Institute® Standards. (2) Most of the ethics questions will likely come directly from the text and examples in the *Standards of Practice Handbook*. You will be much better off if you read both our summaries of the Standards *and* the original Handbook and all the examples presented in it.

The CFA Institute Professional Conduct Program is covered by the CFA Institute Bylaws and the Rules of Procedure for Proceedings Related to Professional Conduct. The Disciplinary Review Committee of the CFA Institute Board of Governors has overall responsibility for the Professional Conduct Program and enforcement of the Code and Standards.

The CFA Institute Designated Officer, through the Professional Conduct staff, conducts inquiries related to professional conduct. Several circumstances can prompt such an inquiry:

* Self-disclosure by members or candidates on their annual Professional Conduct Statements of involvement in civil litigation or a criminal investigation, or that the member or candidate is the subject of a written complaint.

- Written complaints about a member or candidate's professional conduct that are received by the Professional Conduct staff.
- Evidence of misconduct by a member or candidate that the Professional Conduct staff received through public sources, such as a media article or broadcast.
- A report by a CFA exam proctor of a possible violation during the examination.

Once an inquiry is begun, the Professional Conduct staff may request (in writing) an explanation from the subject member or candidate, and may:

- Interview the subject member or candidate.
- Interview the complainant or other third parties.
- Collect documents and records relevant to the investigation.

The Designated Officer may decide:

- That no disciplinary sanctions are appropriate.
- To issue a cautionary letter.
- To discipline the member or candidate.

In a case where the Designated Officer finds a violation has occurred and proposes a disciplinary sanction, the member or candidate may accept or reject the sanction. If the member or candidate chooses to reject the sanction, the matter will be referred to a panel of CFA Institute members for a hearing. Sanctions imposed may include condemnation by the member's peers or suspension of the candidate's continued participation in the CFA Program.

## Code and Standards

Questions about the Code and Standards will most likely be application questions. You will be given a situation and be asked to identify whether or not a violation occurs, what the violation is, or what the appropriate course of action should be. You are not required to know the Standards by number, just by name.

One of the first Learning Outcome Statements (LOS) in the Level I curriculum is to state the six components of the Code of Ethics. Candidates should *memorize* the Code of Ethics.

Members of the CFA Institute [including Chartered Financial Analyst® (CFA®) charterholders] and candidates for the CFA designation (Members and Candidates) must:

- Act with integrity, competence, diligence, respect, and in an ethical manner with the public, clients, prospective clients, employers, employees, colleagues in the investment profession, and other participants in the global capital markets.

- Place the integrity of the investment profession and the interests of clients above their own personal interests.
- Use reasonable care and exercise independent, professional judgment when conducting investment analysis, making investment recommendations, taking investment actions, and engaging in other professional activities.
- Practice and encourage others to practice in a professional and ethical manner that will reflect credit on members and their profession.
- Promote the integrity of, and uphold the rules governing, capital markets.
- Maintain and improve their professional competence and strive to maintain and improve the competence of other investment professionals.

## STANDARDS OF PROFESSIONAL CONDUCT

The following is a list of the Standards of Professional Conduct. Candidates should focus on the purpose of the Standard, applications of the Standard, and proper procedures of compliance for each Standard.

The following is intended to offer a useful summary of the current Standards of Practice, but certainly does not take the place of careful reading of the Standards themselves, the guidance for implementing the Standards, and the examples in the Handbook.

1. Know the law relevant to your position.

    *I Professionalism*

    - Comply with the most strict law or Standard that applies to you.
    - Don't solicit gifts.
    - Don't compromise your objectivity or independence.
    - Use reasonable care.
    - Don't lie, cheat, or steal.
    - Don't continue association with others who are breaking laws, rules, or regulations.
    - Don't use others' work or ideas without attribution.
    - Don't guarantee investment results or say that past results will be certainly repeated.
    - Don't do things outside of work that reflect poorly on your integrity or professional competence.

2. Do not act or cause others to act on material nonpublic information.

   *II capital markets*

    - Do not manipulate market prices or trading volume with the intent to mislead others.

3. Act solely for the benefit of your client and know to whom a fiduciary duty is owed with regard to trust accounts and retirement accounts.
    - Treat clients fairly by attempting simultaneous dissemination of investment recommendations and changes.
    - Do not personally take shares in oversubscribed IPOs.

*III Duties to clients*

When in an advisory relationship:

- Know your client.
- Make suitable recommendations/take suitable investment action (in a total portfolio context).
- Preserve confidential client information unless it concerns illegal activity.
- Do not try to mislead with performance presentation.
- Vote nontrivial proxies in clients' best interests.

4. Act for the benefit of your employer.

*IV Duties to employers*

- Do not harm your employer.
- Obtain written permission to compete with your employer or to accept additional compensation from clients contingent on future performance.
- Disclose (to employer) any gifts from clients.
- Don't take material with you when you leave employment (you can take what is in your brain).
- Supervisors must take action to both prevent *and* detect violations.
- Don't take supervisory responsibility if you believe procedures are inadequate.

5. Thoroughly analyze investments.   *V Investment analysis, Recommendation and actions*

- Have reasonable basis.
- Keep records.
- Tell clients about investment process.
- Distinguish between facts and opinions.
- Review the quality of third-party research and the services of external advisers.
- In quantitative models, consider what happens when their inputs are outside the normal range.

6. Disclose potential conflicts of interest (let others judge the effects of any conflict for themselves).

*VI Conflicts of Interest*

- Disclose referral arrangements.
- Client transactions come before employer transactions which come before personal transactions.
- Treat clients who are family members just like any client.

7. Don't cheat on *any* exams (or help others to).

- Don't reveal CFA exam questions or disclose what topics were tested or not tested.
- Don't use your Society position or any CFA Institute position or responsibility to *improperly* further your personal or professional goals.
- Don't use the CFA designation improperly (it is *not* a noun).
- Don't put CFA in bold or bigger font than your name.

*VII Responsibilities as a CFA Institute Member*

- Don't imply or say that holders of the CFA Charter produce better investment results.
- Don't claim that passing all exams on the first try makes you a better investment manager than others.
- Don't claim CFA candidacy unless registered for the next exam or awaiting results.
- There is no such thing as a CFA Level I (or II, or III).

My goodness! What *can* you do?

- You can use information from recognized statistical sources without attribution.
- You can be wrong (as long as you had a reasonable basis at the time).
- You can use several pieces of nonmaterial, nonpublic information to construct your investment recommendations (mosaic theory).
- You can do large trades that may affect market prices as long as the intent of the trade is not to mislead market participants.
- You can say that Treasury securities are without default risk.
- You can always seek the guidance of your supervisor, compliance officer, or outside counsel.
- You can get rid of records after seven years.
- You can accept gifts from clients and referral fees as long as properly disclosed.
- You can call your biggest clients first (after fair distribution of investment recommendation or change).
- You can accept compensation from a company to write a research report if you disclose the relationship and nature of compensation.
- You can get drunk when not at work and commit misdemeanors that do not involve fraud, theft, or deceit.
- You can say you have passed the Level I, II, or III CFA exam (if you really have).
- You can accurately describe the nature of the examination process and the requirements to earn the right to use the CFA designation.

## GLOBAL INVESTMENT PERFORMANCE STANDARDS (GIPS®)
Cross-Reference to CFA Institute Assigned Readings #3 & 4

Performance presentation is an area of constantly growing importance in the investment management field and an important part of the CFA curriculum. Repeated exposure is the best way to learn the material. GIPS appears to be relatively easy, but still requires a reasonable amount of time for it to sink in.

GIPS were created to provide a uniform framework for presenting historical performance results for investment management firms to serve existing and prospective clients. Compliance with GIPS is voluntary, but partial compliance cannot be referenced. There is only one acceptable statement for those firms that claim complete compliance with GIPS.

To claim compliance, a firm must present GIPS-compliant results for a minimum of five years or since firm inception. The firm must be clearly defined as the distinct business entity or subsidiary that is held out to clients in marketing materials. Performance is presented for "composites" which must include all fee-paying discretionary account portfolios with a similar investment strategy, objective, or mandate. After reporting five years of compliant data, one year of compliant data must be added each year to a minimum of ten years.

The idea of GIPS is to provide and gain global acceptance of a set of standards that will result in consistent, comparable, and accurate performance presentation information that will promote fair competition among, and complete disclosure by, investment management firms.

Verification is voluntary and is not required to be GIPS compliant. Independent verification provides assurance that GIPS have been applied correctly on a firm-wide basis. Firms that have had compliance verified are encouraged to disclose that they have done so, but must include periods for which verification was done.

There are nine major sections of the GIPS, which include:

0. Fundamentals of Compliance.

1. Input Data.

2. Calculation Methodology.

3. Composite Construction.

4. Disclosures.

5. Presentation and Reporting.

6. Real Estate.

7. Private Equity.

8. Wrap Fee/Separately Managed Account (SMA) Portfolios.

## Fundamentals of Compliance

GIPS must be applied on a firm-wide basis. Total firm assets are the market value of all accounts (fee-paying or not, discretionary or not). Firm performance will include the performance of any subadvisors selected by the firm, and changes in the organization of the firm will not affect historical GIPS performance.

Firms are encouraged to use the broadest definition of the firm and include all offices marketed under the same brand name. Firms must have written documentation of all procedures to comply with GIPS.

The only permitted statement of compliance is "XYZ has prepared and presented this report in compliance with the Global Investment Performance Standards (GIPS)." There may be no claim that methodology or performance calculation of any composite or account is in compliance with GIPS (except in communication to clients about their individual accounts by a GIPS compliant firm).

The firm must provide every potential client with a compliant presentation. The firm must present a list of composites for the firm and descriptions of those composites (including composites discontinued less than five years ago) to prospective clients *upon request*. Firms are encouraged to comply with recommended portions of GIPS and must comply with updates and clarifications to GIPS.

Current recommendations that will become requirements are: (1) quarterly valuation of real estate, (2) portfolio valuation on the dates of all large cash flows (to or from the account), (3) month-end valuation of all accounts, and (4) monthly asset-weighting of portfolios within composites, not including carve-out returns in any composite for a single asset class.

# Quantitative Methods

| | |
|---|---|
| Weight on Exam | 12% |
| SchweserNotes™ Reference | Book 1, Pages 97–362 |

## Study Session 2: Quantitative Methods—Basic Concepts

### The Time Value of Money
Cross-Reference to CFA Institute Assigned Reading #5

Understanding time value of money (TVM) computations is essential for success not only for quantitative methods, but also other sections of the Level I exam. TVM is actually a larger portion of the exam than simply quantitative methods because of its integration with other topics. For example, any portion of the exam that requires discounting cash flows will require TVM calculations. This includes evaluating capital projects, using dividend discount models for stock valuation, valuing bonds, and valuing real estate investments. No matter where TVM shows up on the exam, the key to any TVM problem is to draw a timeline and be certain of when the cash flows will occur so you can discount those cash flows appropriately.

An interest rate can be interpreted as a required rate of return, a discount rate, or as an opportunity cost; but it is essentially the price (time value) of money for one period. When viewed as a required (equilibrium) rate of return on an investment, a nominal interest rate consists of a real risk-free rate, a premium for expected inflation, and other premiums for sources of risk specific to the investment, such as uncertainty about amounts and timing of future cash flows from the investment.

Interest rates are often stated as simple annual rates, even when compounding periods are shorter than one year. With $m$ compounding periods per year and a stated annual rate of $i$, the effective annual rate is calculated by compounding the periodic rate ($i/m$) over $m$ periods (the number of periods in one year).

$$\text{effective annual rate} = \left(1 + \frac{i}{m}\right)^m - 1$$

With a stated annual rate of 12% (0.12) and monthly compounding, the effective

rate $= \left(1 + \dfrac{0.12}{12}\right)^{12} - 1 = 12.68\%$.

**Future value** (FV) is the amount to which an investment grows after one or more compounding periods.

- *Compounding* is the process used to determine the future value of a current amount.
- The *periodic rate* is the nominal rate (stated in annual terms) divided by the number of compounding periods (i.e., for quarterly compounding, divide the annual rate by four).
- The *number of compounding periods* is equal to the number of years multiplied by the frequency of compounding (i.e., for quarterly compounding, multiply the number of years by four).

$$\text{future value} = \text{present value} \times (1 + \text{periodic rate})^{\text{number of compounding periods}}$$

**Present value** (PV) is the current value of some future cash flow.

- *Discounting* is the process used to determine the present value of some future amount.
- *Discount rate* is the periodic rate used in the discounting process.

$$\text{present value} = \frac{\text{future value}}{(1 + \text{periodic rate})^{\text{number of compounding periods}}}$$

For *non-annual compounding* problems, divide the interest rate by the number of compounding periods per year, $m$, and multiply the number of years by the number of compounding periods per year.

An *annuity* is a stream of equal cash flows that occur at equal intervals over a given period. A corporate bond combines an annuity (the equal semiannual coupon payments) with a lump sum payment (return of principal at maturity).

- *Ordinary annuity.* Cash flows occur at the end of each compounding period.
- *Annuity due.* Cash flows occur at the beginning of each period.

**Present value of an ordinary annuity.** Answers the question: How much would an annuity of $\$X$ every (month, week, quarter, year) cost today if the periodic rate is $I\%$?

The present value of an annuity is just the sum of the present values of all the payments. Your calculator will do this for you.

- N = number of periods.
- I/Y = interest rate per period.
- PMT = amount of each periodic payment.
- FV = 0.
- Compute (CPT) present value (PV).

In other applications, any four of these variables can be entered in order to solve for the fifth. When both present and future values are entered, they typically must be given different signs in order to calculate N, I/Y, or PMT.

**Future value of an ordinary annuity.** Just change to PV = 0 and CPT → FV.

If there is a mismatch between the period of the payments and the period for the interest rate, adjust the interest rate to match. Do not add or divide payment amounts. If you have a *monthly payment*, you need a *monthly interest rate*.

## Present and Future Value of an Annuity Due

When using the TI calculator in END mode, the PV of an annuity is computed as of t = 0 (one period prior to the first payment date, t = 1) and the FV of an annuity is calculated as of time = N (the date of the last payment). With the TI calculator in BGN mode, the PV of an annuity is calculated as of t = 0 (which is now the date of the first payment) and the FV of an annuity is calculated as of t = N (one period after the last payment). In BGN mode the N payments are assumed to come at the beginning of each of the N periods. An annuity that makes N payments at the beginning of each of N periods, is referred to as an annuity due.

Once you have found the PV(FV) of an ordinary annuity, you can convert the discounted (compound) value to an annuity due value by multiplying by one plus the periodic rate. This effectively discounts (compounds) the ordinary annuity value by one less (more) period.

$$PV_{annuity\ due} = PV_{ordinary\ annuity} \times (1 + periodic\ rate)$$

$$FV_{annuity\ due} = FV_{ordinary\ annuity} \times (1 + periodic\ rate)$$

*Perpetuities* are annuities with infinite lives:

$$PV_{perpetuity} = \frac{periodic\ payment}{periodic\ interest\ rate}$$

*Preferred stock* is an example of a perpetuity (equal payments indefinitely).

Present (future) values of any series of cash flows is equal to the sum of the present (future) values of each cash flow. This means you can break up cash flows any way

---

that is convenient, take the PV or FV of the pieces, and add them up to get the PV or FV of the whole series of cash flows.

## DISCOUNTED CASH FLOW APPLICATIONS
Cross-Reference to CFA Institute Assigned Reading #6

### Net Present Value (NPV) of an Investment Project

For a typical investment or capital project, the NPV is simply the present value of the expected future cash flows, minus the initial cost of the investment. The steps in calculating an NPV are:

- *Identify* all outflows/inflows associated with the investment.
- *Determine* discount rate appropriate for the investment.
- *Find PV* of the future cash flows. Inflows are positive and outflows are negative.
- *Compute* the sum of all the discounted future cash flows.
- *Subtract* the initial cost of the investment or capital project.

$$NPV = \frac{CF_1}{(1+r)} + \frac{CF_2}{(1+r)^2} + ... + \frac{CF_{t-1}}{(1+r)^{t-1}} + \frac{CF_t}{(1+r)^t} - NI$$

where:
$CF_t$ = the expected net cash flow at time $t$
$r$ = the discount rate = opportunity cost of capital
$NI$ = the net (time = 0) investment in the project

With uneven cash flows, use the CF function.

### Computing IRR

IRR is the discount rate that equates the PV of cash inflows with the PV of the cash outflows. This also makes IRR the discount rate that results in NPV equal to zero. In other words, the IRR is the $r$ that, when plugged into the above NPV equation, makes the NPV equal zero.

When given a set of equal cash inflows, such as an annuity, calculate IRR by solving for I/Y.

When the cash inflows are uneven, use CF function on calculator.

**Example:**

Project cost is $100, $CF_1$ = $50, $CF_2$ = $50, $CF_3$ = $90. What is the NPV at 10%? What is the IRR of the project?

**Answer:**

Enter CF0 = –100, C01 = 50, F01 = 2, C02 = 90, F02 = 1.

NPV, 10, enter, ↓, CPT, display 54.395.

IRR, CPT, display 35.71 (%).

## NPV vs. IRR

- *NPV decision rule*: For independent projects, adopt all projects with NPV > 0. These projects will increase the value of the firm.
- *IRR decision rule*: For independent projects, adopt all projects with IRR > required project return. These projects will also add value to the firm.

NPV and IRR rules give the same decision for independent projects.

When NPV and IRR rankings differ, rely on NPV for choosing between or among projects.

## Money-Weighted vs. Time-Weighted Return Measures

Time-weighted and money-weighted return calculations are standard tools for analysis of portfolio performance.

- *Money-weighted return* is affected by cash flows into and out of an investment account. It is essentially a portfolio IRR.
- *Time-weighted return* is preferred as a manager performance measure because it is not affected by cash flows into and out of an investment account. It is calculated as the geometric mean of subperiod returns.

## Various Yield Calculations

*Bond-equivalent yield* is two times the semiannually compounded yield. This is because U.S. bonds pay interest semiannually rather than annually.

*Yield to maturity* (YTM) is the IRR on a bond. For a semiannual coupon bond, YTM is two times semiannual IRR. In other words, it is the discount rate that equates the present value of a bond's cash flows with its market price. We will revisit this topic again in the debt section.

*Bank discount yield* is the annualized percentage discount from face value:

$$\text{bank discount yield} = r_{BD} = \frac{\$\text{discount}}{\text{face value}} \times \frac{360}{\text{days}}$$

*Holding period yield* (HPY), also called holding period return (HPR):

$$\text{holding period yield} = \text{HPY} = \frac{P_1 - P_0 + D_1}{P_0} \quad \text{or} \quad \frac{P_1 + D_1}{P_0} - 1$$

For common stocks, the cash distribution ($D_1$) is the dividend. For bonds, the cash distribution is the interest payment.

HPR for a given investment can be calculated for any time period (day, week, month, or year) simply by changing the end points of the time interval over which values and cash flows are measured.

*Effective annual yield* converts a *t*-day holding period yield to a compound annual yield based on a 365-day year:

$$\text{effective annual yield} = \text{EAY} = (1 + \text{HPY})^{365/t} - 1$$

Notice the similarity of EAY to *effective annual rate*:

$$\text{EAR} = (1 + \text{periodic rate})^m - 1$$

where *m* is the number of compounding periods per year and the periodic rate is the stated annual rate/m.

*Money market yield* is annualized (without compounding) based on a 360-day year:

$$\text{money market yield} = r_{MM} = \text{HPY} \times \frac{360}{t}$$

EAY and $r_{MM}$ are two ways to annualize an HPY. Different instruments have different conventions for quoting yields. In order to compare the yields on instruments with different yield conventions, you must be able to convert the yields to a common measure. For instance, to compare a T-bill yield and a LIBOR yield, you can convert the T-bill yield from a bank discount yield to a money market yield and compare it to the LIBOR yield (which is already a money market yield). In order to compare yields on other instruments to the yield (to maturity) of a semi-annual pay bond, we simply calculate the effective semiannual yield and double it. A yield calculated in this manner is referred to as a *bond equivalent yield* (BEY).

## STATISTICAL CONCEPTS AND MARKET RETURNS
Cross-Reference to CFA Institute Assigned Reading #7

The two key areas you should concentrate on in this reading are measures of central tendency and measures of dispersion. Measures of central tendency include the arithmetic mean, geometric mean, weighted mean, median, and mode. Measures of dispersion include the range, mean absolute deviation, variance, and standard deviation. When describing investments, measures of central tendency provide an indication of an investment's expected value or return. Measures of dispersion indicate the riskiness of an investment (the uncertainty about its future returns or cash flows).

### Measures of Central Tendency

*Arithmetic mean.* A population average is called the population mean (denoted $\mu$). The average of a sample (subset of a population) is called the sample mean (denoted $\bar{x}$). Both the population and sample means are calculated as arithmetic means (simple average). We use the sample mean as a "best guess" approximation of the population mean.

*Median.* Middle value of a data set, half above and half below. With an even number of observations, median is the average of the two middle observations.

*Mode.* Value occurring most frequently in a data set. Data set can have more than one mode (bimodal, trimodal, etc.) but only one mean and one median.

*Geometric mean:*

- Used to calculate compound growth rates.
- If returns are constant over time, geometric mean equals arithmetic mean.
- The greater the variability of returns over time, the greater the difference between arithmetic and geometric mean (arithmetic will always be higher).

- When calculating the geometric mean for a returns series, it is necessary to add one to each value under the radical, and then subtract one from the result.
- The geometric mean is used to calculate the time-weighted return, a performance measure.

$$\text{geometric mean return} = R_G = \sqrt[n]{(1+R_1)\times(1+R_2)\times...\times(1+R_n)} - 1$$

**Example:**

A mutual fund had the following returns for the past three years: 15%, –9%, and 13%. What is the arithmetic mean return, the 3-year holding period return, and the average annual compound (geometric mean) return?

**Answer:**

arithmetic mean: $\dfrac{15\% - 9\% + 13\%}{3} = 6.333\%$

holding period return: $1.15 \times 0.91 \times 1.13 - 1 = 0.183 = 18.3\%$

geometric mean: $R_G = \sqrt[3]{(1+0.15)\times(1-0.09)\times(1+0.13)} - 1$

$= \sqrt[3]{1.183} - 1 = 1.0575 - 1 = 0.0575 = 5.75\%$

Geometric mean return is useful for finding the yield on a zero-coupon bond with a maturity of several years or for finding the average annual growth rate of a company's dividend or earnings across several years. Geometric mean returns are a compound return measure.

*Weighted mean.* Mean in which different observations are given different proportional influence on the mean:

$$\text{weighted mean} = \overline{X}_w = \sum_{i=1}^{n} w_i X_i = (w_1 X_1 + w_2 X_2 + ... + w_n X_n)$$

where:
$X_1, X_2, ..., X_n$ = observed values
$w_1, w_2, ..., w_n$ = corresponding weights for each observation, $\sum w_i = 1$

Weighted means are used to calculate the actual or expected return on a portfolio, given the actual or expected returns for each portfolio asset (or asset class). For portfolio returns, the weights in the formula are the percentages of the total portfolio value invested in each asset (or asset class).

**Example: Portfolio return**

A portfolio is 20% invested in Stock A, 30% invested in Stock B, and 50% invested in Stock C. Stocks A, B, and C experienced returns of 10%, 15%, and 3%, respectively. Calculate the portfolio return.

**Answer:**

$$R_p = 0.2(10\%) + 0.3(15\%) + 0.5(3\%) = 8.0\%$$

A weighted mean is also used to calculate the expected return given a probability model. In that case, the weights are simply the probabilities of each outcome.

**Example: Expected portfolio return**

A portfolio of stocks has a 15% probability of achieving a 35% return, a 25% chance of achieving a 15% return, and a 60% chance of achieving a 10% return. Calculate the expected portfolio return.

**Answer:**

$$E(R_p) = 0.15(35) + 0.25(15) + 0.60(10) = 5.25 + 3.75 + 6 = 15\%$$

Note that an arithmetic mean is a weighted mean in which all of the weights are equal to 1/n (where *n* is the number of observations).

## Measures of Dispersion

*Range* is the difference between the largest and smallest value in a data set and is the simplest measure of dispersion. You can think of the dispersion as measuring the width of the distribution. The narrower the range, the less dispersion.

For a population, *variance* is defined as the average of the squared deviations from the mean.

**Example:**

Stocks A, B, and C had returns of 10%, 30%, and 20%, respectively. Calculate the population variance (denoted $\sigma^2$) and sample variance (denoted $s^2$).

**Answer:**

The process begins the same for population and sample variance.

*Step 1:* Calculate the mean expected return: $\dfrac{(10+30+20)}{3} = 20$

*Step 2:* Calculate the squared deviations from the mean and add them together:
$(10 - 20)^2 + (30 - 20)^2 + (20 - 20)^2 = 100 + 100 + 0 = 200$

*Step 3:* Divide by number of observations (n = 3) for the population variance and by the number of observations minus one for the sample variance:

$$\text{population variance} = \sigma^2 = \frac{200}{3} = 66.67$$

$$\text{sample variance} = s^2 = \frac{200}{3-1} = \frac{200}{2} = 100$$

$$\sigma^2 = \frac{\sum\limits_{i=1}^{N}(X_i - \mu)^2}{N} \qquad\qquad s^2 = \frac{\sum\limits_{i=1}^{n}(X_i - \overline{X})^2}{n-1}$$

*Standard deviation* is the square root of variance. On the exam, if the question is asking for the standard deviation, do not forget to take the square root!

*Coefficient of variation* expresses how much dispersion exists relative to the mean of a distribution and allows for direct comparison of the degree of dispersion across different data sets. It measures risk per unit of expected return.

$$CV = \frac{\text{standard deviation of returns}}{\text{mean return}}$$

When comparing two investments using the CV criterion, the one with the lower CV is the better choice.

The *Sharpe ratio* is widely used to evaluate investment performance and measures excess return per unit of risk. Portfolios with large Sharpe ratios are preferred to portfolios with smaller ratios because it is assumed that rational investors prefer higher excess returns (returns in excess of the risk-free rate) and dislike risk.

$$\text{Sharpe ratio} = \frac{\text{excess return}}{\text{risk}} = \frac{R_{portfolio} - R_{risk\text{-}free}}{\sigma_p}$$

If you are given the inputs for the Sharpe ratio for two portfolios and asked to select the best portfolio, calculate the Sharpe ratio, and choose the portfolio with the higher ratio.

## Skewness and Kurtosis

*Skewness* represents the extent to which a distribution is not symmetrical.

A *right-skewed* distribution has positive skew (or skewness) and a mean that is greater than the median, which is greater than the mode.

A *left-skewed* distribution has negative skewness and a mean that is less than the median, which is less than the mode.

The attributes of normal and skewed distributions are summarized in the following illustration.

# Figure 1: Skewed Distributions

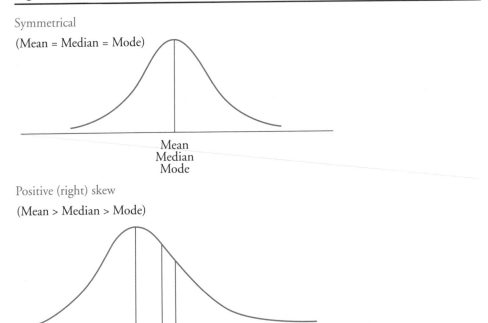

Symmetrical
(Mean = Median = Mode)

Mean
Median
Mode

Positive (right) skew
(Mean > Median > Mode)

Mean
Median
Mode

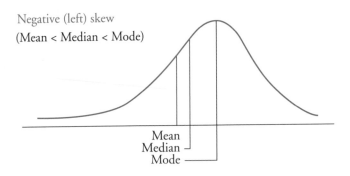

Negative (left) skew
(Mean < Median < Mode)

Mean
Median
Mode

To remember the relations, think of "pulling on the end" of a normal distribution, which is symmetrical with the mean, median, and mode equal. If you pull on the right or positive end, you get a right-skewed (positively skewed) distribution. If you can remember that adding extreme values at one end of the distribution has the greatest effect on the mean, and doesn't affect the mode or high point of the distribution, you can remember the relations illustrated in the preceding graph.

*Kurtosis* is a measure of the degree to which a distribution is more or less peaked than a normal distribution, which has kurtosis of 3.

*Excess kurtosis* is kurtosis relative to that of a normal distribution. A distribution with kurtosis of 4 has excess kurtosis of 1. It is said to have positive excess kurtosis. A distribution with positive excess kurtosis (a leptokurtic distribution) will have more returns clustered around the mean and more returns with large deviations from the mean (fatter tails). In finance, positive excess kurtosis is a significant issue in risk assessment and management, because fatter tails means an increased probability of extreme outcomes, which translates into greater risk.

An illustration of the shapes of normal and leptokurtic distribution is given in the following graph.

**Figure 2: Kurtosis**

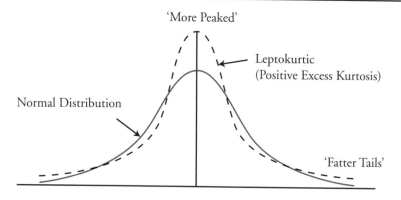

## PROBABILITY CONCEPTS
Cross-Reference to CFA Institute Assigned Reading #8

The ability to apply probability rules is important for the exam. Be able to calculate and interpret widely used measures such as expected value, standard deviation, covariance, and correlation.

### Important Terms

- *Random variable.* Uncertain quantity/number.
- *Outcome.* Realization of a random variable.
- *Event.* Single outcome or a set of outcomes.
- *Mutually exclusive events.* Cannot both happen at same time.
- *Exhaustive set of events.* Set that includes all possible outcomes.

The probability of any single outcome or event must not be less than zero (will not occur) and must not be greater than one (will occur with certainty). A *probability function* (for a discrete probability distribution) defines the probabilities that each outcome will occur. To have a valid probability function, it must be the case that the sum of the probabilities of any set of outcomes or events that is both mutually exclusive and exhaustive is 1 (it is certain that a random variable will take on one of its possible values). An example of a valid probability function is:

$$\text{Prob }(x) = x/15 \text{ for possible outcomes, } x = 1, 2, 3, 4, 5$$

## Odds For and Against

If the probability of an event is 20%, it will occur, on average, one out of five times. The "odds for" are 1-to-4 and the "odds against" are 4-to-1.

## Multiplication Rule for Joint Probability

$$P(AB) = P(A \mid B) \times P(B) = P(B \mid A) \times P(A)$$

The probability that A and B will both (jointly) occur is the probability of A given that B occurs, multiplied by the (unconditional) probability that B will occur.

## Addition Rule

$$P(A \text{ or } B) = P(A) + P(B) - P(AB)$$

If A and B are mutually exclusive, $P(AB)$ is zero and $P(A \text{ or } B) = P(A) + P(B)$

Used to calculate the probability that at least one (one or both) of two events will occur.

## Total Probability Rule

$$P(R) = P(R \mid I) \times P(I) + P(R \mid I^C) \times P(I^C)$$

where: I and $I^C$ are *mutually exclusive and an exhaustive set of events* (i.e., if I occurs, then $I^C$ cannot occur and one of the two must occur).

A tree diagram shows a variety of possible outcomes for a random variable, such as an asset price or earnings per share.

©2011 Kaplan, Inc.

**Figure 3: A Tree Diagram for an Investment Problem**

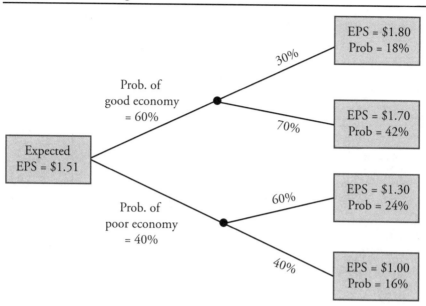

We can illustrate several probability concepts with a tree diagram. The (unconditional) expected EPS is the sum of the possible outcomes, weighted by their probabilities.

$$0.18 \times 1.80 + 0.42 \times 1.70 + 0.24 \times 1.30 + 0.16 \times 1.00 = \$1.51$$

The (conditional) expectation of EPS, given that the economy is good, is $1.73 = 0.3(1.80) + 0.7(1.70)$. Expected EPS, given that the economy is poor, is $0.6(1.30) + 0.4(1.00) = \$1.18$.

The probabilities of each of the EPS outcomes are simply the product of the two probabilities along the (branches) of the tree [e.g., P(EPS = $1.80) = 0.6 \times 0.3 = 18\%$].

## Covariance

The *covariance* between two variables is a measure of the degree to which the two variables tend to move together. It captures the linear relationship between one random variable and another.

A *positive covariance* indicates that the variables tend to move together; a *negative covariance* indicates that the variables tend to move in opposite directions relative to their means. Covariance indicates the direction of the relationship and does not directly indicate the strength of the relationship. Therefore, if you compare the covariance measures for two sets of (paired) random variables and the second is twice the value of the first, the relationship of the second set isn't necessarily twice as strong as the first because the variance of the variables may be quite different as well.

**Example:**

Covariance can be calculated using a joint probability table as follows:

|  | $R_X = 15\%$ | $R_X = 10\%$ |
|---|---|---|
| $R_Y = 20\%$ | 0.30 | 0 |
| $R_Y = 5\%$ | 0 | 0.70 |

First, find the expected returns on X and Y:

$$E(R_X) = 0.30(15) + 0.70(10) = 11.5\%$$
$$E(R_Y) = 0.30(20) + 0.70(5) = 9.5\%$$

Next calculate the covariance:

$$Cov(R_X, R_Y) = [0.3(15.0 - 11.5)(20.0 - 9.5)] + [0.7(10.0 - 11.5)(5.0 - 9.5)]$$
$$= 11.025 + 4.725 = 15.75$$

## Correlation

The *correlation coefficient, r,* is a standardized measure (unlike covariances) of the strength of the linear relationship between two variables. The correlation coefficient can range from −1 to +1.

$$r = corr(R_i, R_j) = \frac{Cov(R_i, R_j)}{\sigma(R_i)\sigma(R_j)}$$

A correlation of +1 indicates a perfect positive correlation. In that case, knowing the outcome of one random variable would allow you to predict the outcome of the other with certainty.

## Expected Return and Variance of a Portfolio of Two Stocks

Know how to compute the *expected return and variance for a portfolio of two assets* using the following formulas:

$$E(R_p) = w_A R_A + w_B R_B$$

$$Var_p = w_A^2 \sigma_A^2 + w_B^2 \sigma_B^2 + 2w_A w_B \sigma_A \sigma_B \rho_{A,B}$$

$$Var_p = w_A^2 \sigma_A^2 + w_B^2 \sigma_B^2 + 2w_A w_B Cov_{A,B}$$

Note that $\sigma_A \sigma_B \rho_{A,B} = Cov_{A,B}$ so the formula for variance can be written either way.

## STUDY SESSION 3: QUANTITATIVE METHODS—APPLICATIONS

## COMMON PROBABILITY DISTRIBUTIONS
Cross-Reference to CFA Institute Assigned Reading #9

Critical topics to understand include the normal distribution and areas under the normal curve, the *t*-distribution, skewness, kurtosis, and the binomial distribution. Be able to calculate confidence intervals for population means based on the normal distribution.

*Discrete random variable*: A limited (finite) number of possible outcomes and each has a positive probability. They can be counted (e.g., number of days without rain during a month).

*Continuous random variable*: An infinite number of possible outcomes. The number of inches of rain over a month can take on an infinite number of values, assuming we can measure it with infinite precision.

*Probability function*, p(x), specifies the probability that a random variable equals a particular value, *x*.

A *probability density function* describes a continuous distribution. For a continuous distribution, the probability that the random variable will take on any single one (of the infinite number) of the possible values is zero. A probability density function is used to calculate the probability that a continuous random variable will take on a value between two given values.

A *cumulative density function* (CDF), for either a discrete or continuous distribution, gives the probability that a random variable will take on a value *less than or equal to* a specific value, that is, the probability that the value will be between minus infinity and the specified value.

For the probability density function, Prob(x) = x/15 for x = 1, 2, 3, 4, 5, the CDF is:

$$\sum_{x=1}^{X} \frac{x}{15}, \text{ so that F(3) or Prob (x } \leq \text{ 3) is } 1/15 + 2/15 + 3/15 = 6/15 \text{ or } 40\%$$

This is simply the sum of the probabilities of 1, 2, and 3. Note that Prob (x = 3, 4) can be calculated as $F(4) - F(2) = \dfrac{10}{15} - \dfrac{3}{15} = \dfrac{7}{15}$.

## Uniform Distributions

With a uniform distribution, the probabilities of the outcomes can be thought of as equal. They are equal for all possible outcomes with a discrete uniform distribution, and equal for equal-sized ranges of a uniform continuous distribution.

For example, consider the *discrete uniform probability distribution* defined as X = {1, 2, 3, 4, 5}, p(x) = 0.2. Here, the probability for each outcome is equal to 0.2 [i.e., p(1) = p(2) = p(3) = p(4) = p(5) = 0.2]. Also, the cumulative distribution function for the *n*th outcome, $F(x_n) = np(x)$, and the probability for a range of outcomes is p(x)k, where *k* is the number of possible outcomes in the range.

A *continuous uniform distribution* over the range of 1 to 5 results in a 25% probability [1 / (5 − 1)] that the random variable will take on a value between 1 and 2, 2 and 3, 3 and 4, or 4 and 5, since 1 is one-quarter of the total range of the random variable.

## The Binomial Distribution

A **binomial random variable** may be defined as the number of "successes" in a given number of trials where the outcome can be either "success" or "failure." You can recognize problems based on a binomial distribution from the fact that there are only two possible outcomes (e.g., the probability that a stock index will rise over a day's trading). The probability of success, *p*, is constant for each trial, the trials are independent, and the probability of failure (no success) is simply 1 − p. A binomial distribution is used to calculate the number of successes in $n$ trials. The probability of $x$ successes in $n$ trials is:

$$p(x) = P(X = x) = (_nC_r)p^x(1 - p)^{n - x}$$

and the expected number of successes is $np$.

If the probability of a stock index increasing each day ($p$) is 60%, the probability (assuming independence) that the index will increase on exactly three of the next five days (and not increase on two days) is $(_5C_3)0.6^3(1 - 0.6)^2 = 0.3456$.

A binomial tree to describe possible stock price movement for $n$ periods shows the probabilities for each possible number of successes over $n$ periods. Additionally, assuming that the stock price over any single period will either increase by a factor $U$ or decrease by a factor $1/U$, a binomial tree shows the possible $n$-period outcomes for the stock price and the probabilities that each will occur.

## Normal Distribution: Properties

- Completely described by mean and variance.
- Symmetric about the mean (skewness = 0).
- Kurtosis (a measure of peakedness) = 3.
- Linear combination of jointly, normally distributed random variables is also normally distributed.

Many properties of the normal distribution are evident from examining the graph of a normal distribution's probability density function:

### Figure 4: Normal Distribution Probability Density Function

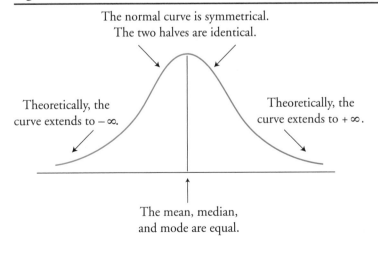

The normal curve is symmetrical. The two halves are identical.

Theoretically, the curve extends to $-\infty$.

Theoretically, the curve extends to $+\infty$.

The mean, median, and mode are equal.

## Calculating Probabilities Using the Standard Normal Distribution

The *z-value* "standardizes" an observation from a normal distribution and represents the number of standard deviations a given observation is from the population mean.

$$z = \frac{\text{observation} - \text{population mean}}{\text{standard deviation}} = \frac{x - \mu}{\sigma}$$

## Confidence Intervals: Normal Distribution

A *confidence interval* is a range of values around an expected outcome within which we expect the actual outcome to occur some specified percentage of the time.

The following graph illustrates confidence intervals for a standard normal distribution, which has a mean of 0 and a standard deviation of 1. We can interpret the values on the x-axis as the number of standard deviations from the mean. Thus, for any normal distribution we can say, for example, that 68% of the outcomes will be within one standard deviation of the mean. This would be referred to as a 68% confidence interval.

**Figure 5: The Standard Normal Distribution and Confidence Intervals**

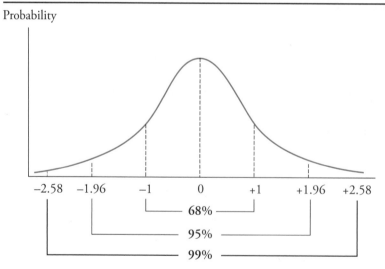

Be prepared to calculate a confidence interval on the Level I exam. Consider a normal distribution with mean $\mu$ and standard deviation $\sigma$. Each observation has an expected value of $\mu$. If we draw a sample of size $n$ from the distribution, the mean of the sample has an expected value of $\mu$. The larger the sample, the closer to $\mu$ we expect the sample mean to be. The standard deviation of the means of samples of size $n$ is simply $\sigma/\sqrt{n}$ and is called standard error of the sample mean. This allows us to construct a confidence interval for the sample mean for a sample of size $n$.

**Example:**

Calculate a 95% confidence interval for the mean of a sample of size 25 drawn from a normal distribution with a mean of 8 and a standard deviation of 4.

**Answer:**

The standard deviation of the means of samples of size 25 is:

$$\frac{4}{\sqrt{25}} = \frac{4}{5} = 0.8$$

A 95% confidence interval will extend 1.96 standard deviations above and below the mean, so our 95% confidence interval is:

$8 \pm 1.96 \times 0.8, 6.432$ to $9.568$

We believe the mean of a sample of 25 observations will fall within this interval 95% of the time.

With a known variance, the formula for a confidence interval is:

$$\bar{x} \pm z_{\alpha/2}\frac{\sigma}{\sqrt{n}}$$

In other words, the confidence interval is equal to the mean value, plus or minus the z-score that corresponds to the given significance level multiplied by the standard error.

- Confidence intervals and z-scores are very important in hypothesis testing, a topic that will be reviewed shortly.

**Shortfall Risk and Safety-First Ratio**

*Shortfall risk.* The probability that a portfolio's return or value will be below a specified (target) return or value over a specified period.

*Roy's safety-first criterion* states that the optimal portfolio minimizes the probability that the return of the portfolio falls below some minimum acceptable "threshold" level.

*Roy's safety-first ratio* (SFRatio) is similar to the Sharpe ratio. In fact, the Sharpe ratio is a special case of Roy's ratio where the "threshold" level is the risk-free rate of return.

Under both the Sharpe and Roy criteria, the best portfolio is the one that has the largest ratio.

Roy's safety-first ratio can be calculated as:

$$\text{SFRatio} = \frac{E\left(R_p\right) - R_L}{\sigma_p}$$

With approximate normality of returns, the SFR is like a *t*-statistic. It shows how many standard deviations the expected return is above the threshold return ($R_L$). The greater the SFR, the lower the probability that returns will be below the threshold return (i.e., the lower the shortfall risk).

## Lognormal Distribution

If *x* is normally distributed, $Y = e^x$ is lognormally distributed. Values of a lognormal distribution are always positive so it is used to model asset prices (rather than rates of return, which can be negative). The lognormal distribution is positively skewed as shown in the following figure.

**Figure 6: Lognormal Distribution**

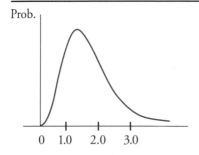

## Continuously Compounded Returns

If we increase the number of compounding periods (*n*) for an annual rate of return, the limit as *n* goes toward infinity is continuous compounding. For a specific

©2011 Kaplan, Inc.

holding period return (HPR), the relation to the continuously compounded return (CCR) over the holding period is as follows:

$$CCR = \ln(1 + HPR) = \ln\left(\frac{\text{ending value}}{\text{beginning value}}\right)$$

$$HPR = \frac{\text{ending value}}{\text{beginning value}} - 1 = e^{CCR} - 1$$

When the holding period is one year, so that HPR is also the effective annual return, CCR is the annual continuously compounded rate of return.

One property of continuously compounded rates is that they are additive over multiple periods. If the continuously compounded rate of return is 8%, the holding period return over a 2-year horizon is $e^{2(0.08)} - 1$, and \$1,000 will grow to $1{,}000\ e^{2.5(0.08)}$ over two and one-half years.

## Simulation

*Historical simulation* of outcomes (e.g., changes in portfolio values) is done by randomly selecting changes in price or risk factors from actual (historical) past changes in these factors and modeling the effects of these changes on the value of a current portfolio. The results of historical simulation have limitations since future changes may not necessarily be distributed as past changes were.

*Monte Carlo simulation* is performed by making assumptions about the distributions of prices or risk factors and using a large number of computer-generated random values for the relevant risk factors or prices to generate a distribution of possibly outcomes (e.g., project NPVs, portfolio values). The simulated distributions can only be as accurate as the assumptions about the distributions of and correlations between the input variables assumed in the procedure.

## SAMPLING AND ESTIMATION
Cross-Reference to CFA Institute Assigned Reading #10

Know the methods of sampling, sampling biases, and the central limit theorem, which allows us to use sampling statistics to construct confidence intervals around point estimates of population means.

- *Sampling error*: Difference between the sample statistic and its corresponding population parameter:

$$\text{sampling error of the mean} = \bar{x} - \mu$$

- *Simple random sampling*: Method of selecting a sample such that each item or person in the population has the *same likelihood of being included* in the sample.
- *Stratified random sampling*: Separate the population into groups based on one or more characteristics. Take a random sample from each class based on the group size. In constructing bond index portfolios, we may first divide the bonds by maturity, rating, call feature, etc., and then pick bonds from each group of bonds in proportion to the number of index bonds in that group. This insures that our "random" sample has similar maturity, rating, and call characteristics to the index.

### Sample Biases

- *Data-mining bias* occurs when research is based on the previously reported empirical evidence of others, rather than on the testable predictions of a well-developed economic theory. Data mining also occurs when analysts repeatedly use the same database to search for patterns or trading rules until one that "works" is found.
- *Sample selection bias* occurs when some data is systematically excluded from the analysis, usually because of the lack of availability.
- *Survivorship bias* is the most common form of sample selection bias. A good example of survivorship bias is given by some studies of mutual fund performance. Most mutual fund databases, like Morningstar's, only include funds currently in existence—the "survivors." Since poorly performing funds are more likely to have ceased to exist because of failure or merger, the survivorship bias in the data set tends to bias average performance upward.
- *Look-ahead bias* occurs when a study tests a relationship using sample data that was not available on the test date.
- *Time-period bias* can result if the time period over which the data is gathered is either too short or too long.

## Central Limit Theorem

The *central limit theorem* of statistics states that in selecting simple random samples of size $n$ from a *population* with a mean $\mu$ and a finite variance $\sigma^2$, the sampling distribution of the sample mean approaches a normal probability distribution with mean $\mu$ and a variance equal to $\sigma^2/n$ as the sample size becomes large.

The central limit theorem is extremely useful because the normal distribution is relatively easy to apply to hypothesis testing and to the construction of confidence intervals.

Specific inferences about the population mean can be made from the sample mean, *regardless of the population's distribution*, as long as the sample size is sufficiently large.

## Student's *t*-Distribution

- Symmetrical (bell shaped).
- Defined by single parameter, degrees of freedom (df), where df = n − 1 for hypothesis tests and confidence intervals involving a sample mean.
- Has fatter tails than a normal distribution; the lower the df, the fatter the tails and the wider the confidence interval around the sample mean for a given probability that the interval contains the true mean.
- As sample size (degrees of freedom) increases, the *t*-distribution approaches normal distribution.

*Student's t-distribution* is similar in concept to the normal distribution in that it is bell-shaped and symmetrical about its mean. The *t-distribution* is appropriate when working with small samples (n < 30) from populations with *unknown variance* and normal, or approximately normal, distributions. It may also be appropriate to use the *t*-distribution when the population variance is unknown and the sample size is large enough that the central limit theorem will assure the sampling distribution is approximately normal.

## Figure 7: Student's *t*-Distribution and Degrees of Freedom

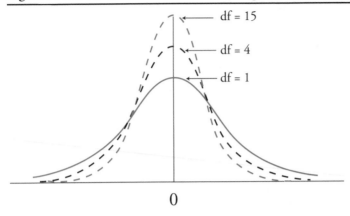

For questions on the exam, make sure you are working with the correct distribution. You should memorize the following table:

## Figure 8: Criteria for Selecting Test Statistic

| When sampling from a: | Test Statistic | |
| --- | --- | --- |
| | Small Sample (n < 30) | Large Sample (n ≥ 30) |
| *Normal* distribution with *known* variance | z-statistic | z-statistic |
| *Normal* distribution with *unknown* variance | t-statistic | t-statistic* |
| *Nonnormal* distribution with *known* variance | not available | z-statistic |
| *Nonnormal* distribution with *unknown* variance | not available | t-statistic** |

\*   The z-statistic is the standard normal, ±1 for 68% confidence, et cetera.
\*\* The z-statistic is theoretically acceptable here, but use of the t-statistic is more conservative.

## HYPOTHESIS TESTING
Cross-Reference to CFA Institute Assigned Reading #11

*Hypothesis.* Statement about a population parameter that is to be tested. For example, "The mean return on the S&P 500 Index is equal to zero."

### Steps in Hypothesis Testing
- State the hypothesis.
- Select a test statistic.

- Specify the level of significance.
- State the decision rule for the hypothesis.
- Collect the sample and calculate statistics.
- Make a decision about the hypothesis.
- Make a decision based on the test results.

## Null and Alternative Hypotheses

The *null hypothesis*, designated as $H_0$, is the hypothesis the researcher wants to reject. It is the hypothesis that is actually tested and is the basis for the selection of the test statistics. Thus, if you believe (seek to show that) the mean return on the S&P 500 Index is different from zero, the null hypothesis will be that the mean return on the index *equals* zero.

The *alternative hypothesis*, designated $H_a$, is what is concluded if there is sufficient evidence to reject the null hypothesis. It is usually the alternative hypothesis you are really trying to support. Why? Since you can never really prove anything with statistics, when the null hypothesis is rejected, the implication is that the (mutually exclusive) alternative hypothesis is valid.

## Two-Tailed and One-Tailed Tests

*Two-tailed test.* Use this type of test when testing a parameter to see if it is different from a specified value:

$$H_0: \mu = 0 \text{ versus } H_a: \mu \neq 0$$

**Figure 9: Two-Tailed Test: Significance = 5%, Confidence = 95%**

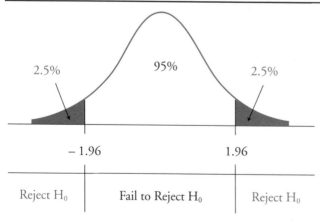

*One-tailed test.* Use this type of test when testing a parameter to see if it is *above* or *below* a specified value:

$$H_0: \mu \le 0 \text{ versus } H_a: \mu > 0, \text{ or}$$
$$H_0: \mu \ge 0 \text{ versus } H_a: \mu < 0$$

With respect to the first hypothesis, $\mu \le 0$, we will reject it only if the test statistic is significantly greater than zero (in the right-hand tail of the distribution). Thus, we call it a one-tailed test.

**Figure 10: One-Tailed Test: Significance = 5%, Confidence = 95%**

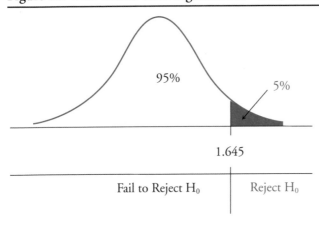

**Test Statistic**

A *test statistic* is calculated from sample data and is compared to a critical value to evaluate $H_0$. The most common test statistics are the $z$-statistic and the $t$-statistic. Which statistic you use to perform a hypothesis test will depend on the properties of the population and the sample size as noted above.

- Critical values come from tables and are based on the researcher's desired level of significance. As the level of significance (the $\alpha$) gets smaller, the critical value gets larger and it becomes more difficult to reject the null hypothesis.
- If the test statistic exceeds the critical value (or is outside the range of critical values), the researcher rejects $H_0$.

**Type I and Type II Errors**

When testing a hypothesis, there are two possible types of errors:

- *Type I error.* Rejection of the null hypothesis when it is actually true.
- *Type II error.* Failure to reject the null hypothesis when it is actually false.

The *power of a test* is $1 - P(\text{Type II error})$. The more likely that a test will reject a false null, the more powerful the test. A test that is unlikely to reject a false null hypothesis has little power.

## Significance Level ($\alpha$)

The *significance level* is the probability of making a Type I error (rejecting the null when it is true) and is designated by the Greek letter alpha ($\alpha$). You can think of this as the probability that the test statistic will exceed or fall below the critical values by chance even though the null hypothesis is true. A significance level of 5% ($a = 0.05$) means there is a 5% chance of rejecting a true null hypothesis.

### Figure 11: Errors in Hypothesis Testing

| | *Type I and Type II Errors in Hypothesis Testing* | |
|---|---|---|
| Decision | True Condition | |
| | $H_0$ is true | $H_0$ is false |
| Do not reject $H_0$ | Correct decision | Incorrect decision<br>Type II error |
| Reject $H_0$ | Incorrect decision<br>Type I error<br>Significance level, $\alpha$,<br>$= P(\text{Type I error})$ | Correct decision<br>Power of the test<br>$= 1 - P(\text{Type II error})$ |

## Economically Meaningful Results

A test may indicate a significant statistical relationship (a statistically meaningful result) which is not economically significant. This is often the case when the gains from exploiting the statistical relation are small in an absolute sense so that the costs of a strategy to exploit the relation are greater than the expected gains from the strategy.

## Other Hypothesis Tests

A test of the equality of the means of two independent normally distributed populations is a *t*-test based on the difference in sample means divided by a standard deviation which is calculated in one of two ways, depending on whether the variances of the two populations are assumed to be equal or not.

When random variables from two populations are dependent, the appropriate test is a *mean differences* or *paired comparisons* test. The test statistic is a *t*-statistic based on the average (mean) of the differences in the sample of the paired values of the two random variables, divided by the standard deviation of the differences between the sample pairs.

A test of whether the population variance of a normal distribution is equal to a specific value is based on the ratio of the sample variance to the hypothesized variance. The test statistic follows a Chi-square distribution and is a two-tailed test.

A test of whether the variances of two normal populations are equal is based on the ratio of the larger sample variance to the smaller sample variance. The appropriate test is an *F*-test (two-tailed), but by putting the larger sample variance in the numerator, values of the test statistic below the lower critical value are ruled out, and only the upper critical value of the *F*-statistic need be considered.

## Parametric and Nonparametric Tests

*Parametric tests,* like the *t*-test, *F*-test, and chi-square test, make assumptions regarding the distribution of the population from which samples are drawn.

*Nonparametric tests* either do not consider a particular population parameter or have few assumptions about the sampled population. Runs tests (which examine the pattern of successive increases or decreases in a random variable) and rank correlation tests (which examine the relation between a random variable's relative numerical rank over successive periods) are examples of nonparametric tests.

## TECHNICAL ANALYSIS
Cross-Reference to CFA Institute Assigned Reading #12

This topic review presents many different technical analysis tools. Don't try to memorize them all. Focus on the basics of technical analysis and its underlying assumptions.

## Assumptions of Technical Analysis

- Values, and thus prices, are determined by supply and demand.
- Supply and demand are driven by both rational and irrational behavior.
- Price and volume reflect the collective behavior of buyers and sellers.
- While the causes of changes in supply and demand are difficult to determine, the actual shifts in supply and demand can be observed in market price behavior.

## Advantages of Technical Analysis

- Based on observable data (price and volume) that are not based on accounting assumptions or restatements.
- Can be used for assets that do not produce cash flows, such as commodities.
- May be more useful than fundamental analysis when financial statements contain errors or are fraudulent.

## Disadvantages of Technical Analysis

- Less useful for markets that are subject to outside intervention, such as currency markets, and for markets that are illiquid.
- Short covering can create positive technical patterns for stocks of bankrupt companies.
- Cannot produce positive risk-adjusted returns over time when markets are weak-form efficient.

## Types of Charts

Except for point and figure charts, all of the following chart types plot price or volume on the vertical axis and time (divided into trading periods) on the horizontal axis. Trading periods can be daily, intraday (e.g., hourly), or longer term (e.g., weekly or monthly).

*Line chart*: Closing prices for each trading period are connected by a line.

*Bar chart*: Vertical lines from the high to the low price for each trading period. A mark on the left side of the line indicates the opening price and a mark on the right side of the vertical line indicates the closing price.

*Candlestick chart*: Bar chart that draws a box from the opening price to the closing price on the vertical line for each trading period. The box is empty if the close is higher than the open and filled if the close is lower than the open.

*Volume chart*: Vertical line from zero to the number of shares (bonds, contracts) exchanged during each trading period. Often displayed below a bar or candlestick chart of the same asset over the same range of time.

*Point and figure chart*: Displays price trends on a grid. Price is on the vertical axis, and each unit on the horizontal axis represents a change in the direction of the price trend.

*Relative strength chart*: Line chart of the ratios of closing prices to a benchmark index. These charts illustrate how one asset or market is performing relative to another. Relative strength charts are useful for performing intermarket analysis and for identifying attractive asset classes and assets within each class that are outperforming others.

## Trend, Support, and Resistance

A market is in an uptrend if prices are consistently reaching higher highs and retracing to higher lows. An uptrend indicates demand is increasing relative to supply. An upward sloping trendline can be drawn that connects the low points for a stock in an uptrend.

A market is in a downtrend if prices are consistently reaching lower lows and retracing to lower highs. A downtrend means supply is increasing relative to demand. A downward sloping trendline can be drawn that connects the high points in a downtrend.

Support and resistance levels are prices at which technical analysts expect supply and demand to equalize. Past highs are viewed as resistance levels, and past lows are viewed as support levels. Trendlines are also thought to indicate support and resistance levels.

The *change in polarity principle* is based on a belief that breached support levels become resistance levels, and breached resistance levels become support levels.

## Figure 12: Trendlines, Support, and Resistance

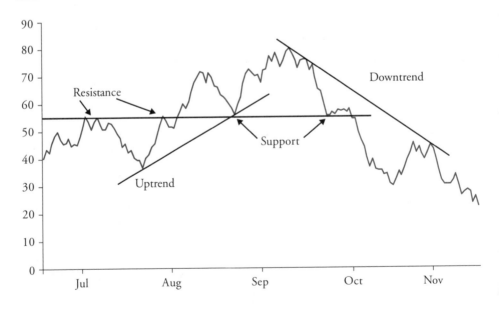

## Common Chart Patterns

*Reversal patterns*: Head-and-shoulders; double top; triple top; inverse head-and-shoulders; double bottom; triple bottom. These price patterns are thought to indicate that the preceding trend has run its course and a new trend in the opposite direction is likely to emerge.

*Continuation patterns*: Triangles; rectangles; flags; pennants. These indicate temporary pauses in a trend which is expected to continue (in the same direction).

Technical analysts often use the sizes of both of these types of patterns to estimate subsequent target prices for the next move.

## Price-based Indicators

*Moving average lines* are a frequently used method to smooth the fluctuations in a price chart. A 20-day moving average is the arithmetic mean of the last 20 closing prices. The larger number of periods chosen, the smoother the resulting moving average line will be. Moving average lines can help illustrate trends by smoothing short-term fluctuations, but when the number of periods is large, a moving average line can obscure changes in trend.

*Bollinger bands* are drawn a given number of standard deviations above and below a moving average line. Prices are believed to have a higher probability of falling (rising) when they are near the upper (lower) band.

*Momentum oscillators* include the rate of change oscillator, the Relative Strength Index (RSI), moving average convergence/divergence (MACD) lines, and stochastic oscillators.

Technical analysts use price-based indicators to identify market conditions that are overbought (prices have increased too rapidly and are likely to decrease in the near term) or oversold (prices have decreased too rapidly and are likely to increase in the near term). They also use charts of momentum oscillators to identify convergence or divergence with price trends. Convergence occurs when the oscillator shows the same pattern as prices (e.g., both reaching higher highs). Divergence occurs when the oscillator shows a different pattern than prices (e.g., failing to reach a higher high when the price does). Convergence suggests the price trend is likely to continue, while divergence indicates a potential change in trend in the near term.

## Sentiment and Flow of Funds Indicators

Technical analysts also use indicators based on investors' bullish (investors expect prices to increase) or bearish (investors expect prices to decrease) sentiment.

Some technical analysts interpret these indicators from a contrarian perspective. Contrarians believe markets get overbought or oversold because most investors tend to buy and sell at the wrong times, and thus it can be profitable to trade in the opposite direction from current sentiment.

Sentiment indicators include the following:

- *Put/call ratio:* Put option volume divided by call option volume.
- *Volatility index* (VIX): Measure of volatility on S&P 500 stock index options.
- *Short interest ratio:* Shares sold short divided by average daily trading volume.
- Amount of *margin debt* outstanding.
- *Opinion polls* that attempt to measure investor sentiment directly.

High levels of the put/call ratio, VIX, and short interest ratio indicate bearish market sentiment, which contrarians interpret as bullish. High levels of margin debt indicate bullish sentiment, which contrarians interpret as bearish.

Indicators of the flow of funds in the financial markets can be useful for identifying changes in the supply and demand for securities. These include the Arms index or short-term trading index (TRIN), which measures funds flowing into advancing and declining stocks; margin debt (also used as a sentiment indicator); new and secondary equity offerings; and mutual fund cash as a percentage of net assets.

## Cycles and Elliott Wave Theory

Some technical analysts apply cycle theory to financial markets in an attempt to identify cycles in prices. Cycle periods favored by technical analysts include 4-year presidential cycles related to election years in the United States, decennial patterns or 10-year cycles, 18-year cycles, and 54-year cycles called Kondratieff waves.

One of the more developed cycle theories is the Elliott wave theory which is based on an interconnected set of cycles that range from a few minutes to centuries. According to Elliott wave theory, in an uptrend the upward moves in prices consist of five waves and the downward moves occur in three waves. If the prevailing trend is down, the downward moves have five waves and the upward moves have three waves. Each of these waves is composed of smaller waves that exhibit the same pattern.

The sizes of these waves are thought to correspond with ratios of Fibonacci numbers. Fibonacci numbers are found by starting with 0 and 1, then adding each of the previous two numbers to produce the next (0, 1, 1, 2, 3, 5, 8, 13, 21, and so on). Ratios of consecutive Fibonacci numbers converge to 0.618 and 1.618 as the numbers in the sequence get larger.

# Economics

| | |
|---|---|
| Weight on Exam | 10% |
| SchweserNotes™ Reference | Book 2, Pages 1–206 |

## Study Session 4: Economics—Microeconomic Analysis

It is important to remember the difference between a shift in a demand (or supply) curve and movement along the curve. As prices change, quantity demanded will change, moving along the curve. As consumer preferences change, the entire demand curve will shift. In other words, quantity demanded will change at all price levels when the demand curve shifts.

### Elasticity
Cross-Reference to CFA Institute Assigned Reading #13

### Price Elasticity of Demand

- *Price elasticity of demand.* Refers to the change in the quantity demanded of a good in relation to the change in price. As the price of a good increases, the quantity demanded decreases.
- *Elastic demand.* A small price increase causes a large decrease in the quantity demanded.
- *Inelastic demand.* A large price increase causes a small decrease in quantity demanded.
- *Perfectly elastic demand.* A small price increase reduces the quantity demanded to zero (a horizontal demand curve).
- *Perfectly inelastic demand.* A price change does not affect the quantity demanded (a vertical demand curve).

$$\text{price elasticity of demand} = \frac{\text{percentage change in quantity demanded}}{\text{percentage change in price}}$$

$$\textit{Note}: \text{percentage change} = \frac{\text{change in value}}{\text{average value}}$$

Be familiar with the relationship between price and total revenue, based on elasticity of demand. If demand is elastic, a price decrease would lead to higher total revenue, because the percentage increase in the quantity demanded is greater than the percentage decrease in price. When demand is inelastic, price and total revenue move in the same direction.

Price elasticity has *two main determinants:*

- *Availability of substitutes.* If good substitutes are available, consumers may switch to a substitute good if prices rise. The presence of many substitutes will tend to increase demand elasticity.
- *Share of budget spent on product.* Goods that occupy a relatively *small* portion of your budget will tend to be price *inelastic.*

Elasticity is *greater in the long run* as consumers can make more adjustments based on the new price of the good.

## Income Elasticity of Demand

*Income elasticity* is a similar concept that describes the sensitivity of demand to a change in consumer income (holding the price of the good constant).

$$\text{income elasticity} = \frac{\text{percentage change in quantity demanded}}{\text{percentage change in income}}$$

An *inferior good* has negative income elasticity. As income increases (decreases), demand decreases (increases). Inferior goods include such things as bus travel and margarine.

A *normal good* has positive income elasticity; as income increases (decreases), demand for the good increases (decreases). Normal goods include things like bread and tobacco. A *luxury good* is a normal good with an income elasticity of demand greater than one (i.e., a 5% increase in income will increase demand by more than 5%).

## Cross Elasticity of Demand

*Cross elasticity* measures the change in demand for one good in response to a change in the price of another good that is a substitute for it or a complement to it.

$$\text{cross elasticity} = \frac{\text{percent change in quantity demanded}}{\text{percent change in price of substitute or complement}}$$

- If the two goods are *substitutes*, cross elasticity is positive. An example is ice cream and frozen yogurt.
- If the two goods are *complements*, cross elasticity is negative. An example is autos and gasoline.

## Elasticity of Supply

*Price elasticity of supply* measures the responsiveness of the quantity supplied to changes in price.

$$\text{price elasticity of supply} = \frac{\text{percent change in quantity supplied}}{\text{percent change in price}}$$

Elasticity of supply has *two main determinants:*

- *Available substitutes for resource inputs used to produce the good.* Elasticity of supply will be lower (supply curve closer to vertical) if the good can only be produced with rare or unique inputs.
- *Time that has elapsed since the price change.* Elasticity of supply can be viewed in three different time frames:
    1. *Momentary supply.* If producers cannot change the output of the good immediately (e.g., oranges), momentary supply is highly inelastic. If they can change output quickly (e.g., electricity), momentary supply is highly elastic.
    2. *Short-term supply.* The supply curve becomes more elastic as producers adjust their production processes, for example by changing the amount of labor they hire.
    3. *Long-term supply.* Elasticity of supply is most elastic in the long run, when producers have made all possible adjustments, including projects such as building factories and distribution systems.

Considering a linear demand curve, the elasticity will be different at different points on the curve (i.e., constant slope does not imply constant elasticity). At lower quantities (higher prices), the percentage change in quantity is relatively larger than the percentage change in price. When this is the case, demand elasticity is greater than one (in absolute value), demand is said to be elastic, and an increase in price will decrease total revenue (P × Q). At higher quantities (lower prices), the percentage change in quantity is relatively smaller than the percentage change in price. When this is the case, demand elasticity is less than one (in absolute value), demand is said to be inelastic, and an increase in price will increase total revenue (P × Q). At the point on the demand curve where total revenue (P × Q) is at a maximum, either an increase or decrease in price will decrease total revenue, demand elasticity is equal to −1 and is said to be unitary elastic or to have unitary elasticity.

# EFFICIENCY AND EQUITY
Cross-Reference to CFA Institute Assigned Reading #14

*Marginal benefit* is the benefit an individual gets from consuming one more unit of a good or service. Marginal benefit decreases as the amount of the good consumed increases (diminishing marginal utility).

*Marginal cost* is the cost of producing one more unit of output. This is also called the opportunity cost because it represents the value of resources in their next-best use other than producing this output.

When marginal benefit is greater than marginal cost, consumers are willing to pay more for the next unit of output than it will cost to produce it. Therefore, value is created by producing more units of this good. This requires resources to be diverted from producing other, less highly valued goods.

If marginal benefit is less than marginal cost, producers are using resources to produce the next unit of output that cost more than consumers are willing to pay for it. Therefore, value is created by producing fewer units of the output and diverting the resources to producing other, more highly-valued goods.

Total value created is maximized at the output level where *marginal benefit equals marginal cost*. This is the *efficient quantity* of output.

## Consumer Surplus and Producer Surplus

*Consumer surplus* is the difference between what a consumer is willing to pay for a good or service and what he actually pays for it. Because marginal benefit decreases as the amount consumed increases, consumer surplus decreases with each additional unit consumed. For the unit for which consumer surplus is zero, marginal benefit equals price and the consumer will not buy any more units of the good. Thus, the marginal benefit curve is equal to the consumer's demand curve for the good.

The marginal cost, or opportunity cost, of producing an additional unit of a good is the *minimum supply price* at which a producer is willing to supply another unit. The marginal cost curve (above average variable cost) is a producer's supply curve for the good. *Producer surplus* is the difference between the price a producer receives for a unit of output and the minimum supply price for (opportunity cost of) that unit.

## Marginal Social Benefit and Marginal Social Cost

*Marginal social benefit* is the sum of all consumers' marginal benefits from a good or service. The marginal social benefit curve is the market demand curve for the good or service.

*Marginal social cost* is the sum of all producers' marginal costs to supply a good or service. The marginal social cost curve is the supply curve for the good or service.

The *equilibrium price and quantity* for the good or service occurs where the market demand and market supply curves intersect. At this price and quantity, the sum of consumer surplus and producer surplus is at its maximum. Thus, the economic gains to society are maximized when the equilibrium quantity of each good or service is produced.

## Obstacles to Efficient Resource Allocation

- Price controls.
- Taxes, subsidies, and production quotas.
- Monopoly.
- External costs.
- External benefits.
- Public goods and common resources.

## Ideas About Fairness

*Utilitarianism* is the idea that the value of an economy is maximized when each individual owns an equal amount of the resources. This proved to be wrong because transferring wealth from the rich to the poor results in less being produced overall.

The *symmetry principle* implies that when an economy is based on private property and voluntary exchange, individuals get goods and services that are equal in value to their contributions to the economy. The distinction here is between a fair/equal economic outcome (utilitarianism) and fair/equal economic opportunity (symmetry).

## MARKETS IN ACTION
Cross-Reference to CFA Institute Assigned Reading #15

A shock that reduces supply will have different effects in the long run and in the short run. An earthquake that reduces the supply of housing, for example, will lead to a significant short-run increase in equilibrium prices (rents). Higher rents will lead to increases in supply (rebuilding) and decreases in price over time, since long-run supply is more elastic than short-run supply.

## Price Ceilings

A *price ceiling* is an upper limit on the price a seller can charge. If the ceiling is above the equilibrium price, it has no effect. But if the ceiling is below the equilibrium price, it results in a shortage—a larger quantity of the good is demanded at that price than will be supplied. The shortage in turn results in long lines for purchases, discrimination by sellers, bribes to sellers, reduced quality of the good, and black markets.

## Price Floors

A *price floor* is a lower limit on the price that a buyer can offer for a good or service. If the floor is below the equilibrium price, it has no effect. But if the floor is above the equilibrium price, the result is a surplus—a larger quantity of the good is supplied than demanded. Price floors cause inefficiencies as producers divert resources to producing the good but find that they cannot sell all they produce, and consumers substitute away from the good toward less expensive goods.

## Effects of a Minimum Wage

A minimum wage is an example of a price floor. When the minimum wage is above the equilibrium market wage for low-skilled labor:

- Unemployment results because more people are willing to work at that wage than firms are willing to hire.
- Firms substitute more than the efficient amount of capital for labor.
- Employers decrease the non-monetary benefits they offer to workers.

## Taxes on Buyers and Sellers

A tax on a good or service increases its equilibrium price and decreases its equilibrium quantity. A *deadweight loss* results because less than the efficient quantity is produced and consumed.

©2011 Kaplan, Inc.

Whether the *statutory incidence* of the tax is imposed on buyers or on sellers, the *actual incidence* of the tax falls on both buyers and sellers. How much of the revenue effectively comes from the buyers and how much effectively comes from the sellers depends on the elasticities of supply and demand.

## Figure 1: Elasticity of Supply and Tax Incidence

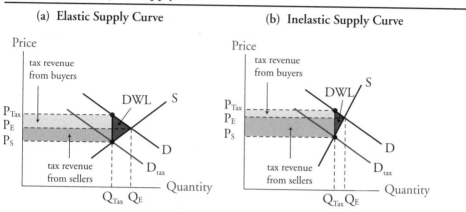

## Figure 2: Elasticity of Demand and Tax Incidence

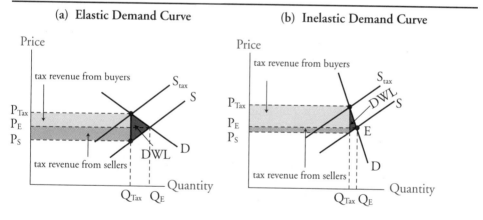

## Subsidies and Quotas

*Subsidies* are government payments to producers. When a good is subsidized, producers supply more than the efficient quantity.

*Quotas* are legal limits on the quantity of a good that can be produced. When the quota amount is less than the equilibrium quantity, quotas increase the price of

---

the good above equilibrium while preventing the efficient quantity from being produced.

## Illegal Goods

If a good is illegal, the demand curve shifts downward (from what it would be if the good were legal) by the value of the expected penalty per unit of the good that buyers incur. The supply curve shifts up by the expected penalty per unit of the good that sellers incur.

## ORGANIZING PRODUCTION
Cross-Reference to CFA Institute Assigned Reading #16

Important concepts related to costs include: *explicit* versus *implicit costs, economic* versus *accounting profit*, and *short- and long-run costs* in production. Be familiar with the various terms related to costs.

### Explicit vs. Implicit Costs; Economic vs. Accounting Profit

*Explicit costs* are the measurable costs of doing business that are reflected on a firm's accounting statement.

*Implicit costs* include the opportunity costs of a firm's equity and owner-provided services.

In practice, *accounting profit* only includes explicit costs and ignores implicit costs such as the opportunity cost of equity capital.

*Economic profit* considers both the explicit and implicit costs. When the firm's revenues are just equal to its costs (explicit and implicit, including the normal rate of return), economic profits are zero and equity capital earns a competitive rate of return.

- *Economic costs*. Reflect explicit and implicit costs.
- *Accounting costs*. Reflect only explicit costs.

### Constraints on Profit Maximization

- *Technology constraints*. Additional profit from increasing output and revenue is limited by the cost of adopting new technology to do so.
- *Information constraints*. A firm will expend resources to acquire information for decision making only up to the point where the cost of acquiring it equals the additional revenue from using it.

- *Market constraints.* Prices consumers are willing to pay for a product, pricing and marketing activity by competitors, and prices and availability of resources constrain a firm's potential growth.

## Technological and Economic Efficiency

A production process is *technologically efficient* compared to other processes if it uses the least amount of specific inputs to produce a given output.

A process is *economically efficient* if it produces the output at the lowest possible cost. If a process is not technologically efficient, it cannot be economically efficient. However, a process can be technologically efficient and still not be economically efficient.

## Command Systems and Incentive Systems

A *command system* organizes production by a managerial chain of command.

An *incentive system* organizes production by creating a system of rewards to motivate workers to perform in the way that maximizes profits. Command and incentive systems are often mixed within an organization. Command systems work best when it is easy to monitor employees' performance. Incentive systems work best when employees' activities are difficult or costly to monitor.

The *principal-agent problem* occurs when the incentives of managers and workers are not the same as the incentives of the firm's owners. For example, workers often have an incentive to shirk, while managers often have an incentive to maximize their own income rather than that of the firm.

Three methods of reducing the principal-agent problem are:

1. Give managers and workers an *ownership interest* in the firm.

2. Provide *incentive pay* based on performance.

3. Establish *long-term contracts* with firms' CEOs to encourage them to maximize the firms' profits over a long period.

## Types of Business Organization

*Proprietorship.* Single owner; unlimited liability for firm's obligations; firm income is personal income to the owner.

- Advantages: Easy to establish, simple decision making, profits only taxed once.
- Disadvantages: Decisions not checked by consensus, owner's wealth exposed to risk, firm may die with owner, difficult and expensive to raise capital.

---

*Partnership.* Two or more owners; unlimited liability for firm's obligations; firm income allocated to partners based on ownership proportion.

- Advantages: Easy to establish, decision making diversified among partners, firm may survive death of a partner, profits taxed only once.
- Disadvantages: Consensus decisions can be difficult to achieve, partners' wealth exposed to risk, capital shortfall if a partner leaves or dies.

*Corporation.* Owned by stockholders; liability limited to amount invested; firm pays corporate tax on its income.

- Advantages: Limited liability, inexpensive capital available, management expertise not limited to owners, unlimited life, able to enter long-term labor contracts.
- Disadvantages: Complex management structure, double taxation of income paid out as dividends.

## Measures of Concentration

The *four-firm concentration ratio* is the percentage of total industry sales made by the industry's four largest firms. The ratio is near zero for a highly competitive industry and 100% for a monopoly. A ratio below 40% indicates a competitive market. A ratio above 60% indicates an oligopoly.

The *Herfindahl-Hirschman Index* is the sum of the squared percentage market shares of the 50 largest firms in an industry. The ratio is very low for a highly competitive industry and 10,000 for a monopoly. An index above 1,800 indicates that the market is not competitive.

The usefulness of these measures is limited because they do not account for the geographical scope of the market, barriers to entry and firm turnover, or the relationship between a market and an industry.

## Coordinating Economic Activity

*Market coordination* means purchasing the various components of a final product or service from firms that specialize in producing them, then assembling the final product. Outsourcing is an example of market coordination.

*Firm coordination* occurs when firms can coordinate activity more efficiently than markets can. Firms can often achieve lower transactions costs and realize economies of scale, scope, and team production.

# Output and Costs
Cross-Reference to CFA Institute Assigned Reading #17

## Short-Run and Long-Run Costs

In the *short run*, it is difficult to alter production methods. The short run is defined as that time period in which the size of plant and equipment cannot be changed. The length of the short run varies from industry to industry.

The *long run* is the period of time necessary for the firm to change its production methods, scale of operation, and resource uses. In the long run, all resources (costs) are variable.

## Types of Costs

- *Fixed costs*, sometimes called sunk costs, remain unchanged in the short run and are therefore not considered when making short-run production decisions. They are related to the passage of time, not the level of production.
- *Average fixed costs* are total fixed costs divided by output. Average fixed costs decline as output increases.
- *Variable costs* (e.g., wages and raw materials) are incurred when the firm produces output. They are related to the level of production, not the passage of time.
- *Average variable cost* equals the total variable cost divided by output.
- *Average total cost* equals the total costs (fixed and variable) divided by the number of units produced.
- *Marginal cost* is the additional cost of producing one more unit of output.

## Law of Diminishing Returns

The *law of diminishing returns* states that as more of one input (e.g., labor) is devoted to a production process, holding the quantity of other inputs constant, output increases at a decreasing rate. For example, if an acre of corn needs to be picked, the addition of a second and third worker is highly productive. But if you already have 30 workers in the field, the additional output of the 31st worker is likely to be less than that of the 30th worker.

Diminishing marginal returns are evidenced at the point where variable costs begin to increase at an increasing rate.

## Figure 3: Total Cost and Variable Cost

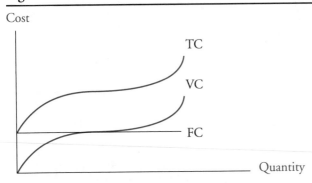

## Key Points About the Cost Curves

- The AFC curve slopes downward.
- The distance between the ATC and AVC curves is equal to AFC.
- MC declines initially, then increases.
- MC intersects AVC and ATC at their minimums.
- ATC and AVC are U-shaped.

## Figure 4: Average and Marginal Costs

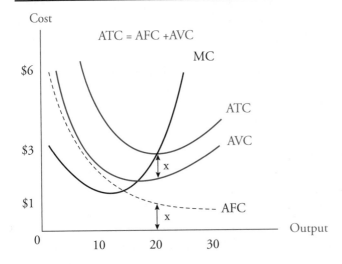

©2011 Kaplan, Inc.

## STUDY SESSION 5: ECONOMICS—MARKET STRUCTURE AND MACROECONOMIC ANALYSIS

## PERFECT COMPETITION; MONOPOLY; MONOPOLISTIC COMPETITION AND OLIGOPOLY
Cross-Reference to CFA Institute Assigned Readings #18, 19, & 20

For study purposes, the material dealing with all four types of economic markets can be combined, as the underlying concepts are similar.

## Types of Economic Markets

- *Perfect competition.* All firms in the market produce identical products; large number of independent firms, each small relative to size of market; no barriers to entry or exit; individual firms face perfectly elastic demand.
- *Monopolistic competition.* Large number of competitors with slightly differentiated products; downward sloping demand for firms.
- *Oligopoly.* Small number of competitors producing similar or differentiated products; interdependence among competitors; significant barriers to entry including large economies of scale.
- *Monopoly.* Single seller of specific, well-defined product that has no good substitutes; high barriers to entry.

"To maximize profits, *produce at the quantity where marginal revenue equals marginal cost.*" This applies to all producers in all types of markets. The marginal revenue curve will be horizontal and equal to price for pure competition/price takers, and downward sloping and below the demand curve for a price searcher, whether under monopolistic competition, oligopoly, or monopoly.

In economics, we measure efficiency compared to perfect or idealized market outcomes. Here, we examine price and output decisions relative to those that would be produced in perfectly competitive markets or under "pure competition."

Purely competitive (price-taker) markets are ones in which:

- All the firms in the market produce a homogeneous product.
- There is a large number of independent firms.
- Each seller is small relative to the total market.
- There are no barriers to entry or exit.

*Price takers* produce a small amount of output relative to the market and face a horizontal (perfectly elastic) demand curve. They *take* the market price as given.

They can sell all of their output at the prevailing market price, but if they set their output price higher than the market price, they will not make any sales.

The marginal revenue of a price taker is therefore the market selling price. The term "price-taker market" means the same thing as "purely competitive market;" a producer takes the price he can sell at as given.

*Price searchers* have downward sloping demand curves and must search for the price (and output) combination that maximizes profits. To sell additional units, a price searcher must charge a lower price. Since we assume that all units are sold at the same price, the marginal revenue curve lies below the demand curve.

A monopoly firm will maximize profits at a higher price and lower quantity than in a competitive market. If *price discrimination* is possible, where different groups of consumers pay different prices for the product, the firm can earn greater economic profits and will produce a greater quantity of output compared to a single-price monopolist. For price discrimination to work:

- The firm must face a downward sloping demand curve.
- Identifiable groups of consumers must have different price elasticities of demand.
- The firm must be able to prevent consumers from reselling the product across groups.

Under monopolistic competition, markets have:

- A *large* number of *independent sellers*.
- Sellers that each produce (slightly) *differentiated products*.
- *Low barriers to entry*.
- Producers that face *downward sloping demand curves* although demand is elastic.

Firms under monopolistic competition pursue *product innovation* because they can earn economic profits in the short run by being first to market with a new or improved product. Competitors will quickly copy those popular innovations that they can and reduce or eliminate economic profits in the process.

*Advertising* costs are high as firms try to increase the perception of differentiated products. *Branding* is an important means of informing consumers about the quality of the branded product. Some argue that the amounts of advertising, branding, and product differentiation are greater than optimal and an inefficient use of resources. However, consumers do benefit from the increased information they receive about products as well as from having a variety of products from which to choose.

## Barriers to Entry

Markets with high barriers to entry have the potential for firms to earn economic profits, even over the long run. Barriers to entry take the form of:

- Economies of scale (very large costs to produce at the efficient scale).
- Government licensing and legal barriers.
- Patents or exclusive rights.
- Control of resources.

## Monopoly vs. Oligopoly

A *monopoly* is a market structure characterized by a single firm that sells a well-defined product for which there are no good substitutes and high entry barriers. Monopolists are price searchers and can earn positive economic profits in the long run.

An *oligopoly* is characterized by a small number of firms. With an oligopoly, decisions made by one firm affect the demand, price, and profit of others in the industry.

If oligopolies could collude "perfectly," they could set the same price and output as a profit-maximizing monopolist and earn the same profits. They would need to agree both on the price and how much each producer would sell, which serves to allocate the (monopoly) profits. In practice, there are many obstacles to collusion that limit firms' economic profits in an oligopoly market structure.

## Traditional Oligopoly Models

In the *kinked demand curve model*, each firm believes its competitors will not follow price increases, but will follow price decreases. The *dominant firm oligopoly model* assumes one firm has a significant cost advantage and produces such a large share of the industry's output that it can effectively set the market price, while the other firms in the industry are essentially price takers.

*Prisoners' dilemma* is a model used to analyze oligopoly output restrictions. It implies that the best course of action for each firm in a collusive agreement is to cheat, regardless of whether the other firm honors the agreement or not.

## MARKETS FOR FACTORS OF PRODUCTION
Cross-Reference to CFA Institute Assigned Reading #21

*Marginal revenue* is the addition to total revenue from selling one more unit of output. *Marginal revenue product* is the addition to total revenue gained by selling the additional output from employing one more unit of a productive resource (input).

### Labor Demand

A firm will hire additional units of labor until the marginal revenue product of labor equals its price in order to maximize profits. An increase (decrease) in the price of the firm's output will increase (decrease) its demand for labor. An increase (decrease) in the price of a factor of production that is a substitute for labor will increase (decrease) demand for labor. An increase (decrease) in the price of a factor of production that is a complement to labor will decrease (increase) demand for labor. Demand for labor is more elastic in the long run than in the short run.

### Labor Supply

The labor supply has increased over time as the accumulation of capital goods in the home has allowed more people to work outside the home. The *supply (curve) of labor* depends on the size of the adult working-age population while the *quantity of labor supplied* depends on the wage rate. Since a worker who is supplying an hour of work is giving up an hour of leisure, we can view the wage rate as either the payment for supplying labor or as the opportunity cost of consuming more leisure. If the wage rate increases, there is a substitution effect to consume less leisure because the opportunity cost of leisure is increased. A wage increase also has an income effect because increases in incomes cause workers to consume more leisure. The effects are in opposite directions and either one can dominate the other.

### Labor Unions

Unionized workers bargain for wages as a group (collective bargaining). The effect of collective bargaining is to restrict the supply of labor and increase compensation compared to what it would be without the union, so that wages are higher and fewer workers are employed.

Unions can offset part of this reduction in labor employed by increasing the demand for union labor. Strategies to achieve this include:

- Increasing the marginal product of labor through increased training.
- Using advertising to increase the demand for union-made products.

©2011 Kaplan, Inc.

- Advocating trade restrictions on foreign goods that compete with union-made domestic goods.
- Reducing the supply or increasing the price of substitutes for union labor (higher minimum wages, immigration restrictions).

## Monopsony Labor Markets

A monopsony market is one with a single buyer. Monopsony in the labor market results when there is only one major employer in a geographic area. Because the marginal cost of an additional worker is greater than the wage rate offered, a monopsonist will employ less labor than in a competitive labor market, and at a wage lower than the equilibrium wage rate in a competitive labor market.

In sum, both labor unions and monopsonist employers reduce the quantity of labor employed, compared to competitive labor markets. Union bargaining results in a higher wage rate than a competitive market, while monopsony results in a lower wage rate. If a union bargains collectively with a monopsonist employer, the resulting wage will be between these higher and lower wage rates.

## Physical and Financial Capital

*Physical capital* is a firm's physical assets (plant, property, equipment, and inventory). The greater the demand for physical capital, the greater the demand for financial capital to purchase it. A firm will employ physical capital until its marginal revenue product is equal to the cost to the firm of the financial capital required to purchase it. At higher (lower) interest rates, firms demand less (more) financial capital. Financial capital is supplied by savings. Savings increase when interest rates and current incomes increase, and decrease when expected future incomes increase.

## Renewable and Non-renewable Resources

*Renewable resource* (e.g., water): Supply is perfectly inelastic (vertical) and price is determined by demand.

*Non-renewable resource* (e.g., oil): Supply is perfectly elastic (horizontal), quantity supplied is determined by demand, and current price is the present value of the expected price next period.

## Economic Rent and Opportunity Cost

*Economic rent* is the difference between what a worker earns and his opportunity cost. *Opportunity cost* of a worker is what he could earn in his next highest paying employment.

## MONITORING JOBS AND THE PRICE LEVEL
Cross-Reference to CFA Institute Assigned Reading #22

## Key Labor Market Indicators

- *Rate of unemployment.* Number of unemployed divided by number in labor force.
- *Labor-force participation rate.* Civilian labor force divided by civilian population age 16 or older.
- *Employment-to-population ratio.* Percentage of working-age population who are employed.
- *Aggregate hours.* Total hours worked in a year by all employed people.
- *Real wage rate.* Money wages adjusted for changes in the price level.

## Three Types of Unemployment

1. *Frictional unemployment* results from constant changes in the economy that prevent *qualified* workers from being matched with existing job openings in a timely manner.

2. *Structural unemployment* is caused by structural changes in the economy that eliminate some jobs while generating job openings for which unemployed workers are not qualified. Structural unemployment differs from frictional unemployment in that workers do not currently have the skills needed to perform the newly created jobs.

3. *Cyclical unemployment* is caused by a change in the general level of economic activity. When the economy is operating at *less than* full capacity, positive levels of cyclical unemployment will be present. At levels above full capacity, negative cyclical unemployment can exist in the short run.

# Inflation

*Inflation* is a protracted period of rising prices. The rate of inflation is the rate of change in a price index over a given period of time:

$$\text{inflation rate} = \frac{\text{this year's price index} - \text{last year's price index}}{\text{last year's price index}}$$

The consumer price index (CPI) is the best known indicator of U.S. inflation. The CPI is believed to overstate inflation by about 1% per year because the CPI does not account for quality improvements in or substitution between goods.

## AGGREGATE SUPPLY AND AGGREGATE DEMAND
Cross-Reference to CFA Institute Assigned Reading #23

*Short-run aggregate supply* (SAS) is a function of the price level—higher prices bring greater supply because in the short run we hold workers' inflation expectations constant. *Long-run aggregate supply* (LAS) is potential GDP, the full-employment real output of the economy.

LAS increases (decreases) with increases (decreases) in:

- Quantity of labor in the economy.
- Quantity of capital in the economy.
- Technology the economy possesses.

The *aggregate demand curve* shows the relation between the price level and the real quantity of final goods and services demanded. It has four components:

1. Consumption.
2. Investment.
3. Government spending.
4. Net exports (exports minus imports).

Three factors that affect aggregate demand are:

1. Expectations about incomes, inflation, and profits.
2. Fiscal and monetary policy.
3. The growth rate of the world economy.

## Short-Run and Long-Run Equilibrium

The economy is in long-run equilibrium at the price level where the aggregate demand curve intersects the LAS curve. At a higher price level there is excess supply and downward pressure on production and prices. At a lower price level there is excess demand and upward pressure on production and prices.

The economy can be in short-run equilibrium at a level of output above or below full-employment GDP (or LAS). If this occurs below full employment GDP, the economy is in recession and will experience downward pressure on wages and prices. If short-run equilibrium occurs above full employment GDP, real output is temporarily greater than full-employment GDP, and the economy will experience inflationary pressure on wages and prices. The changes in money wages (and other resource prices) cause SAS to shift, bringing the economy back to long-run equilibrium.

### Figure 5: Long-Run Disequilibrium

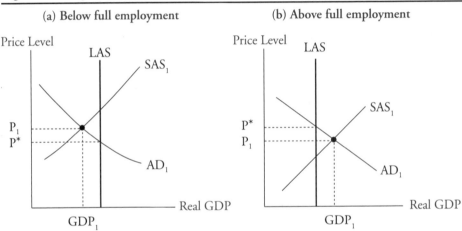

## Main Schools of Macroeconomic Thought

- *Classical:* Shifts in aggregate supply and demand are driven by changes in technology. Adjustment of money wages restores long-run equilibrium quickly. Taxes are the primary impediment to long-run equilibrium at full-employment GDP.
- *Keynesian:* Shifts in aggregate demand are caused by changes in expectations. Wages are "downward sticky" so SAS adjusts slowly to bring the economy from recession to long-run equilibrium. Recommend increasing aggregate demand directly through fiscal or monetary policy.
- *Monetarist:* Unpredictable changes in monetary policy are the primary cause of deviations from full-employment GDP. Recommend steady predictable increases in the money supply and low marginal tax rates to keep prices stable and to maximize real GDP growth.

# STUDY SESSION 6: ECONOMICS—MONETARY AND FISCAL ECONOMICS

The macroeconomics material is not that difficult, but exam questions may require that you identify the effect of a policy change on some economic variable. The effect may be indirect—you might have to reason out how the policy change would affect overall economic conditions and how those conditions would affect the variable in question, employment for example.

## MONEY, THE PRICE LEVEL, AND INFLATION
Cross-Reference to CFA Institute Assigned Reading #24

### Functions of Money

*   Medium of exchange.
*   Unit of account.
*   Store of value.

### Money Supply Measures

M1 refers to all currency not held at banks, travelers' checks, and checking account deposits of individuals and firms. M2 refers to M1 plus time deposits, savings deposits, and money-market mutual fund balances.

Checks represent a claim to a component of M1 (checking accounts) and credit card purchasing power is simply the ability to borrow money, so neither is counted as an additional part of the money supply.

### Functions of Depository Institutions

*   *Create liquidity*. Use short-term deposits to make long-term loans.
*   *Act as financial intermediaries*. Lend at lower cost than borrowers could achieve by seeking out individual lenders.
*   *Pool default risks*. Hold a portfolio of loans and monitor their risks.

### Money Creation with a Fractional Reserve Banking System

With a fractional reserve system of banking, banks must keep a minimum percentage of depositors' money as reserves. A bank's **reserves** consist of the currency and coins that it holds and its deposits with the Federal Reserve. The ratio of a bank's reserves to its total deposits is its **reserve ratio**.

When a bank's **actual reserve ratio** is greater than its **desired reserve ratio**, it is said to have **excess reserves** and will seek to make more loans.

The **monetary base** consists of currency and coins in circulation plus banks' deposits with the Federal Reserve. Because the desired reserve ratio is less than one, an increase in the monetary base will result in a larger increase in the money supply, by a factor called the **money multiplier**. We can describe this relationship simply as:

$$\Delta \text{ money supply} = \Delta \text{ monetary base} \times \text{money multiplier}$$

Consider a case where a bank with a desired reserve ratio of 10% has excess reserves and makes a loan equal to 90% of these excess reserves. Subsequently, the loan proceeds are deposited into a bank that loans out 90% of that amount, which is deposited in a bank that loans out 90% of that amount, and so on. Assuming the maximum effect of these transactions, the money multiplier is:

1 / desired reserve ratio = 1 / 10% = 10

Since borrowers, on average, choose to hold some cash as well as bank deposits, there is a **currency drain**, which reduces the money multiplier. Given the desired reserve ratio and the **currency drain ratio** (equal to the ratio of currency held outside the banking system to deposits), we can express the money multiplier as:

$$\text{money multiplier} = \frac{1+c}{d+c}$$

where:
$c$ = currency as a percentage of deposits
$d$ = desired reserve ratio

Note that the lower the desired reserve ratio and the lower the currency drain, the greater is the money multiplier.

## Federal Reserve Policy Tools

- *Discount rate.* The rate at which banks can borrow reserves from the Fed. Lower discount rates tend to increase the money supply and decrease interest rates; higher rates tend to decrease the money supply and increase interest rates.
- *Reserve requirement.* Higher percentage reduces the money supply and increases interest rates; lower percentage increases the money supply and decreases interest rates.
- *Open market operations.* Fed buying and selling of Treasury securities. Fed purchases increase cash available for lending, decreasing interest rates. Fed sales remove cash, increasing interest rates.

## The Fed's Balance Sheet

- *Assets:* Primarily Treasury securities, but also gold, deposits with other central banks, IMF special drawing rights, loans to banks at the discount rate.
- *Liabilities:* U.S. currency in circulation; bank reserve deposits.

## What Determines the Demand for Money?

- *Interest rates.* Most critical.
- *Inflation.* Increases the demand for nominal money.
- *Real GDP growth.* Also increases the demand for money (nominal and real).

## Supply of Money

The supply of money is determined by the central bank and is independent of the interest rate. The supply curve is vertical:

### Figure 6: Supply and Demand for Money

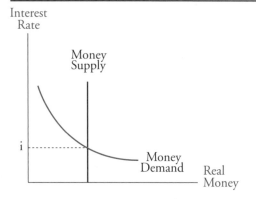

## Quantity Theory of Money: Implications for Inflation

**Equation of exchange:** MV = PY must hold by definition.

money supply × velocity = price level × real output

*Velocity* is the average number of times per year each dollar is used to buy goods and services (velocity = GDP / money).

If we assume that velocity and real output don't change all that much, the equation of exchange leads us to the *quantity theory of money: an increase in the money supply will cause a proportional increase in prices*. We can refine this to: growth in the money supply in excess of the growth rate of real GDP is inflationary.

## U.S. Inflation, Unemployment, and Business Cycles
Cross-Reference to CFA Institute Assigned Reading #25

*Demand-pull inflation* results from increases in aggregate demand that increase equilibrium GDP above full-employment GDP in the short run. Unemployment falls below its natural rate, leading to upward pressure on real wages. Increasing real wages shift (decrease) short-run aggregate supply, resulting in a new equilibrium at full-employment GDP and a higher price level. Demand-pull inflation will continue only if the government continues the fiscal or monetary policies that are increasing aggregate demand.

*Cost-push inflation* results from unexpected increases in the real price of factor inputs such as wages or energy. Short-run aggregate supply decreases (shifts up and to the left), which results in short-run equilibrium below full-employment GDP and with a higher price level. If the government responds with monetary or fiscal policy that increases aggregate demand, equilibrium GDP can be increased to full-employment GDP, but at a still higher price level. Sustained cost-push inflation happens when input costs continue to increase and the government continues to make policy changes that further increase aggregate demand, as occurred when oil prices underwent sustained increases in the 1970s.

### Inflation and Unemployment

In the short run, unanticipated increases (decreases) in actual inflation coincide with decreases (increases) in unemployment. This relationship is illustrated by the *short-run Phillips curve*, which is constructed holding workers' inflation expectations constant. In the long run, expected and actual inflation are equal and the economy reaches equilibrium at the natural rate of unemployment so that the long-run Phillips curve is vertical at full-employment real GDP.

In the following figure, Point 1 (Point 2) represents a short-run equilibrium with less (more) unemployment when actual inflation is greater (less) than expected.

©2011 Kaplan, Inc.

## Figure 7: Long-Run and Short-Run Phillips Curve

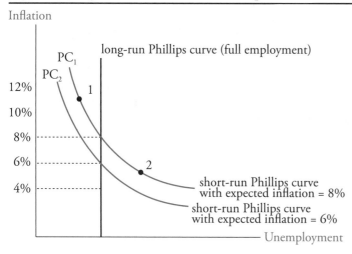

## Business Cycles

A business cycle is characterized by fluctuations in economic activity and has two phases (contraction and expansion) and two turning points (trough and peak).

Key variables used to determine the phase of cycle are:

*   Real GDP.
*   Real income.
*   Employment.
*   Industrial production.
*   Wholesale-retail sales.

## Figure 8: Phases of the Business Cycle

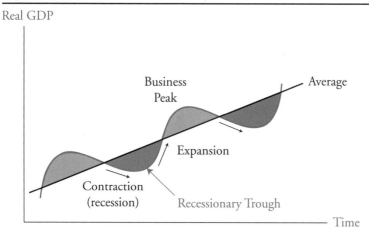

## Business Cycle Theories

Mainstream business cycle theories, which include the classical, Keynesian, and monetarist schools of thought, hold that business cycles are caused by variations in aggregate demand, while long-run aggregate supply (potential GDP) increases at a fairly stable rate over time. An alternative view, called *real business cycle theory*, proposes that the growth rate of potential GDP fluctuates in response to fluctuations in the rate of technological change and its impact on labor productivity, which increases rapidly over some periods and more slowly over others.

## FISCAL POLICY
Cross-Reference to CFA Institute Assigned Reading #26

The effects of changes in fiscal policy (changes in taxes and changes in government expenditures) on aggregate supply are referred to as *supply-side effects*. Both an increase in taxes on expenditures and an increase in income taxes can cause consumers to supply less labor, since the goods and services obtained for an hour's labor are decreased in either case. A decrease in labor supplied reduces aggregate supply, real GDP, and potential real GDP.

The *Laffer curve* illustrates the relation between tax rates and total taxes collected. It shows that tax revenues will initially increase with an increase in the tax rate, but will reach a maximum at some tax rate, and then decrease as the reduction in tax revenue from the decrease in economic activity at higher tax rates outweighs any increase in revenues from the increase in the tax rate.

**Figure 9: Laffer Curve**

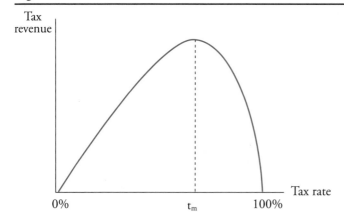

©2011 Kaplan, Inc.

Higher taxes on capital income result in lower private savings, making less capital available for investment and reducing potential real GDP and the growth rate of real GDP.

## Sources of Investment Financing

- National savings.
- Borrowing from foreigners.
- Government savings.

The *crowding-out effect* occurs when budget deficits and the consequent government borrowing (negative government savings) caused by expansionary fiscal policy lead to higher interest rates and lower private investment. Government borrowing increases demand for loanable funds, which increases real interest rates, in turn reducing profitability of investment projects. The effect reduces the impact of the expansionary fiscal policy on aggregate demand.

## Generational Effects of Fiscal Policy

The difference between the present value of future benefits promised to voters (such as Medicare insurance in the United States) and the currently collected taxes is referred to as a *generational imbalance*. The *generational effects* of such an imbalance are that workers in a future generation must either pay higher taxes or accept large cuts in government spending (services) in order to make up for the current imbalance.

## Fiscal Multipliers

When government expenditures are increased, aggregate demand and GDP increase by some multiple of the expenditure increase, as wages and payments received by workers and capital owners lead to future increases in aggregate expenditures. This is referred to as the *expenditures (government purchases) multiplier*. When taxes are increased, the resulting decrease in consumption expenditures is also subject to a *tax multiplier effect* as decreases in consumption decrease others' incomes. Since the expenditures multiplier is stronger (greater) than the tax multiplier, an equal increase in both taxes and expenditures (a balanced budget increase) will tend to increase GDP. Because of this, we say the *balanced budget multiplier* is positive.

## Discretionary Fiscal Policy

During recessions, governments can increase spending, reduce taxes, or both, to stimulate aggregate demand. During inflationary booms, they can reduce spending and/or increase taxes to reduce aggregate demand.

Discretionary fiscal policy has multiplier effects:

- *Government purchases multiplier.* A dollar of government spending causes more than a $1 increase in aggregate demand.
- *Tax multiplier.* Tax cuts also have magnified effects on aggregate demand, but less so than government purchases because some of the tax cut is saved instead of spent.
- *Balanced budget multiplier.* If a combined program of government purchases and taxes keeps the budget in balance, the multiplier effect from government purchases will be stronger than the multiplier effect from taxes. An increase in spending coupled with an equal increase in taxes will have a positive effect on aggregate demand.

## Importance of Timing in Fiscal Policy

Know these three time lags:

1. *Recognition delay.* Time it takes policymakers to recognize that a policy change is necessary.

2. *Administrative or law-making delay.* Time lag between policy recognition and final passage of law or policy change.

3. *Impact delay.* Time lag between passage of the law or policy and when its impact is felt in the economy.

## Automatic Stabilizers

*Automatic stabilizers* are built-in fiscal devices that ensure deficits in a recession and surpluses during booms. Automatic stabilizers minimize the problem of proper timing. There are two main automatic stabilizers:

1. *Induced taxes.* People drop from the tax rolls during downturns and are added to tax rolls (or enter higher brackets) during booms. Less tax is collected from businesses during economic downturns.

2. *Needs-tested spending.* More money is paid out as more people become unemployed.

# Monetary Policy; An Overview of Central Banks
Cross-Reference to CFA Institute Assigned Readings #27 and 28

The goals set for the U.S. Federal Reserve are to: (1) achieve maximum sustainable output and employment, (2) maintain a stable price level, and (3) maintain moderate long-term interest rates.

The Fed is to achieve these goals by managing the growth rate of the money supply and credit aggregates in line with the growth rate of potential GDP (full-employment GDP). With a target inflation rate of 1% to 2%, the growth rate of monetary aggregates is targeted at 1% to 2% above the growth rate of potential GDP.

The Fed operationalizes these goals by focusing on differences between actual and target inflation rates and between actual and potential GDP. When a change in policy is called for, the Fed either decreases or increases the target federal funds rate by increasing or decreasing the money supply, respectively.

## The Fed's Decision-Making Strategies

The *Taylor rule* is an *instrument rule* based on a target federal funds (overnight) rate that is given as:

target FFR = 2% + actual inflation + 0.5(actual inflation − 2%) + 0.5(output gap)

where 2% is the target inflation rate and the output gap is the difference between actual and potential GDP growth rates.

In contrast to an instrument rule, a *targeting rule* is based on expected inflation. The target FFR is set to the rate that results in an expected rate of inflation equal to the policy makers' target rate.

Under either type of policy rule, the Fed uses *open market operations* as its primary tool to implement policy changes, selling (buying) government securities to decrease (increase) bank reserves, bank lending activity, and the money supply.

## Monetary Policy Transmission Mechanism

Considering the case of a recessionary gap (actual GDP growth less than potential GDP growth) and a resulting policy decision to increase the growth rate of the money supply to increase aggregate demand, the transmission mechanism is as follows:

- Purchases of U.S. Treasury securities increase bank reserves and the willingness of banks to lend, which leads to a decrease in the federal funds rate.
- Other short-term rates fall as a result, as do longer-term rates as long as the premium for expected inflation does not increase.
- The decline in (real) interest rates increases aggregate demand in three ways:
  1. Businesses increase investment spending.
  2. Consumers increase spending on durable goods.
  3. Decreased real rates lead to depreciation of the domestic currency, which increases net exports.

Two types of potential problems with this transmission mechanism are:

1. A loose link between short-term rates, over which the Fed has control, and longer-term rates, which depend on inflationary expectations.

2. Time lags between policy actions and their effects on the economy.

## Alternative Monetary Policy Strategies

The actions of the U.S. Fed seem to conform closely to those suggested by a Taylor rule. Alternative policy strategies include:

1. The *McCallum rule* focuses on a steady growth rate of the monetary base, but fluctuations in the demand for money can lead to fluctuations in interest rates and aggregate demand.

2. A rule targeting the growth rate of the money supply can lead to volatility of interest rates and aggregate demand due to fluctuations in money demand and velocity.

3. A policy which targets a constant foreign exchange rate essentially constrains monetary policy to match that of an exchange partner.

4. Many countries use inflation rate targeting, with results that may or may not be better than those from the Fed's historical policy strategy.

Those countries that use inflation targeting typically set the target rate at 2%, with an acceptable range of 1% to 3%. Various inflation measures are used, including a *core inflation* measure that excludes volatile components such as food and energy. While central bank mandates differ across countries, stable prices are the primary goal and often specific targets are prescribed.

Management of the short-term interbank lending rate is the most often used monetary policy tool. The equivalent of the U.S. federal funds rate is termed the overnight rate, repurchase rate, repo rate, and cash rate in various countries.

Other, less used, tools that central banks can use to manage the money supply are the rate at which it will lend reserves to banks (*discount rate*) and the *reserve requirement* for banks, the percentage of deposits that banks must not lend out (must keep as reserves). Decreasing the discount rate or the reserve requirement will tend to increase the money supply, decrease interest rates, and stimulate aggregate demand.

# FINANCIAL REPORTING AND ANALYSIS

Study Sessions 7, 8, 9, & 10

| | |
|---|---|
| Approximate Weight on Exam | 20% |
| SchweserNotes™ Reference | Book 3, Pages 1–322 |

## STUDY SESSION 7: FINANCIAL REPORTING AND ANALYSIS—AN INTRODUCTION

Study Session 7 introduces the sources of financial information on which an analyst can draw when making investment recommendations. This session outlines the basic principles of recording financial transactions and events and discusses the role of standard setting bodies in determining how transactions and events should be recorded.

## FINANCIAL STATEMENT ANALYSIS: AN INTRODUCTION
Cross-Reference to CFA Institute Assigned Reading #29

The **income statement** reports on the financial performance of the firm over a period of time. The elements of the income statement include revenues, expenses, gains, and losses.

- *Revenues* are inflows from delivering or producing goods, rendering services, or other activities that constitute the entity's ongoing major or central operations.
- *Expenses* are outflows from delivering or producing goods or services that constitute the entity's ongoing major or central operations.
- *Gains and losses* are increases (decreases) in equity or net assets from peripheral or incidental transactions.

The **balance sheet** reports the firm's financial position at a point in time. The balance sheet consists of three elements:

1. *Assets* are probable current and future economic benefits obtained or controlled by a particular entity as a result of past transactions or events.

2. *Liabilities* are probable future sacrifices of economic benefits. They arise from present obligations of a particular entity to transfer assets or provide services to other entities in the future as a result of past transactions or events.

3. *Owners' equity* is the residual interest in the assets of an entity that remains after deducting its liabilities.

©2011 Kaplan, Inc.

Transactions are measured so that the fundamental accounting equation holds:

$$\text{assets} = \text{liabilities} + \text{owners' equity}$$

The **cash flow statement** reports the company's cash receipts and outflows. These cash flows are classified as follows:

- *Operating cash flows* include the cash effects of transactions that involve the normal business of the firm.
- *Investing cash flows* are those resulting from acquisition or sale of property, plant, and equipment, of a subsidiary or segment, and purchase or sale of investments in other firms.
- *Financing cash flows* are those resulting from issuance or retirement of debt and equity securities and dividends paid to stockholders.

The **statement of changes in owners' equity** reports the amounts and sources of changes in equity investors' investment in the firm.

**Financial statement notes** (footnotes) include disclosures that offer further detail about the information summarized in the financial statements. Footnotes allow users to improve their assessments of the amount, timing, and uncertainty of the estimates reported in the financial statements. Footnotes:

- Provide information about accounting methods and the assumptions and estimates used by management.
- Are audited, whereas other disclosures, such as supplementary schedules, are not audited.
- Provide additional information on such items as fixed assets, inventory, income taxes, pensions, debt, contingencies and commitments, marketable securities, significant customers, sales to related parties, and export sales.
- Often contain disclosures relating to contingent losses.

**Supplementary schedules** contain additional information. Examples of such disclosures are:

- Operating income or sales by region or business segment.
- Reserves for an oil and gas company.
- Information about hedging activities and financial instruments.

**Management's Discussion and Analysis** (MD&A) provides an assessment of the financial performance and condition of a company from the perspective of its management. For publicly held companies in the United States, the MD&A is required to discuss:

- Results from operations, with a discussion of trends in sales and expenses.
- Discussion of significant effects of currently known trends, events, and uncertainties (may voluntarily disclose forward-looking data).

- Capital resources and liquidity, with a discussion of trends in cash flows.
- A general business overview based on known trends.

Management's Discussion and Analysis can also include the following:

- Discontinued operations, extraordinary items, and other unusual or infrequent events.
- Extensive disclosures in interim financial statements.
- Disclosures of a segment's need for cash flows or contribution to revenues or profit.

## Audit Reports

An **audit** is an independent review of an entity's financial statements. Public accountants conduct audits and examine the financial reports and supporting records. The objective of an audit is to enable the auditor to provide an opinion on the fairness and reliability of the financial reports.

The independent certified public accountant employed by the board of directors is responsible for seeing that the financial statements conform to Generally Accepted Accounting Principles (GAAP). The auditor examines the company's accounting and internal control systems, confirms assets and liabilities, and generally tries to be confident that there are no material errors in the financial statements and that they conform to applicable reporting standards. The auditor's report is an important source of information.

The **standard auditor's opinion** contains three parts, stating that:

1. Whereas the financial statements are prepared by management and are its responsibility, the auditor has performed an independent review.
2. Generally accepted auditing standards were followed, thus providing *reasonable assurance* that the financial statements contain no material errors.
3. The auditor is satisfied that the statements were prepared in accordance with GAAP and that the accounting principles chosen and estimates made are reasonable. The auditor's report must also contain additional explanation when accounting methods have not been used consistently between periods.

An *unqualified opinion* indicates that the auditor believes the statements are free from material omissions and errors. If the statements make any exceptions to GAAP, the auditor may issue a *qualified opinion* and explain these exceptions in the audit report. The auditor can issue an *adverse opinion* if the statements are not presented fairly or are materially nonconforming with GAAP.

The auditor's opinion will also contain an explanatory paragraph when a material loss is probable but the amount cannot be reasonably estimated. These "uncertainties" may relate to the *going concern assumption* (financial statements assume the firm will continue to operate), the valuation or realization of assets, or to litigation. This type of disclosure may be a signal of serious problems and call for closer examination by the analyst.

Under U.S. GAAP, the auditor must state an opinion on the company's **internal controls**, the processes by which the company ensures that it presents accurate financial statements. Internal controls are the responsibility of the firm's management. Under the Sarbanes-Oxley Act, management is required to provide a report on the company's internal control system that includes the following elements:

- A statement that the firm's management is responsible for implementing and maintaining effective internal controls.
- A description of how management evaluates the internal control system.
- An assessment by management of the effectiveness over the most recent year of the firm's internal controls.
- A statement that the firm's auditors have assessed management's report on internal controls.
- A statement certifying that the firm's financial statements are presented fairly.

An analyst should examine a company's *quarterly or semiannual reports* which typically update the major financial statements and footnotes, but are not necessarily audited.

## Other Information Sources

Securities and Exchange Commission filings are available from EDGAR (Electronic Data Gathering, Analysis, and Retrieval System, *www.sec.gov*). These include Form 8-K, which a company must file to report events, such as acquisitions and disposals of major assets, or changes in its management or corporate governance. Companies' annual and quarterly financial statements are also filed with the SEC (Form 10-K and Form 10-Q respectively).

**Proxy statements** are issued to shareholders when there are matters that require a shareholder vote. These statements, which are also filed with the SEC and available from EDGAR, are a good source of information about the election of (and qualifications of) board members, compensation, management qualifications, and the issuance of stock options.

*Corporate reports and press releases* are written by management and are often viewed as public relations or sales materials. Not all of the material is independently reviewed by outside auditors. Such information can often be found on the company's Web site.

An analyst should also review information on the economy and the company's industry and compare the company to its competitors. This information can be acquired from sources such as trade journals, statistical reporting services, and government agencies.

The **financial statement analysis framework**[1] consists of six steps:
1. State the objective and context.
2. Gather data.
3. Process the data.
4. Analyze and interpret the data.
5. Report the conclusions or recommendations.
6. Update the analysis.

# FINANCIAL REPORTING MECHANICS
Cross-Reference to CFA Institute Assigned Reading #30

**Financial statement elements** are the major classifications of assets, liabilities, owners' equity, revenues, and expenses. **Accounts** are the specific records within each element where specific transactions are entered. **Contra accounts** are used for entries that offset other accounts.

**Assets** are the firm's economic resources. Examples of assets include the following:

- *Cash and cash equivalents.* Risk-free securities with original maturities of 90 days or less.
- *Accounts receivable.* Accounts receivable often have an "allowance for bad debt expense" as a contra account.
- *Inventories.*
- *Financial assets* such as marketable securities.
- *Prepaid expenses.* Items that will show up on future income statements as expenses.
- *Property, plant, and equipment.* Includes a contra-asset account for accumulated depreciation.
- *Investment in affiliates* accounted for using the equity method.
- *Deferred tax assets.*
- *Intangible assets.* Economic resources of the firm that do not have a physical form, such as patents, trademarks, licenses, and goodwill.

---

1   Hennie Van Greunung and Sonja Brajovic Bratanovic, *Analyzing and Managing Banking Risk: Framework for Assessing Corporate Governance and Financial Risk,* International Bank for Reconstruction and Development, April 2003, p. 300.

**Liabilities** are claims that creditors have on the company's resources. Examples of liabilities include the following:

- Accounts payable and trade payables.
- Financial liabilities such as short-term notes payable.
- Unearned revenue. Items that will show up on future income statements as revenues.
- Income taxes payable. The taxes accrued during the past year but not yet paid.
- Long-term debt such as bonds payable.
- Deferred tax liabilities.

**Owners' equity** is the claim that the firm's owners have on its resources, which is the amount by which assets exceed liabilities. Owners' equity includes the following:

- *Capital.* Par value of common stock.
- *Additional paid-in capital.* Proceeds from common stock sales above par value. (Share repurchases that the company has made are represented in the contra account *Treasury stock.*)
- *Retained earnings.* Cumulative income that has not been distributed as dividends.
- *Other comprehensive income.* Changes in carrying amounts of assets and liabilities.

**Revenue** represents inflows of economic resources and includes the following:

- *Sales.* Revenue from the firm's day-to-day activities.
- *Gains.* Increases in assets or equity from transactions incidental to the firm's day-to-day activities.
- *Investment income* such as interest and dividend income.

**Expenses** are outflows of economic resources and include the following:

- *Cost of goods sold.*
- *Selling, general, and administrative expenses.* These include such expenses as advertising, salaries, rent, and utilities.
- *Depreciation* and *amortization.*
- *Tax expense.*
- *Interest expense.*
- *Losses.* Decreases in assets or equity from transactions incidental to the firm's day-to-day activities.

## The Accounting Equation

The basic accounting equation (what balances in a balance sheet):

assets = liabilities + owners' equity

The expanded accounting equation shows the components of owners' equity:

assets = liabilities + contributed capital + ending retained earnings

The expanded accounting equation can also be stated as:

assets  = liabilities
+ contributed capital
+ beginning retained earnings
+ revenue
− expenses
− dividends

Keeping the accounting equation in balance requires **double-entry accounting**, in which a transaction has to be recorded in at least two accounts. An increase in an asset account, for example, must be balanced by a decrease in another asset account or by an increase in a liability or owners' equity account.

## Accruals and Adjustments

Revenues and expenses are not always recorded at the same time cash changes hands. The principle of **accrual accounting** requires that revenue is recorded when the firm earns it, and expenses are recorded when the firm incurs them, regardless of whether cash has actually been paid. Accruals fall into four categories:

1. *Unearned revenue:* Cash increases and a liability for the goods or services the firm must provide in the future is recorded in the same amount.
2. *Accrued revenue:* Revenue is recorded for credit sales, accounts receivable increases, and inventory decreases.
3. *Prepaid expenses:* Cash decreases and an asset (prepaid expenses) increases. The asset decreases and expenses increase when the expense is actually incurred.
4. *Accrued expenses:* The firm owes cash for expenses it has incurred but has not paid. A liability for accrued expenses, such as wages payable, increases.

With unearned revenue and prepaid expenses, cash changes hands first and the revenue or expense is recorded later. With accrued revenue and accrued expenses, the revenue or expense is recorded first. In all these cases, the effect of accrual accounting is to recognize revenues or expenses in the appropriate period.

Most assets are recorded on the financial statements at their historical cost. In some cases, however, accounting standards require balance sheet values of certain assets to reflect their current market values. Accounting entries that update these assets' values are called **valuation adjustments**. To keep the accounting equation in balance, changes in asset values are also changes in owners' equity, through gains or losses on the income statement or in other comprehensive income.

Information flows through an accounting system in four steps:

1. *Journal entries* record every transaction, showing which accounts are changed by what amounts.
2. The *general ledger* sorts the journal entries by account.
3. At the end of the accounting period, an *initial trial balance* is prepared that shows the balances in each account. If any adjusting entries are needed, they will be recorded and reflected in an *adjusted trial balance*.
4. The account balances from the adjusted trial balance are presented in the financial statements.

An analyst doesn't have access to the detailed information that flows through a company's accounting system, but only sees the financial statements. The analyst needs to understand the various accruals, adjustments, and management assumptions that went into the financial statements. These are often explained in the footnotes to the statements and in Management's Discussion and Analysis.

Because these adjustments and assumptions are to some extent at the discretion of management, the possibility exists that management may manipulate or misrepresent the company's financial performance and/or condition.

## FINANCIAL REPORTING STANDARDS
Cross-Reference to CFA Institute Assigned Reading #31

Given the variety and complexity of possible transactions, and the estimates and assumptions a firm must make when presenting its performance, financial statements could potentially take any form if reporting standards didn't exist. Reporting standards ensure that the information is "useful to a wide range of users," including security analysts, by making financial statements comparable to one another and narrowing the range within which management's estimates can be seen as reasonable.

**Standard-setting bodies** are professional organizations of accountants and auditors that establish financial reporting standards. **Regulatory authorities** are government agencies that have the legal authority to enforce compliance with financial reporting standards.

The two primary standard-setting bodies are the *Financial Accounting Standards Board* (FASB) and the *International Accounting Standards Board* (IASB). In the United States, the FASB sets forth Generally Accepted Accounting Principles (U.S. GAAP). Outside the United States, the IASB establishes International Financial Reporting Standards (IFRS). Many national standard-setting bodies, including the FASB, are working toward convergence with IFRS.

Regulatory authorities, such as the *Securities and Exchange Commission* (SEC) in the United States and the *Financial Services Authority* (FSA) in the United Kingdom, are established by national governments to enforce accounting standards.

Most national authorities belong to the *International Organization of Securities Commissions* (IOSCO). Because of the increasing globalization of securities markets, IOSCO is seeking to attain uniform financial regulations across countries.

## Barriers to Developing a Single Set of Standards

One barrier to developing one universally accepted set of accounting standards (referred to as convergence) is simply that different standard-setting bodies and the regulatory authorities of different countries disagree on what the best treatment of the item or issue is. Other barriers result from the political pressures that regulatory bodies face from business groups and others that will be affected by changes in their reporting standards.

The ideas on which the IASB bases its standards are expressed in its "Framework for the Preparation and Presentation of Financial Statements." The IASB framework details the objective of financial statements, defines the qualitative characteristics they should have, and specifies the reporting elements that are required. The framework also notes certain constraints and assumptions that are involved in financial statement preparation.

The objective of financial reporting according to the IFRS framework is "to provide information about the financial position, performance, and changes in financial position of an entity; this information should be useful to a wide range of users for the purpose of making economic decisions." Stated another way, the objective of financial statements is the fair presentation of a company's financial performance.

# Qualitative Characteristics

To meet the objectives of fairness and usefulness, financial statements should be the following.

*Understandable.* Users with a basic knowledge of business and accounting, and who make a reasonable effort to study the financial statements, should be able to readily understand the information they present.

*Relevant.* Financial statements are relevant if the information in them can influence users' economic decisions or affect users' evaluations of past events or forecasts of future events. To be relevant, information should also be timely and sufficiently detailed.

*Reliable.* Information is reliable if it reflects economic reality, is unbiased, and is free of material errors. Specific factors that support reliability include the following:

- *Faithful representation* of transactions and events.
- *Substance over form*, presenting not only the legal form of a transaction or event, but its economic reality.
- *Neutrality* (i.e., absence of bias).
- *Prudence* and conservatism in making estimates.
- *Completeness*, within the limits of cost and materiality.

*Comparable.* Financial statement presentations should be consistent among firms and across time periods.

# Constraints and Assumptions

One of the constraints on financial statement preparation is the need to balance reliability, in the sense of being free of error, with the timeliness that makes the information relevant. Cost is also a constraint; the benefit that users gain from the information should be greater than the cost of presenting it. A third constraint is the fact that intangible and non-quantifiable information cannot be captured directly in financial statements.

The two primary assumptions that underlie financial statements are the accrual basis and the going concern assumption. The accrual basis requires that revenue be recognized when earned and expenses recognized when incurred, regardless of when cash is actually paid. The going concern assumption presumes that the company will continue to operate for the foreseeable future.

## Required Financial Statements

The *required financial statements* are as follows:

- Balance sheet.
- Statement of comprehensive income.
- Cash flow statement.
- Statement of changes in owners' equity.
- Explanatory notes, including a summary of accounting policies.

The fundamental *principles for preparing financial statements* as stated in IAS No. 1:

- *Fair presentation*—faithfully representing the effects of the entity's transactions and events according to the standards.
- *Going concern basis*—financial statements assume the firm will continue to exist unless its management intends to (or must) liquidate it.
- *Accrual basis*—revenues recognized when earned and expenses recognized when incurred.
- *Consistency*—between periods in how items are presented and classified.
- *Materiality*—financial statements should be free of misstatements or omissions that could influence the decisions of those who use the statements.

Also stated in IAS No. 1 are *principles for presenting financial statements*:

- *Aggregation* of similar items and separation of dissimilar items.
- No *offsetting* of assets against liabilities or income against expenses unless a specific standard permits or requires it.
- Most entities should present a *classified balance sheet* showing current and noncurrent assets and liabilities.
- *Minimum information* is required on the face of each financial statement and in the notes.
- *Comparative information* for prior periods should be included unless a specific standard states otherwise.

## IFRS vs. U.S. GAAP

U.S. GAAP consists of standards issued by the FASB along with numerous other pronouncements and interpretations. Both the IASB and the FASB have frameworks for preparing and presenting financial statements. The two organizations are working toward a common framework, but the two frameworks differ in several aspects at present.

Until these frameworks converge, analysts will need to interpret financial statements that are prepared under different standards. In many cases, however, a company will present a **reconciliation statement** showing what their financial results would have been under an alternative reporting system.

Even when a unified framework emerges, special reporting standards that apply to particular industries (e.g., insurance, banking) will continue to exist.

A *coherent financial reporting framework* is one that fits together logically. Such a framework should be transparent, comprehensive, and consistent.

- *Transparency*—full disclosure and fair presentation reveal the underlying economics of the company to the financial statement user.
- *Comprehensiveness*—all types of transactions that have financial implications should be included, including new kinds that emerge.
- *Consistency*—similar transactions should be accounted for in similar ways across companies, geographic areas, and time periods.

Barriers to creating a coherent financial reporting framework include issues related to valuation, standard setting, and measurement.

- *Valuation*—The different measurement bases for valuation involve a trade-off between relevance and reliability. Bases that require little judgment, such as historical cost, tend to be more reliable, but may be less relevant than a base like fair value that requires more judgment.
- *Standard setting*—Three approaches to standard setting are a "principles-based" approach that relies on a broad framework, a "rules-based" approach that gives specific guidance about how to classify transactions, and an "objectives-oriented" approach that blends the other two approaches. IFRS is largely a principles-based approach. U.S. GAAP has traditionally been more rules-based, but FASB is moving toward an objectives-oriented approach.
- *Measurement*—Another trade-off in financial reporting is between properly valuing the elements at one point in time (as on the balance sheet) and properly valuing the changes between points in time (as on the income statement). An "asset/liability" approach, which standard setters have largely used, focuses on balance sheet valuation. A "revenue/expense" approach would tend to focus on the income statement.

As financial reporting standards continue to evolve, analysts need to monitor how these developments will affect the financial statements they use. An analyst should be aware of new products and innovations in the financial markets that generate new types of transactions. These might not fall neatly into the existing financial reporting standards.

To keep up to date on the evolving standards, an analyst can monitor professional journals and other sources, such as the IASB (*www.iasb.org*) and FASB (*www.fasb.org*) Web sites. CFA Institute produces position papers on financial reporting issues through the CFA Centre for Financial Market Integrity (*www.cfainstitute.org/cfacentre*).

---

An analyst should use the disclosures about financial standards in the footnotes and MD&A to evaluate what policies are discussed, whether they cover all the relevant data in the financial statements, which policies required management to make estimates, and whether the disclosures have changed since the prior period. In disclosing the likely impact of implementing recently issued accounting standards, management can discuss the impact of adopting the standard, conclude that the standard does not apply or will not affect the financial statements materially, or state that they are still evaluating the effects of the new standards.

# STUDY SESSION 8: FINANCIAL REPORTING AND ANALYSIS—THE INCOME STATEMENT, BALANCE SHEET, AND CASH FLOW STATEMENT

## UNDERSTANDING THE INCOME STATEMENT
Cross-Reference to CFA Institute Assigned Reading #32

The income statement reports the revenues and expenses of the firm for a period of time. The income statement is sometimes referred to as the "statement of operations," the "statement of earnings," or the "profit and loss statement (P&L)."

The income statement equation is:

$$revenues - expenses = net\ income$$

**Revenues** are the amounts reported from the sale of goods and services in the normal course of business. **Expenses** are the amounts incurred to generate revenue, such as cost of goods sold, operating expenses, interest, and taxes. Expenses are grouped together by their nature or function.

The income statement also includes **gains and losses**, which result from incidental transactions outside the firm's normal business activities.

## Presentation Formats

A firm can present its income statement using a single-step or multi-step format. In a single-step statement, all revenues are grouped together and all expenses are grouped together. A multi-step format includes subtotals such as gross profit and operating profit.

**Gross profit** is the amount that remains once the cost of a product or service is subtracted from revenue. Subtracting operating expenses, such as selling, general

©2011 Kaplan, Inc.

and administrative expenses, from gross profit results in another subtotal known as **operating profit** or operating income.

For *nonfinancial firms*, operating profit is the amount that remains before financing costs and income taxes are considered. Subtracting interest expense and income taxes from operating profit results in the firm's **net income**, sometimes referred to as "earnings" or the "bottom line." For *financial firms*, interest expense is usually considered an operating expense.

If a firm has a controlling interest in a subsidiary and consolidates the subsidiary's results with its own, the pro-rata share of the subsidiary's income for the portion of the subsidiary that the firm does not own is reported in the firm's income statement as **noncontrolling interest** or **minority owners' interest**.

## General Principles of Revenue Recognition

Under the accrual method of accounting, revenue is recognized when earned, and expenses to produce that revenue are recognized when incurred. Accrual accounting does not necessarily coincide with the receipt or payment of cash, so firms can manipulate net income through their choices about revenue and expense recognition. The Securities and Exchange Commission (SEC) provides additional guidance by listing four criteria to determine whether revenue should be recognized.[2]

1.  There is evidence of an arrangement between the buyer and seller.
2.  The product has been delivered or the service has been rendered.
3.  The price is determined or determinable.
4.  The seller is reasonably sure of collecting money.

Revenue is usually recognized at delivery, but revenue may be recognized before delivery occurs or after delivery takes place in some circumstances.

## Long-Term Contracts

The **percentage-of-completion method** and the **completed-contract method** are used for contracts (often related to construction projects) that extend beyond one accounting period. In certain cases involving service contracts or licensing agreements, the firm may simply recognize revenue equally over the term of the contract or agreement.

---

2    SEC Staff Accounting Bulletin 101.

The *percentage-of-completion method* is appropriate when the outcome of the project can be reliably estimated. Revenue, expense, and profit are recognized in proportion to the total cost incurred to date, divided by the total expected cost of the project.

The *completed-contract method* is used when the outcome of a project cannot be reliably measured or the project is short-term. Revenue, expense, and profit are only recognized when the contract is complete.

Under International Financial Reporting Standards (IFRS), if the firm cannot reliably measure the outcome of the project, revenue is recognized to the extent of contract costs, costs are expensed when incurred, and profit is recognized at completion.

As compared to the completed contract method, the percentage-of-completion method is considered more aggressive because revenue is reported sooner. The percentage-of-completion method provides smoother earnings and results in better matching of revenues and expenses. Cash flow is the same under both methods.

An **installment sale** occurs when a firm finances a sale and payments are expected to be received over an extended period. If collectability is certain, revenue is recognized at the time of sale. If collectability cannot be reasonably estimated, the **installment method** is used, and if collectability is highly uncertain, the **cost recovery method** is used.

Under the *installment method*, profit recognized is the proportion of cash collected multiplied by the total expected profit. The installment method is used in limited circumstances, usually involving the sale of real estate. Under the *cost recovery method*, profit is recognized only when, and to the extent that, cash collections exceed estimated total costs.

In a **barter transaction**, two parties exchange goods or services without any cash payment. According to U.S. GAAP, revenue can be recognized at fair value only if the firm has historically received cash payments for such services and can use this historical experience to determine fair value.[3] Under IFRS, revenue from barter transactions must be measured based on the fair value of revenue from similar non-barter transactions with unrelated parties.[4]

---

3   Emerging Issues Task Force EITF 99–17, "Accounting for Advertising Barter Transactions."

4   IASB, SIC Interpretation 31, Revenue – Barter Transactions Involving Advertising Services, paragraph 5.

## Gross vs. Net Revenue Reporting

Under **gross revenue reporting**, the selling firm reports sales revenue and cost of goods sold separately. Under **net revenue reporting**, only the difference between sales and cost is reported. While profit is the same, reported sales are higher using gross revenue reporting. Firms disclose their revenue recognition policies in the financial statement footnotes.

Users of financial information must consider two points when analyzing a firm's revenue: (1) how conservative the firm's revenue recognition policies are (recognizing revenue sooner rather than later is more aggressive), and (2) to what extent the firm's policies rely on estimates and judgments.

## Recognition of Expense

Under the accrual method of accounting, expense recognition is based on the *matching principle,* whereby expenses for producing goods and services are recognized in the period in which the revenue for the goods and services is recognized. Expenses that are not tied directly to generating revenue, such as administrative costs, are called *period costs* and are expensed in the period incurred.

The cost of long-lived assets must also be matched with revenues. The allocation of cost over an asset's useful life is known as **depreciation** or **amortization** expense.

If a firm sells goods or services on credit or provides a warranty to the customer, the matching principle requires the firm to estimate bad-debt expense and/or warranty expense. Since estimates are involved, it is possible for firms to delay the recognition of expense. Delayed expense recognition increases net income and is, therefore, more aggressive.

## Depreciation

Most firms use the **straight-line depreciation** method for financial reporting purposes. However, most assets generate proportionally more benefits in their early years and an **accelerated depreciation** method is more appropriate for matching revenues and expenses. In the early years of an asset's life, the straight-line method will result in lower depreciation expense and higher net income than accelerated methods.

*Straight-line depreciation* (SL) allocates an equal amount of depreciation each year over the asset's useful life as follows:

$$\text{SL depreciation expense } = \frac{\text{cost } - \text{residual value}}{\text{useful life}}$$

The most common *accelerated method* of depreciation is the **double-declining balance method** (DDB), which uses 200% of the straight-line rate, applied against the declining balance (value net of depreciation). If an asset's life is 10 years, the straight-line rate is 1/10 or 10%. The DDB rate for this asset is 2/10 or 20%.

$$\text{DDB depreciation} = \left(\frac{2}{\text{useful life}}\right)(\text{asset cost} - \text{accumulated depreciation})$$

DDB does not use the residual value in the calculations, but depreciation stops once residual value has been reached.

## Inventory

Under the **first-in, first-out** (FIFO) method, the first item purchased is the first item sold. FIFO is appropriate for inventory that has a limited shelf life. Under the **last-in, first-out** (LIFO) method, the last item purchased is the first item sold. LIFO is appropriate for inventory that does not deteriorate with age. For example, a coal mining company will sell coal off the top of the pile. The **average cost** method, which allocates the average cost of all inventory to each unit sold, is popular because of its ease of use.

In the United States, LIFO is popular because of the income tax benefits. LIFO results in higher cost of goods sold in an inflationary environment. Higher cost of goods sold results in lower taxable income, and thus lower income taxes. LIFO inventory accounting is not permitted under IFRS.

## Intangible Assets

**Amortization expense** of intangible assets with limited lives is similar to depreciation; the expense should match the benefits/value used over the period. Most firms, however, use the straight-line method. Goodwill and other intangible assets with *indefinite lives* are not amortized. However, they must be tested for impairment at least annually. If the asset is impaired, an expense is recognized in the income statement.

## Operating and Nonoperating Components of the Income Statement

*Operating* and *nonoperating transactions* are usually reported separately in the income statement. For a nonfinancial firm, nonoperating transactions may result from investment income and financing expenses (interest). The income from and the gains and losses on the sale of these securities are not a part of the firm's normal business operations. For a financial firm, such income, gains, and losses may be considered operating income.

## Discontinued Operations

A *discontinued operation* (must be physically and operationally distinct from the rest of the firm) is one that management has decided to dispose of, but either has not yet done so, or disposed of in the current period after the operation had generated income or losses. Income and losses from discontinued operations are reported separately in the income statement, net of tax, after income from continuing operations. While discontinued operations do not affect net income from continuing operations, the analyst must decide their effect on firm earnings and cash flows in the future.

**Unusual or infrequent items** are recorded for events that are either unusual in nature *or* infrequent in occurrence, but *not* both. Unusual or infrequent items are included in income from continuing operations. Examples include:

*   Gains or losses from the sale of assets or part of a business (that do not qualify as discontinued operations).
*   Impairments, write-offs, write-downs, and restructuring costs.

An analyst must review these to determine their effect, if any, on future income.

## Extraordinary Items

Under U.S. GAAP, an *extraordinary item* is both unusual and infrequent in occurrence (e.g., losses from an expropriation of assets or uninsured losses from natural disasters). Extraordinary items are reported separately in the income statement, net of tax, after income from continuing operations. IFRS does not allow extraordinary treatment in the income statement.

Although extraordinary items do not affect income from continuing operations, an analyst may want to review them to determine whether some portion should be included when forecasting future income (i.e., they may not be *that* extraordinary).

## Accounting Changes

A **change in accounting principle** refers to the change from one GAAP or IFRS method to another method and requires retrospective application so all of the prior period financial statements currently presented are restated to reflect the change.

Generally, a **change in accounting estimate** is the result of a change in management's judgment, usually due to new information. For example, management may change the estimated useful life of an asset because new information indicates the asset has a longer life than originally expected. A change in estimate is applied prospectively and does not require the restatement of prior financial statements. Accounting changes typically do not affect cash flow. An analyst should review accounting principle changes and changes in accounting estimates to determine the impact on future operating results.

A change from an incorrect accounting method to one that is acceptable under GAAP or IFRS, or the correction of an accounting error, is reported as a **prior-period adjustment**. Prior-period adjustments are made by restating results for all prior period statements presented in the current financial statements. Disclosure of the nature of the adjustment and of its effect on net income is also required.

Prior-period adjustments usually involve errors or new accounting standards and typically do not affect cash flow unless tax accounting is also affected. Analysts should review adjustments carefully because errors may indicate weaknesses in the firm's internal control system.

## Earnings Per Share

The following basic definitions are essential.

*Potentially dilutive securities.* These securities include stock options, warrants, convertible debt, and convertible preferred stock.

*Dilutive securities.* Those securities that would *decrease EPS* if exercised and converted to common stock.

*Antidilutive securities.* Those securities that would *increase EPS* if exercised and converted to common stock.

*Simple capital structure.* A capital structure that contains *no potentially dilutive* securities. This structure contains only common stock, nonconvertible debt, and nonconvertible preferred stock.

*Complex capital structures.* Complex structures contain *potentially dilutive securities* such as options, warrants, or convertible securities.

*Weighted average number of shares outstanding.* Each share issue is weighted by the portion of the year it was outstanding. Stock splits and stock dividends are applied retroactively to the beginning of the year, so "old" shares are converted to "new" shares for consistency.

## Basic EPS

The basic EPS calculation *does not* consider the effects of any dilutive securities in the computation of EPS. It is the only EPS presented for firms with simple capital structures and is one of the two EPS calculations presented for firms with complex capital structures.

$$\text{basic EPS} = \frac{\text{net income} - \text{preferred dividends}}{\text{weighted average number of common shares outstanding}}$$

## Diluted EPS

If a firm has a complex capital structure (contains potentially dilutive securities), both basic and diluted EPS must be reported. To calculate diluted EPS, treat any *dilutive* securities as if they were converted to common stock from the first of the year (or when issued if issued during the current year).

Each potentially dilutive security must be considered separately to determine whether or not it is actually dilutive for the current reporting period. Only income from continuing operations (excluding discontinued operations, extraordinary items, and accounting changes) is considered in determining diluted EPS.

To determine whether a convertible security is dilutive, calculate:

$$\frac{\text{convertible pfd. dividends}}{\text{\# shares from conversion of pfd.}} \quad \text{or} \quad \frac{\text{convertible debt interest}\,(1 - \text{tax rate})}{\text{\# shares from conversion of debt}}$$

If the calculated amount is less than basic EPS, the security is dilutive.

When considering dilutive securities, the denominator is the basic EPS denominator adjusted for the equivalent number of common shares created by the conversion of all outstanding dilutive securities (convertible bonds, convertible preferred shares, plus options and warrants).

$$\text{diluted EPS} = \frac{\text{adjusted income available for common shares}}{\text{weighted-average common and potential common shares outstanding}}$$

where adjusted income available for common shares is:
earnings available for common shares
+ dividends on dilutive convertible preferred stock
+ after-tax interest on dilutive convertible debt

Therefore, diluted EPS is:

$$\text{diluted EPS} = \frac{\left[\text{net income} - \text{preferred dividends}\right] + \left(\begin{array}{c}\text{convertible}\\\text{preferred}\\\text{dividends}\end{array}\right) + \left(\begin{array}{c}\text{convertible}\\\text{debt}\\\text{interest}\end{array}\right)(1-t)}{\left(\begin{array}{c}\text{weighted}\\\text{average}\\\text{shares}\end{array}\right) + \left(\begin{array}{c}\text{shares from}\\\text{conversion of}\\\text{conv. pfd. shares}\end{array}\right) + \left(\begin{array}{c}\text{shares from}\\\text{conversion of}\\\text{conv. debt}\end{array}\right) + \left(\begin{array}{c}\text{shares}\\\text{issuable from}\\\text{stock options}\end{array}\right)}$$

With respect to convertible bonds, remember that what you are looking for is a reduction in EPS. The denominator is rising due to the increased number of shares, and the numerator is rising due to the after-tax interest cost savings. When the denominator is rising faster than the numerator, conversion is dilutive.

## Treasury Stock Method

The *treasury stock method* assumes that the hypothetical funds received by the company from the exercise of options or warrants are used to purchase shares of the company's common stock at the average market price over the reporting period.

Options and warrants are dilutive whenever the exercise price is less than the average stock price over the reporting period.

$$\text{new shares (treasury stock method)} = \frac{\text{avg. mkt. price} - \text{exercise price}}{\text{average market price}} \times \text{\# of shares covered by options/warrants}$$

## Financial Ratios Based on the Income Statement

A vertical **common-size income statement** expresses all income statement items as a percentage of sales. This format is useful for time-series and cross-sectional analysis and facilitates the comparison of firms of different sizes.

It is usually more meaningful to present income tax expense as an effective rate, equal to income tax expense divided by pre-tax income, than as a percentage of sales.

**Profitability ratios** examine how well management has done at generating profits from sales. The different ratios are designed to isolate specific costs. Generally, higher margin ratios are desirable.

**Gross profit margin** is the ratio of gross profit (sales less cost of goods sold) to sales:

$$\text{gross profit margin} = \frac{\text{gross profit}}{\text{revenue}}$$

Gross profit margin can be increased by raising sales prices or lowering per-unit cost.

**Net profit margin** is the ratio of net income to sales:

$$\text{net profit margin} = \frac{\text{net income}}{\text{revenue}}$$

Net profit margin can be increased by raising sales prices or cutting costs.

Any subtotal presented in the income statement can be expressed in terms of a margin ratio (to revenues). For example, *operating profit margin* is equal to operating income divided by revenue. *Pre-tax margin* is equal to pre-tax earnings divided by revenue.

## Items Excluded from the Income Statement that Affect Owners' Equity

*Transactions with owners:*

1. Issuing or reacquiring stock.
2. Dividends paid.

*Transactions included in other comprehensive income:*

1. Foreign currency translation gains and losses.
2. Adjustments for minimum pension liability.
3. Unrealized gains and losses from *cash flow hedging* derivatives.
4. Unrealized gains and losses from *available-for-sale* securities.

**Comprehensive income** is a measure that includes all changes to equity other than owner contributions and distributions.

## UNDERSTANDING THE BALANCE SHEET
Cross-Reference to CFA Institute Assigned Reading #33

The balance sheet shows the values of the assets and liabilities of the firm at a point in time. Values may be historical values, fair market values, or historical values adjusted for amortization of premiums or discounts. Balance sheet items can be divided into assets, liabilities, and equity.

$$\text{assets} = \text{liabilities} + \text{owners' equity}$$

Some common ways of presenting balance sheet data are:

- The **account format**—assets are presented on the left side of the page and liabilities and equity are presented on the right side.
- The **report format**—assets, liabilities, and equity are presented in one column.
- A **classified balance sheet** groups together similar items (current assets, current liabilities, current liabilities, noncurrent liabilities) to arrive at significant subtotals. These groupings should be used unless a liquidity-based presentation is more relevant, as for a financial institution.

### Accrual Process

The accrual method of accounting also creates assets and liabilities.

- Cash received in advance of recognizing revenue results in an increase in assets (cash) and an increase in liabilities (unearned revenue).
- Recognizing revenue before cash is received results in an increase in assets (accounts receivable) and an increase in equity (retained earnings). Cash paid in advance of recognizing expense results in a decrease in one asset (cash) and an increase in another asset (prepaid expenses) by the same amount.
- Recognizing an expense before cash is paid results in an increase in liabilities (accrued expenses) and a decrease in equity (retained earnings).

## Current and Noncurrent Assets and Liabilities

**Current assets** include cash and other assets that will be converted into cash or used up within one year or operating cycle, whichever is greater.

**Current liabilities** are obligations that will be satisfied within one year or operating cycle, whichever is greater. More specifically, a liability that meets any of the following criteria is considered current:

- Settlement is expected during the normal operating cycle.
- It is held for trading purposes.
- Settlement is expected within one year.
- There is no unconditional right to defer settlement for at least one year.

Current assets minus current liabilities equals **working capital**.

**Noncurrent assets** do not meet the definition of current assets; that is, they will not be converted into cash or used up within one year or operating cycle.

**Noncurrent liabilities** do not meet the criteria of current liabilities.

If a firm includes (consolidates) balance sheet accounts of a subsidiary that is not 100% owned, the firm reports a **noncontrolling interest** or **minority interest** in its consolidated balance sheet. The noncontrolling interest is the pro-rata share of the subsidiary's net assets (equity) not owned by the parent company. Noncontrolling interest is reported in the equity section of the consolidated balance sheet.

## Measurement Bases of Assets and Liabilities

Balance sheet assets and liabilities are valued using both **historical cost** and **fair value**.

- *Historical cost* is the value that was exchanged at the acquisition date. Historical cost is objective (highly reliable), but its relevance to an analyst declines as values change.
- *Fair value* is the amount at which an asset could be bought or sold, or a liability can be incurred or settled, between knowledgeable, willing parties in an arm's length transaction.

The financial statement footnotes should include the following information about the measurement of its assets and liabilities:

- Basis for measurement.
- Carrying value of inventory by category.
- Amount of inventory carried at fair value less costs to sell.

- Write-downs and reversals, with a discussion of the circumstances that led to the reversal.
- Inventories pledged as collateral for liabilities.
- Inventories recognized as an expense.

Some of the more common **current assets** are:

- **Cash, and cash equivalents**—cash equivalents typically mature in 90 days or less (e.g., 90-day T-bills).
- **Accounts receivable (trade receivables)**—receivables are reported net of any allowance for bad debt.
- **Inventories**—items held for sale or used in the manufacture of goods to be sold. Firms that use the **retail method** measure inventory at retail prices and subtract an expected gross margin to reflect cost.
- **Marketable securities**—debt or equity securities that are traded in a public market.
- **Other current assets**—includes prepaid expenses.

Some examples of **current liabilities** are:

- **Accounts payable (trade payables)**—amounts owed to suppliers.
- **Notes payable**—obligations in the form of promissory notes due to creditors within one year or operating cycle, whichever is greater.
- **Current portion of long-term debt**—the principal portion of debt due within one year or operating cycle, whichever is greater.
- **Taxes payable**—current taxes that have been recognized in the income statement but have not yet been paid.
- **Accrued liabilities (accrued expenses)**—expenses that have been recognized in the income statement but are not yet contractually due.
- **Unearned revenue (income)**—cash collected in advance of providing goods and services. The related liability is to provide those goods and services.

## Tangible Assets

Long-term assets with physical substance are known as *tangible assets*. Tangible assets, such as plant, equipment, and natural resources, are reported on the balance sheet at historical cost less accumulated depreciation or depletion.

Land is also a tangible asset that is reported at historical cost and is not depreciated.

Tangible assets not used in the operations of the firm should be classified as investment assets.

## Intangible Assets

*Intangible assets* are long-term assets that lack physical substance. The cost of an identifiable intangible asset is amortized over its useful life. Examples of identifiable intangible assets include patents, trademarks, and copyrights.

An intangible asset that is *unidentifiable* cannot be purchased separately and may have an infinite life. The best example of an unidentifiable intangible asset is goodwill.

**Goodwill** is created when a business is purchased for more than the fair value of its assets net of liabilities. Goodwill is not amortized, but must be tested for impairment (a decrease in its fair value) at least annually. Since goodwill is not amortized, firms can manipulate net income upward by allocating more of the acquisition price to goodwill and less to the identifiable assets. The result is less depreciation and amortization expense and thus higher net income.

When computing ratios, analysts should eliminate goodwill from the balance sheet and goodwill impairment charges from the income statement for comparability. Also, analysts should evaluate future acquisitions in terms of the price paid relative to the earning power of the acquired firm.

Intangible assets that are purchased are reported on the balance sheet at historical cost less accumulated amortization. Except for certain legal costs, intangible assets that are created internally, including research and development costs, are expensed as incurred under U.S. GAAP and are not shown on the balance sheet.

Under IFRS, a firm must identify the research stage and the development stage. Accordingly, the firm must expense costs during the research stage but *may* capitalize costs incurred during the development stage.

All of the following should be expensed as incurred, and do not create balance sheet assets:

- Start-up and training costs.
- Administrative overhead.
- Advertising and promotion costs.
- Relocation and reorganization costs.
- Termination costs.

Some analysts completely eliminate intangible assets, particularly unidentifiable intangibles, for analytical purposes. This is inadvisable. Analysts should consider the economic value of each intangible asset before making an adjustment.

## Accounting Treatments for Financial Instruments

**Marketable investment securities** are classified as one of the following:

- **Held-to-maturity securities.** Debt securities acquired with the intent to be held to maturity are reported on the balance sheet at amortized cost. Amortized cost is equal to the face (par) value less any unamortized discount or plus any unamortized premium, as it is with debt issued by the firm.
- **Trading securities.** Debt and equity securities acquired with the intent to profit from near-term price fluctuations are reported on the balance sheet at fair value. Unrealized gains and losses are recognized in the income statement.
- **Available-for-sale securities.** Debt and equity securities that are not expected to be held to maturity or traded in the near term are reported on the balance sheet at fair value. Unrealized gains and losses are not recognized in the income statement, but are reported in other comprehensive income as a part of stockholders' equity.

Dividend and interest income, and realized gains and losses (actual gains or losses when the securities are sold), are recognized in the income statement for all three classifications of securities.

### Figure 1: Summary of Investment Security Classifications

|  | Trading | Available-for-sale | Held-to-maturity |
|---|---|---|---|
| Balance sheet | Fair value | Fair value | Amortized cost |
| Income statement | • Dividends<br>• Interest<br>• Realized G/L<br>• Unrealized G/L | • Dividends<br>• Interest<br>• Realized G/L | • Interest<br>• Realized G/L |

## Components of Owners' Equity

**Owners' equity** is the residual interest in assets that remains after subtracting an entity's liabilities. The owners' equity section of the balance sheet includes:

- **Contributed capital**—the total amount received from the issuance of common and preferred stock.
- **Noncontrolling interest** (minority interest)—the minority shareholders' pro-rata share of the net assets (equity) of a consolidated subsidiary that is partially owned by the parent.
- **Retained earnings**—the cumulative net income of the firm since inception that has not been paid out as dividends.
- **Treasury stock**—stock that has been reacquired by the issuing firm but not yet retired. Treasury stock has no voting rights and does not receive dividends.

- **Accumulated other comprehensive income**—includes all changes in stockholders' equity not recognized in the income statement or from issuing stock, reacquiring stock, and paying dividends.

Under U.S. GAAP, the firm can report comprehensive income in the income statement (below net income), in a separate statement of comprehensive income, or in the statement of changes in stockholders' equity. Under IFRS, a firm can include all revenue and expense items in the statement of comprehensive income, or may present a separate income statement and a statement of comprehensive income.

The **statement of changes in stockholders' equity** summarizes all transactions that increase or decrease the equity accounts for the period.

## Analysis of the Balance Sheet

A vertical **common-size balance sheet** expresses all balance sheet accounts as a percentage of total assets and allows the analyst to evaluate the balance sheet changes over time (*time-series analysis*) as well as to compare the balance sheets with other firms, industry, and sector data (*cross-sectional analysis*). Several commercial services provide data for comparison.

**Liquidity ratios** measure the firm's ability to satisfy short-term obligations when due.

- The **current ratio** is the best-known measure of liquidity.

$$\text{current ratio} = \frac{\text{current assets}}{\text{current liabilities}}$$

  A current ratio of less than one means the firm has negative working capital and may be facing a liquidity crisis. Working capital is equal to current assets minus current liabilities.

- The **quick ratio** (acid test ratio) is a more conservative measure of liquidity because it excludes inventories and less liquid current assets from the numerator.

$$\text{quick ratio} = \frac{\text{cash} + \text{marketable securities} + \text{receivables}}{\text{current liabilities}}$$

- The **cash ratio** is the most conservative measure of liquidity.

$$\text{cash ratio} = \frac{\text{cash} + \text{marketable securities}}{\text{current liabilities}}$$

The higher its liquidity ratios, the more likely the firm will be able to pay its short-term bills when due. The ratios differ only in the assumed liquidity of the current assets.

**Solvency ratios** measure a firm's financial risk and measure the firm's ability to satisfy long-term obligations (its solvency). The higher the ratio, the greater the financial leverage and the greater the financial risk.

- The **long-term debt-to-equity ratio** measures long-term financing sources relative to the equity base.

$$\text{long-term debt-to-equity} = \frac{\text{total long-term debt}}{\text{total equity}}$$

- The **debt-to-equity ratio** measures total debt relative to the equity base.

$$\text{debt-to-equity} = \frac{\text{total debt}}{\text{total equity}}$$

- The **total debt ratio** measures the extent to which assets are financed by creditors.

$$\text{total debt ratio} = \frac{\text{total debt}}{\text{total assets}}$$

- The **financial leverage ratio** is a variation of the debt-to-equity ratio that is used as a component of the DuPont model.

$$\text{financial leverage ratio} = \frac{\text{total assets}}{\text{total equity}}$$

## UNDERSTANDING THE CASH FLOW STATEMENT
Cross-Reference to CFA Institute Assigned Reading #34

The **cash flow statement** provides information beyond that available from net income and other financial data. The cash flow statement provides information about a firm's liquidity, solvency, and financial flexibility. The cash flow statement reconciles the beginning and ending balances of cash over an accounting period. The change in cash is a result of the firm's operating, investing, and financing activities as follows:

$$
\begin{array}{rl}
 & \text{Operating activities} \\
+ & \text{Investing activities} \\
+ & \underline{\text{Financing activities}} \\
= & \text{Change in cash balance} \\
+ & \underline{\text{Beginning cash balance}} \\
= & \text{Ending cash balance}
\end{array}
$$

## Figure 2: U.S. GAAP Cash Flow Classifications

### Operating Activities

| *Inflows* | *Outflows* |
| --- | --- |
| Cash collected from customers | Cash paid to employees and suppliers |
| Interest and dividends received | Cash paid for other expenses |
| Sale proceeds from trading securities | Acquisition of trading securities |
| | Interest paid |
| | Taxes paid |

### Investing Activities

| *Inflows* | *Outflows* |
| --- | --- |
| Sale proceeds from fixed assets | Acquisition of fixed assets |
| Sale proceeds from debt & equity investments | Acquisition of debt & equity investments |
| Principal received from loans made to others | Loans made to others |

### Financing Activities

| *Inflows* | *Outflows* |
| --- | --- |
| Principal amounts borrowed from others | Principal paid on amounts from others |
| Proceeds from issuing stock | Payments to reacquire stock |
| | Dividends paid to shareholders |

## Differences Between U.S. GAAP and IFRS

Under IFRS:

- Interest and dividends received may be classified as either CFO or CFI.
- Dividends paid to shareholders and interest paid on debt may be classified as either CFO or CFF.

- Income taxes are reported as operating activities unless the expense can be tied to an investing or financing transaction.

**Noncash investing and financing activities** are not reported in the cash flow statement but must be disclosed in either a footnote or a supplemental schedule to the cash flow statement.

## Direct Method and Indirect Methods Calculating CFO

Two different methods of presenting the cash flow statement are permitted under U.S. GAAP and IFRS: the direct method and the indirect method. The use of the direct method is encouraged by both standard setters. The difference in the two methods relates to the presentation of cash flow from operating activities. Total cash flow from operating activities is exactly the same under both methods, and the presentation of cash flow from investing activities and from financing activities is exactly the same under both methods.

The direct method provides more information than the indirect method. The main advantage of the indirect method is that it focuses on the differences between net income and operating cash flow.

### Direct Method

The direct method presents operating cash flow by taking each item from the income statement and converting it to its cash equivalent by adding or subtracting the changes in the corresponding balance sheet accounts. The following are examples of operating cash flow components:

- Cash collected from sales is the main component of CFO. Cash collections are calculated by adjusting sales for the changes in accounts receivable and unearned (deferred) revenue.
- Cash used in the production of goods and services (cash inputs) is calculated by adjusting cost of goods sold (COGS) for the changes in inventory and accounts payable.

### Indirect Method

Using the indirect method, operating cash flow is calculated in four steps:

*Step 1:* Begin with net income.
*Step 2:* Subtract gains or add losses that resulted from financing or investing cash flows (such as gains from sale of land).
*Step 3:* Add back all noncash charges to income (such as depreciation and amortization) and subtract all noncash components of revenue.

*Step 4:* Add or subtract changes to related balance sheet operating accounts as
follows:
- Increases in the operating asset accounts (uses of cash) are subtracted,
while decreases (sources of cash) are added.
- Increases in the operating liability accounts (sources of cash) are added,
while decreases (uses of cash) are subtracted.

Most firms present the cash flow statement using the indirect method. For
analytical purposes, it may be beneficial to *convert the cash flow statement to the
direct method.* Examples of such conversion for two items are:

*Cash collections from customers:*
1. Begin with net sales from the income statement.
2. Subtract (add) any increase (decrease) in the accounts receivable balance as
reported in the indirect method.
3. Add (subtract) an increase (decrease) in unearned revenue.

*Cash payments to suppliers:*
1. Begin with cost of goods sold (COGS) as reported in the income statement.
2. If depreciation and/or amortization have been included in COGS (they
increase COGS), they must be eliminated when computing the cash paid to
suppliers.
3. Subtract (add) any increase (decrease) in the accounts payable balance as
reported in the indirect method.
4. Add (subtract) any increase (decrease) in the inventory balance as disclosed in
the indirect method.
5. Subtract any inventory write-off that occurred during the period.

## Disclosure Requirements

Under U.S. GAAP, a direct method presentation must also disclose the adjustments
necessary to reconcile net income to cash flow from operating activities. The
reconciliation is not required under IFRS.

Under IFRS, payments for interest and taxes must be disclosed separately in the
cash flow statement under either method (direct or indirect). Under U.S. GAAP,
payments for interest and taxes can be reported in the cash flow statement or
disclosed in the footnotes.

## Investing and Financing Cash Flows

**Investing cash flows** (CFI) are calculated by subtracting expenditures on new assets from the proceeds of asset sales.

When calculating the cash from an asset that has been sold, it is necessary to consider any gain or loss from the sale using the following formula:

cash from asset sold = book value of the asset + gain (or − loss) on sale

**Financing cash flows** (CFF) are determined by measuring the cash flows occurring between the firm and its suppliers of capital. Cash flows between the firm and creditors result from new borrowings and debt repayments. Note that interest paid is technically a cash flow to the creditors, but it is already included in CFO under U.S. GAAP. Cash flows between the firm and the shareholders occur when equity is issued, shares are repurchased, and dividends are paid. CFF is the sum of these two measures:

net cash flows from creditors = new borrowings − principal repaid

net cash flows from shareholders = new equity issued − share repurchases
− cash dividends

## Analysis of the Cash Flow Statement

### 1. Operating Cash Flow

The analyst should identify the major determinants of operating cash flow, primarily the firm's earning-related activities and changes in noncash working capital.

Equality of operating cash flow and net income is an indication of high quality earnings but can be affected by the stage of business cycle and of the firm's life cycle. Earnings that exceed operating cash flow may be an indication of premature recognition of revenues or delayed recognition of expenses.

### 2. Investing Cash Flow

Increasing capital expenditures, a use of cash, is usually an indication of growth. Conversely, a firm may reduce capital expenditures or even sell capital assets in order to conserve or generate cash. This may result in higher cash outflows in the future as older assets are replaced or growth resumes.

## 3. Financing Cash Flow

The financing activities section of the cash flow statement reveals information about whether the firm is generating cash by issuing debt or equity. It also provides information about whether the firm is using cash to repay debt, reacquire stock, or pay dividends.

The cash flow statement can be converted to **common-size format** by expressing each line item as a percentage of revenue. Alternatively, each inflow of cash can be expressed as a percentage of total cash inflows and each outflow of cash can be expressed as a percentage of total cash outflows.

**Free cash flow** is a measure of cash that is available for discretionary purposes; that is, the cash flow that is available once the firm has covered its obligations and capital expenditures.

**Free cash flow to the firm** (FCFF) is the cash available to all investors, including stockholders and debt holders. FCFF can be calculated using net income or operating cash flow as a starting point.

FCFF is calculated from net income as:

$$\text{FCFF} = \text{NI} + \text{non-cash charges} + [\text{interest expense} \times (1 - \text{tax rate})] \\ - \text{net capital investment} - \text{working capital investment}$$

FCFF is calculated from operating cash flow as:

$$\text{FCFF} = \text{CFO} + [\text{interest expense} \times (1 - \text{tax rate})] - \text{net capital expenditure}$$

**Free cash flow to equity** (FCFE) is the cash flow that is available for distribution to the common shareholders; that is, after all obligations have been paid. FCFE can be calculated as follows:

$$\text{FCFE} = \text{CFO} - \text{net capital expenditure} + \text{net borrowing}$$

## Cash Flow Ratios That Measure Performance

- The **cash flow-to-revenue ratio** measures the amount of operating cash flow generated for each dollar of revenue.

$$\text{cash flow-to-revenue} = \frac{\text{CFO}}{\text{net revenue}}$$

- The **cash return-on-assets ratio** measures the return of operating cash flow attributed to all providers of capital.

$$\text{cash return-on-assets} = \frac{\text{CFO}}{\text{average total assets}}$$

## Cash Flow Ratios That Measure Coverage

- The **debt coverage ratio** measures financial risk and leverage.

$$\text{debt coverage} = \frac{\text{CFO}}{\text{total debt}}$$

- The **interest coverage ratio** measures the firm's ability to meet its interest obligations.

$$\text{interest coverage} = \frac{\text{CFO} + \text{interest paid} + \text{taxes paid}}{\text{interest paid}}$$

## FINANCIAL ANALYSIS TECHNIQUES
Cross-Reference to CFA Institute Assigned Reading #35

With respect to analysis of financial statements, there are a number of key ratios that should simply be memorized including:

- Current, quick, and cash ratios.
- All the ratios in the cash conversion cycle (the turnover ratios are more important, like receivables, inventory, and payables turnover).
- Turnover ratios use sales in the numerator, except for payables and inventory turnover ratios, which use purchases and COGS, respectively.
- Gross profit margin, net profit margin, and operating profit margin are readily available from a common-size income statement.

- Return on equity (ROE) is critical. Definitely know the three- and five-component DuPont ROE decompositions.
- Debt-to-equity, total debt, interest coverage, and fixed financial coverage ratios (remember to add lease interest expense to numerator and denominator).
- The retention ratio and growth rate are important concepts that also appear in Corporate Finance and Equity Investments.

## Usefulness and Limitations of Ratio Analysis

Financial ratios provide useful information to analysts, including:

- Insights into the financial relationships that are useful in forecasting future earnings and cash flows.
- Information about the financial flexibility of the firm.
- A means of evaluating management's performance.

Financial ratios have limitations:

- Ratios are not useful when viewed in isolation. Ratios should be interpreted relative to industry averages, economy-wide firm averages, and the company's own historical performance.
- Comparisons with other companies are made more difficult because of different accounting methods. Some of the more common differences include inventory methods (FIFO and LIFO), depreciation methods (accelerated and straight-line), and lease accounting (capital and operating).
- There may be difficulty in locating comparable ratios when analyzing companies that operate in multiple industries.
- Conclusions cannot be made from viewing one set of ratios. Ratios must be viewed relative to one another.
- Judgment is required. Determining the target or comparison value for a ratio is difficult and may require some range of acceptable values.

*Common-size balance sheets and income statements.* These statements normalize balance sheets and income statements and allow the analyst to make easier comparisons of different-sized firms. A vertical common-size balance sheet expresses each balance sheet account as a *percentage of total assets*. A horizontal common-size balance sheet expresses each account as a ratio to the first-year value (e.g., 1.1 indicates an increase of 10% above the first-year value). A vertical common-sized income statement expresses each income statement item as a *percentage of sales*.

*Measures of liquidity:*

$$\text{current ratio} = \frac{\text{current assets}}{\text{current liabilities}}$$

$$\text{quick ratio} = \frac{\text{cash} + \text{marketable securities} + \text{receivables}}{\text{current liabilities}}$$

*Measures of operating performance—turnover ratios and the cash conversion cycle:*

$$\text{receivables turnover} = \frac{\text{annual sales}}{\text{average receivables}}$$

$$\text{inventory turnover} = \frac{\text{cost of goods sold}}{\text{average inventory}}$$

$$\text{payables turnover ratio} = \frac{\text{purchases}}{\text{average trade payables}}$$

$$\text{days of sales outstanding} = \frac{365}{\text{receivables turnover}}$$

$$\text{days of inventory on hand} = \frac{365}{\text{inventory turnover}}$$

$$\text{number of days of payables} = \frac{365}{\text{payables turnover ratio}}$$

$$\begin{array}{c}\text{cash}\\ \text{conversion}\\ \text{cycle}\end{array} = \left(\begin{array}{c}\text{days of sales}\\ \text{outstanding}\end{array}\right) + \left(\begin{array}{c}\text{days of inventory}\\ \text{on hand}\end{array}\right) - \left(\begin{array}{c}\text{number of}\\ \text{days of}\\ \text{payables}\end{array}\right)$$

*Measures of operating performance—operating efficiency ratios:*

$$\text{total asset turnover} = \frac{\text{revenue}}{\text{average total assets}}$$

$$\text{fixed asset turnover} = \frac{\text{revenue}}{\text{average net fixed assets}}$$

$$\text{working capital turnover} = \frac{\text{revenue}}{\text{average working capital}}$$

*Measures of operating performance—operating profitability:*

$$\text{gross profit margin} = \frac{\text{gross profit}}{\text{revenue}}$$

$$\text{operating profit margin} = \frac{\text{operating income}}{\text{revenue}} = \frac{\text{EBIT}}{\text{revenue}}$$

$$\text{net profit margin} = \frac{\text{net income}}{\text{revenue}}$$

*Return on total capital* (ROTC):

$$\text{return on total capital} = \frac{\text{EBIT}}{\text{average total capital}}$$

Total capital includes debt capital, so interest is added back to net income.

*Return on equity* (ROE):

$$\text{return on total equity} = \frac{\text{net income}}{\text{average total equity}}$$

$$\text{return on common equity} = \frac{\text{net income} - \text{preferred dividends}}{\text{average common equity}}$$

Basic EPS

*Measures of solvency:*

$$\text{debt-to-equity ratio} = \frac{\text{total debt}}{\text{total shareholders' equity}}$$

$$\text{debt-to-capital} = \frac{\text{total debt}}{\text{total debt} + \text{total shareholders' equity}}$$

$$\text{debt-to-assets} = \frac{\text{total debt}}{\text{total assets}}$$

$$\text{financial leverage} = \frac{\text{average total assets}}{\text{average total equity}}$$

*Measures of interest coverage:*

$$\text{interest coverage} = \frac{\text{EBIT}}{\text{interest payments}}$$

$$\text{fixed charge coverage} = \frac{\text{EBIT} + \text{lease payments}}{\text{interest payments} + \text{lease payments}}$$

*Growth analysis:*

$$g = \text{retention rate} \times \text{ROE}$$

$$\text{retention rate} = 1 - \frac{\text{dividends declared}}{\text{net income available to common}}$$

*DuPont analysis.* The DuPont method decomposes the ROE to better analyze firm performance. An analyst can see the impact of leverage, profit margin, and turnover on ROE. There are two variants of the DuPont system: the traditional approach and the extended system.

Both approaches begin with:

$$\text{return on equity} = \left(\frac{\text{net income}}{\text{equity}}\right)$$

The *traditional DuPont equation* is:

$$\text{return on equity} = \left(\frac{\text{net income}}{\text{sales}}\right)\left(\frac{\text{sales}}{\text{assets}}\right)\left(\frac{\text{assets}}{\text{equity}}\right)$$

You may also see it presented as:

$$\text{return on equity} = \left(\frac{\text{net profit}}{\text{margin}}\right)\left(\frac{\text{asset}}{\text{turnover}}\right)\left(\frac{\text{leverage}}{\text{ratio}}\right)$$

The traditional DuPont equation is arguably the most important equation in ratio analysis since it breaks down a very important ratio (ROE) into three key components. If ROE is low, it must be that at least one of the following is true: the company has a poor profit margin; the company has poor asset turnover; or the firm is under-leveraged.

The *extended DuPont equation* takes the net profit margin and breaks it down further. The extended DuPont equation can be written as:

$$\text{ROE} = \left(\frac{\text{net income}}{\text{EBT}}\right)\left(\frac{\text{EBT}}{\text{EBIT}}\right)\left(\frac{\text{EBIT}}{\text{revenue}}\right)\left(\frac{\text{revenue}}{\text{total assets}}\right)\left(\frac{\text{total assets}}{\text{total equity}}\right)$$

You may also see it presented as:

$$\text{ROE} = \left(\frac{\text{tax}}{\text{burden}}\right)\left(\frac{\text{interest}}{\text{burden}}\right)\left(\frac{\text{EBIT}}{\text{margin}}\right)\left(\frac{\text{asset}}{\text{turnover}}\right)\left(\frac{\text{financial}}{\text{leverage}}\right)$$

## Pro Forma Financial Statements

Both common-size financial statements and ratio analysis can be used in preparing pro forma financial statements. A forecast of financial results that begins with an estimate of a firm's next-period revenues might use the most recent COGS from a common-size income statement. Similarly, the analyst may believe that certain ratios will remain the same or change in one direction or the other for the next period. In the absence of any information indicating a change, an analyst may choose to incorporate the operating profit margin and other ratios from the prior period into a pro forma income statement for the next period. Beginning with an estimate of next-period sales, the estimated operating profit margin can be used to forecast operating profits for the next period.

Following are three methods of examining the variability of financial outcomes around point estimates:

1. **Sensitivity analysis** is based on "what if" questions, such as: What will be the effect on net income if sales increase by 3% rather than the estimated 5%?

2. **Scenario analysis** is based on specific scenarios (a specific set of outcomes for key variables) and will also yield a range of values for financial statement items.

3. **Simulation** is a technique in which probability distributions for key variables are selected and a computer generates a distribution of outcomes based on repeated random selection of values for the key variables.

## STUDY SESSION 9: FINANCIAL REPORTING AND ANALYSIS—INVENTORIES, LONG-LIVED ASSETS, INCOME TAXES, AND NON-CURRENT LIABILITIES

### INVENTORIES
Cross-Reference to CFA Institute Assigned Reading #36

For a manufacturing firm, raw materials, goods in process, and finished goods are recorded on the balance sheet as a current asset called inventory.

Costs included in inventory on the balance sheet include:

- Purchase cost.
- Conversion cost.
- Allocation of fixed production overhead based on normal capacity levels.
- Other costs necessary to bring the inventory to its present location and condition.

All of these costs for inventory acquired or produced in the current period are added to beginning inventory value and then allocated either to cost of goods sold for the period or to ending inventory.

Period costs, such as unallocated overhead, abnormal waste, most storage costs, administrative costs, and selling costs, are expensed.

©2011 Kaplan, Inc.

## Inventory Cost Allocation Methods

*First-in, first-out* (FIFO) assumes costs incurred for items that are purchased or manufactured first are the first costs to enter the cost of goods sold (COGS) computation. The balance of ending inventory is made up of those costs most recently incurred.

*Last-in, first-out* (LIFO) assumes costs incurred for items that are purchased or manufactured most recently are the first costs to enter the COGS computation. The balance of ending inventory is made up of costs that were incurred for items purchased or manufactured at the earliest time. Note that in the United States, companies using LIFO for tax purposes must also use LIFO in their financial statements, and that LIFO is not permitted under IFRS.

*Weighted average costing* calculates an average cost per unit by dividing cost of goods available by total units available. This average cost is used to determine both COGS and ending inventory.

With the *specific identification* method, individual items in inventory, such as a car dealer's cars in inventory, are carried at their individual costs and added to COGS as they are sold.

All of these methods are permitted under U.S. GAAP, but IFRS do not permit LIFO inventory accounting.

## Inventory Values on the Balance Sheet

Under IFRS, inventories are valued at the lower of cost or net realizable value, which is estimated sales proceeds net of direct selling costs. Inventory "write-up" is allowed, but only to the extent that a previous write-down to net realizable value was recorded.

Under U.S. GAAP, inventories are valued at the lower of cost or market. "Market" is usually equal to replacement cost but cannot exceed net realizable value or be less than net realizable value minus a normal profit margin. No subsequent "write-up" is allowed.

## Periodic and Perpetual Inventory Systems

Firms account for changes in inventory using either a periodic or perpetual system. In a **periodic inventory system**, inventory values and COGS are determined at the end of the accounting period. No detailed records of inventory are maintained;

rather, inventory acquired during the period is reported in a Purchases account. At the end of the period, purchases are added to beginning inventory to arrive at cost of goods available for sale. To calculate COGS, ending inventory is subtracted from goods available for sale.

In a **perpetual inventory system**, inventory values and COGS are updated continuously. Inventory purchased and sold is recorded directly in inventory when the transactions occur. Thus, a Purchases account is not necessary.

For the FIFO and specific identification methods, ending inventory values and COGS are the same whether a periodic or perpetual system is used. However, periodic and perpetual inventory systems can produce different values for inventory and COGS under the LIFO and weighted average cost methods.

## LIFO vs. FIFO

In periods of rising prices and stable or increasing inventory quantities:

| *LIFO results in:* | *FIFO results in:* |
|---|---|
| Higher COGS | Lower COGS |
| Lower gross profit | Higher gross profit |
| Lower inventory balances | Higher inventory balances |

In periods of falling prices:

| *LIFO results in:* | *FIFO results in:* |
|---|---|
| Lower COGS | Higher COGS |
| Higher gross profit | Lower gross profit |
| Higher inventory balances | Lower inventory balances |

For a firm using the (weighted) average cost inventory method, all of these values will be between those for the LIFO and FIFO methods.

## Ratios for Evaluating Inventory Management

Ratios that are directly affected by the choice of inventory accounting method include inventory turnover, days of inventory, and gross profit margin.

High inventory turnover relative to other firms in an industry may indicate too little inventory and low turnover may indicate inventory that is too great. Comparing the firm's revenue growth to that of the industry can provide information on whether inventories are too large (slow moving or obsolete) or too small (so that sales are lost to a significant degree).

## Ratios and Inventory Method

*Profitability.* As compared to FIFO, LIFO produces higher COGS in the income statement and will result in lower earnings. Any profitability measure that includes COGS will be lower under LIFO. For example, higher COGS will result in lower gross, operating, and net profit margins as compared to FIFO.

*Liquidity.* Compared to FIFO, LIFO results in a lower inventory value on the balance sheet. Because inventory (a current asset) is lower under LIFO, the current ratio, a popular measure of liquidity, is also lower under LIFO than under FIFO. Working capital is lower under LIFO as well, because current assets are lower. The quick ratio is unaffected by the firm's inventory cost flow method because inventory is excluded from its numerator.

*Activity.* Inventory turnover (COGS / average inventory) is higher for firms that use LIFO compared to firms that use FIFO. Under LIFO, COGS is valued at more recent, higher costs (higher numerator), while inventory is valued at older, lower costs (lower denominator). Higher turnover under LIFO will result in lower days of inventory on hand (365 / inventory turnover).

*Solvency.* LIFO results in lower total assets compared to FIFO because LIFO inventory is lower. Lower total assets under LIFO result in lower stockholders' equity (assets – liabilities). Because total assets and stockholders' equity are lower under LIFO, the debt ratio and the debt-to-equity ratio are higher under LIFO compared to FIFO.

## LONG-LIVED ASSETS
Cross-Reference to CFA Institute Assigned Reading #37

The purchase cost of assets that will provide economic benefits to the firm over more than one year is typically not taken as an expense in the year of acquisition, but is capitalized (creating an asset on the balance sheet) and spread over an asset's useful economic life by recording depreciation of the asset's value.

Compared to taking the acquisition cost as an expense in the period of acquisition, capitalization decreases expenses (which increases net income), increases assets and equity (which decreases reported leverage), reduces income variability, and increases operating cash flow and decreases investing cash flow in the same amounts, since the cost of a capitalized assets is treated as an investing cash flow rather than an operating cash flow.

The following table summarizes the financial implications of capitalizing versus expensing:

|  | Capitalizing | Expensing |
|---|---|---|
| Income variability | Lower | Higher |
| Profitability—first year (ROA & ROE) and Net Income | Higher | Lower |
| Profitability—later years (ROA & ROE) and Net Income | Lower | Higher |
| Total cash flows (assuming no tax effects) | Same | Same |
| Cash flow from operations | Higher | Lower |
| Cash flow from investing | Lower | Higher |
| Leverage ratios (debt/equity & debt/assets) | Lower | Higher |

*Capitalization of interest.* Interest costs incurred when constructing assets over multiple periods for firm use or for sale must be capitalized under both U.S. GAAP and IFRS, either to the balance sheet asset value or to inventory, respectively. The expense is recognized over time as either asset depreciation or in COGS when a constructed asset is sold.

Capitalization of construction interest reduces interest expense in the period of capitalization and increases either depreciation or COGS. Capitalized interest expense is treated as an investing, rather than operating, cash outflow and an analyst should take account of this difference. To better measure interest coverage, an analyst should add capitalized interest to interest expense and increase EBIT by adding depreciation expense from previously capitalized interest.

## Research and Development (R&D) Costs

IFRS requires expensing of research expenditures and capitalization of development costs after product feasibility has been established. Under U.S. GAAP, research and development expenditures generally must be expensed when incurred. An exception is development costs of software for internal use or external sale. U.S. GAAP requires software development costs subsequent to establishing technological feasibility to be capitalized. However, whether that occurs early in the process or just prior to manufacture is subject to management judgment.

Do not confuse capitalization of expenses (asset created) with capitalization of leases (both an asset and liability are created).

# Depreciation

The historical cost of capitalized physical assets is allocated over their economic (useful) lives by recording depreciation expense. Depreciation methods include straight-line (an equal amount each period), accelerated (greater in the early years of an asset's life), and units-of-production (proportional to asset use).

*Straight-line depreciation:*

$$\text{depreciation expense} = \frac{\text{original cost} - \text{salvage value}}{\text{depreciable life}}$$

*Double-declining balance (an accelerated method):*

$$\text{DDB depreciation in year } x = \frac{2}{\text{asset life in years}} \times \text{book value at beginning of year } x$$

Note that the salvage value is not used to compute annual depreciation under the double-declining balance method. The end-of-period book (carrying) value of an asset, however, is not allowed to go below its estimated salvage value.

*Units of production and service hours depreciation.* Under this method, an asset's depreciable basis is divided by estimated units of production or total service hours. Each period, depreciation is calculated as cost-per-unit (hour) times the number of units produced (hours of service).

## Financial Statement Effects of Depreciation Methods

Compared to straight-line depreciation, an accelerated depreciation method will result in greater depreciation expense in the early years of an asset's life. This will reduce EBIT, net income, assets, and equity, and decrease ROA and ROE, compared to straight-line depreciation. When an accelerated method is used for tax reporting, taxable income is less in the early years of an asset's life, reducing taxes and increasing reported cash flows.

Over an asset's useful life, total depreciation and income are the same under all methods; only the timing of expense and income is affected.

Note that increasing (decreasing) the estimated salvage value or estimated asset life will decrease (increase) periodic depreciation expense, increasing reported income.

## Useful Lives and Salvage Values

Calculating depreciation expense requires estimating an asset's useful life and its salvage (residual) value. Firms can manipulate depreciation expense, and therefore net income, by increasing or decreasing either of these estimates.

A longer estimated useful life decreases annual depreciation and increases reported net income, while a shorter estimated useful life will have the opposite effect. A higher estimate of the salvage value will also decrease depreciation and increase net income, while a lower estimate of the salvage value will increase depreciation and decrease net income.

A change in an accounting estimate, such as useful life or salvage value, is put into effect in the current period and prospectively. That is, the change in estimate is applied to the asset's carrying (book) value and depreciation is calculated going forward using the new estimate. The previous periods are not affected by the change.

## Intangible Assets

Purchased assets that do not have physical substance but have finite lives (e.g., patents and franchises) are reported on the balance sheet at their fair values, which are reduced over their economic lives by amortization (like depreciation of a physical asset).

Internally developed intangible assets are not reported on the balance sheet. Values of intangible assets that do not have finite lives (e.g., goodwill) and of those that can be renewed at minimal cost (e.g., trademarks) are not amortized, but must be checked periodically for impairment.

## Derecognition of Long-lived Assets

Long-lived assets are *derecognized* and removed from the balance sheet when they are sold, exchanged, or abandoned.

When a long-lived asset is sold, the asset is removed from the balance sheet and the difference between the sale proceeds and the carrying value of the asset is reported as a gain or loss in the income statement. The carrying value is equal to original cost minus accumulated depreciation and any impairment charges.

The gain or loss is usually reported in the income statement as a part of other gains and losses, or reported separately if material. Also, if the firm presents its cash flow statement using the indirect method, the gain or loss is removed from net income to compute cash flow from operations because the proceeds from selling a long-lived asset are an investing cash inflow.

If a long-lived asset is abandoned, the treatment is similar to a sale, except there are no proceeds. In this case, the carrying value of the asset is removed from the balance sheet and a loss of that amount is recognized in the income statement.

If a long-lived asset is exchanged for another asset, a gain or loss is computed by comparing the carrying value of the old asset with fair value of the old asset (or the fair value of the new asset if that value is clearly more evident). The carrying value of the old asset is removed from the balance sheet and the new asset is recorded at its fair value.

## Impairments

Under IFRS, the firm must annually assess whether events or circumstances indicate an **impairment** of an asset's value has occurred. For example, there may have been a significant decline in the market value of the asset or a significant change in the asset's physical condition. If so, the asset's value must be tested for impairment.

An asset is impaired when its carrying value (original cost less accumulated depreciation) exceeds the **recoverable amount.** The recoverable amount is the greater of its fair value less any selling costs and its **value in use.** The value in use is the present value of its future cash flow stream from continued use.

If impaired, the asset's value must be written down on the balance sheet to the recoverable amount. An impairment loss, equal to the excess of carrying value over the recoverable amount, is recognized in the income statement.

Under IFRS, the loss can be reversed if the value of the impaired asset recovers in the future. However, the loss reversal is limited to the original impairment loss. Thus, the carrying value of the asset after reversal cannot exceed the carrying value before the impairment loss was recognized.

Under U.S. GAAP, an asset is tested for impairment only when events and circumstances indicate the firm may not be able to recover the carrying value through future use.

Determining an impairment and calculating the loss potentially involves two steps. In the first step, the asset is tested for impairment by applying a **recoverability test.** If the asset is impaired, the second step involves measuring the loss.

**Recoverability.** An asset is considered impaired if the carrying value (original cost less accumulated depreciation) is greater than the asset's future *undiscounted* cash flow stream. Because the recoverability test is based on estimates of future undiscounted cash flows, tests for impairment involve considerable management discretion.

**Loss measurement.** If impaired, the asset's value is written down to fair value on the balance sheet and a loss, equal to the excess of carrying value over the fair value of the asset (or the *discounted* value of its future cash flows if the fair value is not known), is recognized in the income statement.

Under U.S. GAAP, loss recoveries are not permitted.

## Asset Revaluations

Under U.S. GAAP, long-lived assets cannot be revalued upward, except that held-for-sale assets can be revalued upward to the extent of previous impairment writedowns.

Under IFRS, assets may be revalued upward to fair value. Gains reversing previous writedowns are reported on the income statement, and any excess gains are taken as an adjustment to equity in an account called **revaluation surplus**.

The initial effects of upward asset revaluations are to increase assets and stockholders' equity, and net income where gains are taken into income. If a depreciable asset is revalued upward, depreciation will be greater, and income less, in subsequent periods.

## INCOME TAXES
Cross-Reference to CFA Institute Assigned Reading #38

Definitely know this terminology. From the tax return we have:

- *Taxable income:* Income subject to tax as reported on the tax return.
- *Taxes payable:* The tax liability based on taxable income, as shown on the tax return.
- *Income tax paid:* The actual cash outflow for taxes paid during the current period.
- *Tax loss carryforwards:* Losses that could not be deducted on the tax return in the current period but may be used to reduce taxable income and taxes payable in future periods.

On the financial statements, we find *pretax income*, which is income before income tax expense. Pretax income on the income statement is used to calculate:

- *Income tax expense:* A noncash income statement item that includes cash tax expense plus any increase (minus any decrease) in the deferred tax liability minus any increase (plus any decrease) in the deferred tax asset.
- *Deferred income tax expense:* The excess of income tax expense over taxes payable.
- *Valuation allowance:* A contra account that reduces a deferred tax asset for the probability that it will not be realized (U.S. GAAP).

## Deferred Tax Liabilities

Deferred tax liabilities are balance sheet amounts that result from an excess of income tax expense over taxes payable and are expected to result in future cash outflows.

The most common reason for creation of a deferred tax liability is that depreciation expense on the income statement (straight-line) is less than depreciation expense on the tax return (accelerated). Pretax income is therefore greater than taxable income, and income tax expense is greater than income tax payable. The taxes that are "deferred" by using accelerated depreciation on the tax return are carried as a deferred tax liability on the balance sheet.

## Deferred Tax Assets

Deferred tax assets are balance sheet amounts that result when taxes payable are greater than income tax expense. This results when revenues are recognized for tax prior to their recording on the financial statements, or when expenses for financial reporting are recorded prior to recognizing them as deductible expenses for tax. Prior losses in excess of those that can be used to offset previous income represent a tax-loss carryforward, which is an asset as it will reduce future taxes.

An example of an expense item that can give rise to a deferred tax asset is warranty expense. On the income statement, estimated warranty expense is deductible; on the tax return, only warranty expense actually incurred is deductible. Early on, this leads to taxes payable being greater than income tax expense, which gives rise to a deferred tax asset. In future periods, taxes payable will be less than income tax expense, and the "benefit" of the asset will be realized.

*Calculating deferred tax liabilities and assets.* Under the liability method, all temporary differences between taxable income and pretax income are multiplied by the expected future tax rate (typically the current rate) to calculate deferred tax assets and liabilities. They are not netted; deferred tax assets and liabilities can be on the balance sheet simultaneously and separately.

*Financial analysis.* If a company's assets are growing, it may be the case that a deferred tax liability is not expected to reverse in the foreseeable future; an analyst should treat this "liability" as additional equity (decrease the DTL and increase equity). If the liability is expected to reverse, the liability should be adjusted to present value terms to the extent practicable. Decide which is more appropriate on a case-by-case basis.

*Tax basis.* Gains or losses can result when an asset is sold or a liability is paid when there is a difference between the proceeds or payment and the tax basis of the asset or liability. The tax basis for a long-lived asset is its historical cost minus accumulated tax depreciation. The tax basis for debt is historical proceeds adjusted for the amortization of any original discount or premium to par.

*Change in tax rates.* A change in tax rates will be reflected by an adjustment to both deferred tax asset and liability accounts. A decrease (increase) in the tax rate will decrease (increase) both deferred tax assets and liabilities; the net change is reflected in income tax expense for the current period.

## DTL and DTA Calculations

Consider a firm with a 40% tax rate that has $1,000 in financial statement depreciation and $3,000 of tax return depreciation, as well as $500 of warranty expense that cannot be deducted in the current period for taxes.

The firm will report a DTL of $(3,000 - 1,000)(0.40) = \$800$ and a DTA of $(500 - 0)(0.40) = \$200$. Reported income tax expense is greater than taxes payable by $800 - 200 = \$600$.

A change in the firm's expected tax rate from 40% to 30% would reduce the DTL to $600 and the DTA to $150. The reduction of $200 in the DTL and the decrease in the DTA of $50 net to a $150 decrease in liabilities, which will reduce reported income tax expense (taxes payable – net deferred tax liability) by $150. Net income/profitability is increased, equity is increased, and leverage is decreased by the change.

## Permanent vs. Temporary Differences

So far, our examples have been temporary differences between taxable income and pretax income that will potentially reverse over time. In the case of interest income on tax-exempt bonds, for example, pretax income is greater than taxable income, and this will not reverse. There is no deferred asset or liability created, and

## Derecognition of Debt

When bonds mature, no gain or loss is recognized by the issuer. At maturity, any original discount or premium has been fully amortized; thus, the book value of a bond liability and its face value are the same. The cash outflow to repay a bond is reported in the cash flow statement as a financing cash flow.

A firm may choose to **redeem** bonds before maturity because interest rates have fallen, because the firm has generated surplus cash through operations, or because funds from the issuance of equity make it possible (and desirable).

When bonds are redeemed before maturity, a gain or loss is recognized by subtracting the redemption price from the book value of the bond liability at the reacquisition date. For example, consider a firm that reacquires $1 million face amount of bonds at 102% of par when the carrying value of the bond liability is $995,000. The firm will recognize a loss of $25,000 ($995,000 carrying value – $1,020,000 redemption price). Had the carrying value been greater than the redemption price, the firm would have recognized a gain.

Under U.S. GAAP, any remaining unamortized bond issuance costs must be written off and included in the gain or loss calculation. Writing off the cost of issuing the bond will reduce a gain or increase a loss. No write-off is necessary under IFRS because the issuance costs are already accounted for in the book value of the bond liability.

Any gain or loss from redeeming debt is reported in the income statement, usually as a part of continuing operations, and additional information is disclosed separately. Redeeming debt is usually not a part of the firm's day-to-day operations; thus, analysts often eliminate the gain or loss from the income statement for analysis and forecasting.

When presenting the cash flow statement using the indirect method, any gain (loss) is subtracted from (added to) net income in calculating cash flow from operations. The redemption price is reported as an outflow from financing activities.

## Leases

A firm may choose to lease, rather than purchase, assets:

- To conserve cash.
- Because of attractive financing (lower interest costs).
- To avoid risk of asset obsolescence.

- To avoid reporting a balance sheet liability (with an operating lease) and improve leverage ratios.
- Flexibility to design custom lease liability.
- Tax advantage (U.S.) if an off-balance-sheet lease can be treated as ownership for tax (deduct depreciation and interest expense).

## Lease Classification

Under U.S. GAAP, a lease must be classified by the lessee as a *finance (capital) lease* if any one of the following four criteria is met:

- The title is transferred to the lessee at the end of the lease period.
- A bargain purchase option exists.
- The lease period is at least 75% of the asset's life.
- The present value of the lease payments is at least 90% of the fair value of the asset.

If none of the criteria hold, the lease will be classified as an *operating lease*. Lease classification under IFRS is similar (without specific quantitative tests) and a lease must be classified as a finance lease if substantially all of the risks and rewards of ownership are transferred to the lessee.

## Financial Statement Effects of Leases

When a lease is reported as a finance lease, the firm adds a lease asset and a lease liability to its balance sheet in equal amounts. Over time, the firm recognizes interest expense on the lease liability and depreciation expense on the lease asset. The liability decreases each period by the excess of the lease payment over the interest expense.

When a lease is classified as an operating lease, no balance sheet entries are made, and the lease payment is reported as an expense each period.

Because of these differences, compared to a firm reporting a lease as an operating lease, a firm reporting the same lease as a finance lease will report: higher assets, higher liabilities, higher operating cash flow and lower financing cash flow (portion of lease payment that reduces the lease liability is considered a financing cash flow) over the life of the lease. Since the sum of interest expense and depreciation is greater than the lease payment in the early years of a finance lease, reporting a lease as a finance lease will decrease net income and profitability ratios compared to reporting the lease as an operating lease.

The following tables summarize the effects of capital leases compared to operating leases on financial statement items and ratios.

**Figure 3: Effects of Lease Classification (Financial Statement Totals)**

| Financial Statement Totals | Finance Lease | Operating Lease |
|---|---|---|
| Assets | Higher | Lower |
| Liabilities | Higher | Lower |
| Net income (in the early years) | Lower | Higher |
| Cash flow from operations | Higher | Lower |
| Cash flow from financing | Lower | Higher |
| Total cash flow | Same | Same |

**Figure 4: Effects of Lease Classification (Ratios)**

| Ratios | Finance Lease | Operating Lease |
|---|---|---|
| Current ratio (CA/CL) | Lower | Higher |
| Working capital (CA − CL) | Lower | Higher |
| Asset turnover (Sales/TA) | Lower | Higher |
| Return on assets (EAT/TA) | Lower | Higher |
| Return on equity (EAT/E) | Lower | Higher |
| Debt/equity | Higher | Lower |

With a finance lease, the next lease payment is recognized as a current liability, reducing the current ratio and net working capital. Operating income (EBIT) is higher for a finance lease because the interest expense is not subtracted in its calculation. Total net income will be the same over the entire lease term regardless of classification, but net income will be lower in the early years for a finance lease because interest costs are higher in the early years (the sum of depreciation and interest expense exceeds the lease payment).

## Lessor Treatment of Lease Transactions

If the conditions for a finance lease are not met, a lessor reports a lease as an operating lease. A lessor reports the lease payments as income and depreciates the leased asset on its balance sheet.

If the conditions for a finance lease are met, a lessor reports the lease as either a **sales-type lease** or a **direct financing lease**. From a lessor's perspective, when the carrying value of the leased asset is less than the present value of the lease payments, as is the case when the lessor is the manufacturer of the leased asset, the lease is treated as a sales-type lease. In this case, the lessor reports the transaction as if the asset were sold at the lease value (recognizing profit at lease initiation) and as if a loan was provided to the lessee. A lease receivable (asset) is added to the lessor's balance sheet. Interest income and a reduction in the value of the lease receivable asset (future lease payments) are reported as lease payments are received. The interest income is treated as operating cash inflow and the reduction in the asset value is treated as an investing cash inflow.

If the lessor's book value for the leased asset is the same as the present value of the lease, the lease is reported as a direct financing lease. An example would be a leasing company that leases cars to customers, first purchasing the automobiles from various manufacturers. The lessor records interest income over the life of the lease (as if it were purely a loan transaction) and no profit at the inception of the lease. Interest income is reported as an operating cash inflow and reduction in the value of the lease asset is reported as an investing cash inflow, just as with a sales-type lease.

With a sales-type finance lease, recognizing profit at the inception of the lease increases the lessor's net income, retained earnings, and assets compared to an operating lease or direct financing lease. The lessor reports higher net income in the early years for a direct financing lease compared to an operating lease. This pattern results because interest income from the direct financing lease decreases over time, while the payment on the operating lease is level. Over the life of the lease, lessor net income is the same whether a lease is treated as an operating lease or as a direct financing lease.

## Pension Plans

A **defined contribution plan** is a retirement plan in which the firm contributes a sum each period to the employee's retirement account. The firm makes no promise to the employee regarding the future value of the plan assets. The investment decisions are left to the employee, who assumes all of the investment risk. On the income statement, pension expense is simply equal to the employer's contribution. There is no future obligation to report on the balance sheet.

In a **defined benefit plan**, the firm promises to make periodic payments to employees after retirement. The benefit is usually based on the employee's years of service and the employee's compensation at, or near, retirement. For example, an employee might earn a retirement benefit of 2% of her final salary for each year of service. Because the employee's future benefit is defined, the employer assumes the investment risk.

Financial reporting for a defined benefit plan is much more complicated than for a defined contribution plan because the employer must estimate the value of the future obligation to its employees. The obligation involves forecasting a number of variables, such as future compensation levels, employee turnover, retirement age, mortality rates, and an appropriate discount rate.

The present value of the future obligation is known as the **defined benefit obligation**. The defined benefit obligation is the present value of the amount owed to employees for future pension benefits earned to date.

For a defined benefit plan, pension expense consists of the following:

- **Service cost** is the present value of benefits earned by the employees during the current period. Service cost increases the benefit obligation.
- **Interest cost** is the increase in the benefit obligation due to the passage of time. Benefit obligations are similar to borrowing with a promise to make future payments; thus, interest accrues on the obligation each period.
- The **expected return on plan assets** reduces pension expense. Since the expected return and actual return should be equal over the long term, the expected return is used to calculate pension expense in order to reduce the volatility of annual pension expense. If a large enough liability results from a difference between expected and actual returns on plan assets, the firm must amortize the liability over time as part of pension expense.
- **Actuarial gains and losses** are based on assumptions the actuary must make about the benefits to be paid in the future. Changes in assumptions about retirement ages or the rate of salary growth, for example, produce gains and losses that affect pension expense.
- **Prior service costs** are retroactive benefits awarded to employees when a plan is initiated or amended.

IFRS and U.S. GAAP allow firms to smooth the effects of changes in actuarial assumptions and prior service costs over time. Smoothing results in less volatile pension expense.

The difference between the defined benefit obligation and the plan assets is referred to as the **funded status** of the plan. If the value of the plan assets exceeds the present value of the benefit obligation, the plan is said to be **overfunded**. Conversely, if the benefit obligation exceeds the plan assets, the plan is **underfunded**. The funded status represents the economic reality of the plan.

Under U.S. GAAP, the funded status is reported on the balance sheet. Thus, an overfunded amount of a pension is reported as an asset and an underfunded amount is reported as a liability.

Under IFRS, firms remove unrecognized actuarial gains and losses and unrecognized prior service costs from the funded status. The result is a balance sheet amount that does not represent economic reality.

Under IFRS and U.S. GAAP, firms separately disclose the components of the benefit obligation, plan assets, and pension expense. In addition, firms disclose the assumptions used to calculate pension expense, such as the discount rate, the compensation growth rate, and the expected rate of return on plan assets.

# STUDY SESSION 10: FINANCIAL REPORTING AND ANALYSIS— TECHNIQUES, APPLICATIONS, AND INTERNATIONAL STANDARDS CONVERGENCE

## FINANCIAL REPORTING QUALITY: RED FLAGS AND ACCOUNTING WARNING SIGNS
Cross-Reference to CFA Institute Assigned Reading #40

This is a broad, qualitative overview of earnings quality. Keep in mind that management may be motivated to overstate or even understate its earnings.

### Low Earnings Quality

Low earnings quality is often the result of the following:

- Selecting accounting principles that misrepresent the economics of the transaction.
- Structuring transactions to achieve a desired outcome.
- Using aggressive or unrealistic estimates and assumptions.
- Exploiting the intent of an accounting principle.

### Figure 5: The Fraud Triangle

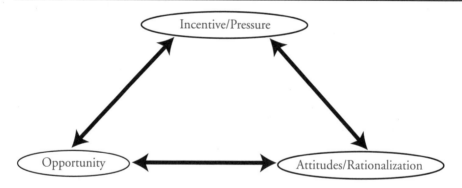

- *Incentive/pressure* is the motive to commit fraud.
- *Opportunities* to commit fraud exist when the firm has a weak internal control system.
- *Attitude/rationalization* is the mindset that fraud is justified.

## Common Warning Signs of Earnings Manipulation

Common warning signs of earnings manipulation include the following:

- Aggressive revenue recognition.
- Different growth rates of operating cash flow and earnings.

- Abnormal comparative sales growth.
- Abnormal inventory growth as compared to sales.
- Moving nonoperating income and nonrecurring gains up the income statement to boost revenue.
- Delaying expense recognition.
- Excessive use of off-balance sheet financing arrangements including leases.
- Classifying expenses as extraordinary or nonrecurring and moving them down the income statement to boost income from continuing operations.
- LIFO liquidations (decreases in inventory levels that result in out-of-date, low costs being recognized in COGS).
- Abnormal comparative margin ratios.
- Aggressive assumptions and estimates.
- Year-end surprises.
- Equity method investments with little or no cash flow.

## ACCOUNTING SHENANIGANS ON THE CASH FLOW STATEMENT
Cross-Reference to CFA Institute Assigned Reading #41

Management has several ways to manipulate operating cash flow, including deciding how to allocate cash flow between categories and changing the timing of receipt of cash flows. Firms can manipulate operating cash flow by classifying operating activities as financing activities and vice versa. Also keep in mind that not all increases in cash flow are sustainable. Examples of the ways management can manipulate operating cash flow include the following:

- *Stretching accounts payable* by delaying payment is not a sustainable source of operating cash flow. Suppliers may refuse to extend additional credit because of the slower payments. Stretching accounts payable can be identified by increases in the number of days in payables. Days-in payables is calculated by dividing the average balance of accounts payable by cost of goods sold (COGS) and multiplying the result by the number of days in the period.
- Another form of delaying cash flows associated with accounts payable is to *finance the payables through a third party*. This allows the firm to alter the timing of payment, as well as treat the payment as a financing activity in the cash flow statement.
- *Securitizing accounts receivable* accelerates the operating cash flow into the current period, but the source of cash is not sustainable. Securitizing receivables may also allow the firm to immediately recognize gains in the income statement.
- Some firms repurchase stock to offset the dilutive effect of employee stock options. The analyst must determine whether the *income tax benefits from employee stock options* provide a sustainable source of operating cash flow. For analytical purposes, reclassify the net cash outflow to repurchase stock from financing activities to operating activities.

## FINANCIAL STATEMENT ANALYSIS: APPLICATIONS
Cross-Reference to CFA Institute Assigned Reading #42

This topic covers the use of common-size financial statements and other ratio analysis to evaluate past performance, prepare projections of future earnings, assess credit quality, and screen for equity investments; and adjusting financial statements to facilitate comparison between companies.

### Analysis Based on Ratios

Trends in financial ratios and differences between a firm's financial ratios and those of its competitors or industry averages can indicate important aspects of a firm's business strategy and whether a strategy is succeeding. Some examples of interpreting ratios are:

- Premium and custom products are usually sold at higher gross margins than less differentiated commodity-like products, so we should expect cost of goods sold to be a higher proportion of sales for the latter.
- We might also expect a company with products that have cutting-edge features and high quality to spend a higher proportion of sales on research and development. This proportion may be quite low for a firm purchasing components from suppliers rather than developing new features and capabilities in-house.
- The ratio of gross profits to operating profits will be larger for a firm that has relatively high research and development and/or advertising expenditures.
- If a firm claims it will improve earnings per share by cutting costs, examination of operating ratios and gross margins over time will reveal whether the firm has actually been able to implement such a strategy.

### Forecasting Financial Performance for a Firm

A forecast of future net income and cash flow often begins with a forecast of future sales based on the top-down approach (especially for shorter horizons).

- Begin with a forecast of GDP growth, often supplied by outside research or an in-house economics group.
- Use historical relationships to estimate the relationship between GDP growth and the growth of industry sales.
- Determine the firm's expected market share for the forecast period, and multiply by industry sales to forecast firm sales.
- In a simple forecasting model, some historical average or trend-adjusted measure of profitability (operating margin, EBT margin, or net margin) can be used to forecast earnings.

- In complex forecasting models, each item on an income statement and balance sheet can be estimated based on separate assumptions about its growth in relation to revenue growth.
- For multi-period forecasts, the analyst typically employs a single estimate of sales growth at some point that is expected to continue indefinitely.
- To estimate cash flows, the analyst must make assumptions about future sources and uses of cash, especially as regards changes in working capital, capital expenditures on new fixed assets, issuance or repayments of debt, and issuance or repurchase of stock.
- A typical assumption is that noncash working capital as a percentage of sales remains constant.
- A first-pass model might indicate a need for cash in future periods, and these cash requirements can then be met by projecting necessary borrowing in future periods. For consistency, interest expense in future periods must also be adjusted for any increase in debt and reflected in the income statement, which must be reconciled with the pro forma balance sheet by successive iterations.

## Role of Financial Statement Analysis in Assessing Credit Quality

The three Cs of credit analysis are:
1. **Character**: *Character* refers to firm management's professional reputation and the firm's history of debt repayment.
2. **Collateral**: The ability to pledge specific *collateral* reduces lender risk.
3. **Capacity**: The *capacity* to repay requires close examination of a firm's financial statements and ratios. Since some debt is for periods of 30 years or longer, the credit analyst must take a very long-term view of the firm's prospects.

Credit rating agencies, such as Moody's and Standard and Poor's, use items to assess firm creditworthiness that can be separated into four general categories:

1. *Scale and diversification.* Larger companies and those with more different product lines and greater geographic diversification are better credit risks.
2. *Operational efficiency.* Such items as operating ROA, operating margins, and EBITDA margins fall into this category. Along with greater vertical diversification, high operating efficiency is associated with better debt ratings.
3. *Margin stability.* Stability of the relevant profitability margins indicates a higher probability of repayment (leads to a better debt rating and a lower interest rate). Highly variable operating results make lenders nervous.
4. *Leverage.* Ratios of operating earnings, EBITDA, or some measure of free cash flow to interest expense or total debt make up the most important part of the credit rating formula. Firms with greater earnings in relation to their debt and in relation to their interest expense are better credit risks.

## Screening for Potential Equity Investments

In many cases, an analyst must select portfolio stocks from the large universe of potential equity investments. Accounting items and ratios can be used to identify a manageable subset of available stocks for further analysis.

Criteria commonly used to screen for attractive equity investments include low P/E, P/CF or P/S; high ROE, ROA, or growth rates of sales and earnings; and low leverage. Multiple criteria are often used because a screen based on a single factor can include firms with other undesirable characteristics.

Analysts should be aware that their equity screens will likely include and exclude many or all of the firms in particular industries.

## Financial Statement Adjustments to Facilitate Comparisons

Differences in accounting methods chosen by firms subject to the same standards, as well as differences in accounting methods due to differences in applicable accounting standards, can make comparisons between companies problematic. An analyst must be prepared to adjust the financial statements of one company to make them comparable to those of another company or group of companies.

Common adjustments required include adjustment for:

- Differences in depreciation methods and assumptions.
- Differences in inventory cost flow assumptions/methods.
- Differences in the treatment of the effect of exchange rate changes.
- Differences in classifications of investment securities.
- Operating leases.
- Capitalization decisions.
- Goodwill.

## INTERNATIONAL STANDARDS CONVERGENCE
Cross-Reference to CFA Institute Assigned Reading #43

The material here covers the IFRS treatment for many items and highlights some differences with U.S. GAAP treatment.

## IFRS Treatments of Assets and Liabilities

### Inventory

Under IFRS, the choice of inventory method is based on the physical flow of the inventory. Two acceptable methods are the first-in, first-out (FIFO) method and the average cost method. The last-in, first-out (LIFO) method is allowed under U.S. GAAP but is not permitted under IFRS.

Under IFRS, inventory is reported on the balance sheet at the lower of cost or net realizable value, and under U.S. GAAP the lower of cost or *market*, which must be between net realizable value and net realizable value minus a normal profit margin. In the United States, once an inventory writedown occurs, any subsequent recovery of value is ignored. Under IFRS, adjustment for a recovery of value is permitted.

## Property and Equipment

Under both IFRS and U.S. GAAP, long-term (fixed) assets are carried on the balance sheet at original cost less accumulated depreciation.

Under IFRS, property and equipment can be revalued upward, but this is not permitted under U.S. GAAP. Under IFRS, the increase in value is reported on the income statement to the extent that a previous downward valuation was reported on the income statement. Increases in value in excess of previous impairment charges are reported as a direct adjustment to equity.

## Intercorporate Investments

Under IFRS, the accounting treatment for intercorporate investments is as follows:

| Method | Ownership | Degree of Influence |
|---|---|---|
| Market | Less than 20% | No significant influence |
| Equity | 20% – 50% | Significant influence |
| Consolidation | More than 50% | Control |
| Proportionate Consolidation (IFRS only) | Shared | Joint control |

In the case of joint control of an investee, such as an ownership interest in a joint venture, IFRS recommends the use of the *proportionate consolidation* method, although the equity method is permitted. Under proportionate consolidation, the investor reports its pro-rata share of the assets, liabilities, and net income of the investee.

Under U.S. GAAP, the equity method is usually required for joint ventures. Proportionate consolidation is not permitted.

## Goodwill

Under IFRS and U.S. GAAP, goodwill is not amortized in the income statement; however, it must be tested at least annually for impairment. Judgment is involved in determining whether goodwill is impaired, so the timing of impairment charges can be used to manage earnings.

For comparability purposes, analysts often make the following adjustments when performing financial analysis:

- Deduct goodwill when computing ratios.
- Exclude goodwill impairment charges from the income statement when analyzing trends.
- Evaluate acquisitions in terms of the price paid relative to the earning power of the acquired assets.

Two other issues affect the comparability of the financial statements of the acquiring firm in a business acquisition.

1. The assets and liabilities of the acquired firm are recorded at fair value at the date of acquisition. As a result, the acquiring firm reports assets and liabilities with a mixture of bases for valuation; the acquiring firm's old assets continue to be reported at historical cost, while the acquired assets are reported at fair value.

2. The revenues and expenses of the acquired firm are included in the acquiring firm's income statement from the acquisition date. There is no restatement of the prior-period income statements, so the acquisition may create the illusion of growth.

## Identifiable Intangible Assets

Under U.S. GAAP and IFRS, acquired intangible assets are reported on the balance sheet at acquisition cost less accumulated amortization. The costs of internally developed intangibles are generally expensed as incurred. U.S. GAAP does not permit upward revaluations of intangible assets.

As with property and equipment, IFRS allows upward revaluations of identifiable intangible assets. In this case, the intangible assets are reported at fair value at the revaluation date less the accumulated amortization since revaluation.

As with property and equipment, any increase in value is reported in the income statement to the extent that a previous downward valuation was included in net income. Any increase in value beyond that is reported as a direct adjustment to equity.

Analysts must be aware that not all intangible assets are reported on the balance sheet. Some intangibles are expensed as incurred. These unrecorded assets must still be considered when valuing a firm.

## Provisions

**Provisions** are nonfinancial liabilities that are uncertain as to their timing or amount. Examples include warranty obligations and contingencies. According to IAS No. 37, a firm should recognize a liability when it has a present obligation that is a result of a past event and the firm can reliably estimate the cost to settle the obligation.

U.S. GAAP does not use the term "provisions." In the United States, if a contingency is probable and can be reasonably estimated, a loss is recognized in the income statement and a liability is reported on the balance sheet.

## Major International Accounting Standards for Income Statement Items

The definitions of revenue and the criteria for recognition between U.S. GAAP and IFRS differ slightly. However, the main principles are the same. U.S. GAAP provides more industry-specific guidance than IFRS.

### Construction Contracts

Under U.S. GAAP, the percentage-of-completion method of revenue recognition is appropriate for contracts that extend beyond one accounting period if the outcome of the project can be reasonably estimated. Accordingly, revenue, expense, and therefore profit are recognized as the work is performed. If the outcome of the project cannot be reasonably estimated, the completed-contract method is required.

Under IFRS, if the firm cannot reliably estimate the outcome of the project, revenue is recognized to the extent that it is probable that contract costs will be recovered.

### Depreciation

Tangible assets (excluding land) are depreciated, intangible assets (except goodwill) are amortized, and natural resources are depleted. A change in an estimate is put into effect prospectively; that is, no cumulative adjustment is made.

In choosing an appropriate allocation method (e.g., straight-line, accelerated), IFRS requires that the method reflect the pattern of expected consumption and the allocation must be made on a systematic basis over the asset's useful life.

### Interest Capitalization

Borrowing costs are generally expensed in the year incurred. Under both IFRS and U.S. GAAP, firms must capitalize construction interest. Interest on non-project-specific borrowing is included to the extent of investment in the project.

### Income Taxes

Both U.S. GAAP and IFRS require firms to recognize temporary differences in tax liabilities arising from differences between financial reporting standards and tax reporting standards. These differences result in deferred tax assets and deferred tax liabilities.

### Nonrecurring Items

Analysts often remove nonrecurring items from the income statement for forecasting purposes. Recurring earnings are usually viewed as more sustainable. Over the past several years, there has been convergence between U.S. GAAP and IFRS in the areas of discontinued operations and changing accounting principles. However, the treatment of extraordinary items still differs.

Under U.S. GAAP, an extraordinary item is a material transaction that is both unusual in nature and infrequent in occurrence. Extraordinary items are reported in the income statement, net of tax, below income from continuing operations.

IFRS does not permit firms to treat items as "extraordinary" in the income statement.

### Dividends and Interest

Under U.S. GAAP, dividends paid to the firm's shareholders are reported as CFF while interest paid is CFO. Interest paid and received and dividends received are all classified as CFO.

IFRS allows more flexibility in the classification of cash flows. Under IFRS, interest and dividends received may be classified as either CFO or CFI. Dividends paid to the firm's shareholders and interest paid on the firm's debt may be classified as either CFO or CFF.

## Effect of International Accounting Differences on Financial Ratios

As an example, consider a U.S. firm that reports using LIFO inventory costing and an IFRS firm that reports using FIFO. By adding the *LIFO reserve* (the difference between LIFO inventory and FIFO inventory, which must be discloed by LIFO firms) to the U.S. firm's inventory balance, the analyst can state the U.S. firm's inventory on a FIFO basis to make it comparable with the IFRS firm. Converting LIFO COGS to FIFO COGS can be accomplished by subtracting the change in the LIFO reserve over the period from LIFO COGS.

These adjustments to LIFO inventory and LIFO COGS will change the following ratios for the LIFO firm (during periods of rising prices):

- Higher gross profit margin [(Revenue – COGS) / Revenue] because of lower COGS.
- Higher operating profit margin (Operating profit / Revenue) because of higher gross profit.
- Higher net profit margin (Net income / Revenue) because of higher operating profit.
- Higher current ratio (Current asset / Current liabilities) because of higher current assets (inventory).
- Lower total asset turnover ratio (Revenue / Average total assets) because of higher total assets (inventory).
- Lower inventory turnover ratio (COGS / Average inventory) because of lower COGS and higher inventory.
- Lower debt-to-equity ratio because of higher equity.

# Corporate Finance

| | |
|---|---|
| Weight on Exam | 8% |
| SchweserNotes™ Reference | Book 4, Pages 1–133 |

For only 8% of the total exam, there is a lot of material to cover. Don't become too immersed in detail.

## Capital Budgeting
Cross-Reference to CFA Institute Assigned Reading #44

**Capital budgeting** is identifying and evaluating projects for which the cash flows extend over a period longer than a year. The process has four steps:

1. Generating ideas.
2. Analyzing project proposals.
3. Creating the firm's capital budget.
4. Monitoring decisions and conducting a post-audit.

*Categories of capital budgeting projects* include:

- Replacement projects to maintain the business.
- Replacement projects to reduce costs.
- Expansion projects to increase capacity.
- New product or market development.
- Mandatory projects, such as meeting safety or environmental regulations.
- Other projects, including high-risk research and development or management pet projects, are not easily analyzed through the capital budgeting process.

## Five Key Principles of Capital Budgeting

1. Decisions are based on *incremental cash flows*. Sunk costs are not considered. Externalities, including *cannibalization* of sales of the firm's current products, should be included in the analysis.

2. Cash flows are based on *opportunity costs*, which are the cash flows the firm will lose by undertaking the project.

3. *Timing* of the cash flows is important.

4. Cash flows are analyzed on an *after-tax basis*.

5. *Financing costs* are reflected in the required rate of return on the project, *not* in the incremental cash flows.

Projects can be *independent* and evaluated separately, or *mutually exclusive*, which means the projects compete with each other and the firm can accept only one of them. In some cases, *project sequencing* requires projects to be undertaken in a certain order, with the accept/reject decision on the second project depending on the profitability of the first project.

A firm with *unlimited funds* can accept all profitable projects. However, when *capital rationing* is necessary, the firm must select the most valuable group of projects that can be funded with the limited capital resources available.

## Capital Budgeting Methods

The *payback period* is the number of years it takes to recover the initial cost of the project. You must be given a maximum acceptable payback period for a project. This criterion ignores the time value of money and any cash flows beyond the payback period.

The *discounted payback period* is the number of years it takes to recover the initial investment in present value terms. The discount rate used is the project's cost of capital. This method incorporates the time value of money but ignores any cash flows beyond the discounted payback period.

The *profitability index* is the present value of a project's future cash flows divided by the initial cash outlay. The decision rule is to accept a project if its profitability index is greater than one, which is the same as the IRR > cost of capital rule and the NPV > 0 rule (since PI = 1 + NPV/Initial Outlay).

*Net present value* for a normal project is the present value of all the expected future cash flows minus the initial cost of the project, using the project's cost of capital. A project that has a positive net present value should be accepted because it is expected to increase the value of the firm (shareholder wealth).

The *internal rate of return* is the discount rate that makes the present value of the expected future cash flows equal to the initial cost of the project. If the IRR is greater than the project's cost of capital, it should be accepted because it is expected to increase firm value. If the IRR is equal to the project's cost of capital, the NPV is zero.

For an independent project, the criteria for acceptance (NPV > 0 and IRR > project cost of capital) are equivalent and always lead to the same decision.

For mutually exclusive projects, the NPV and IRR decision rules can lead to different rankings because of differences in project size and/or differences in the timing of cash flows. The NPV criterion is theoretically preferred, as it directly estimates the effect of project acceptance on firm value.

Be certain you can calculate all of these measures quickly and accurately with your calculator.

Since inflation is reflected in the WACC (or project cost of capital) calculation, future cash flows must be adjusted upward to reflect positive expected inflation, or some wealth-increasing (positive NPV) projects will be rejected.

Larger firms, public companies, and firms where management has a higher level of education tend to use NPV and IRR analysis. Private companies and European firms tend to rely more on the payback period in capital budgeting decisions.

In theory, a positive NPV project should increase the company's stock price by the project's NPV per share. In reality, stock prices reflect investor expectations about a firm's ability to identify and execute positive NPV projects in the future.

## COST OF CAPITAL
Cross-Reference to CFA Institute Assigned Reading #45

Knowing how to calculate the *weighted average cost of capital* (WACC) and all of its components is critical.

$$\text{WACC} = (w_d)[k_d(1 - t)] + (w_{ps})(k_{ps}) + (w_{ce})(k_{cd})$$

Here, the *w*s are the proportions of each type of capital, the *k*s are the current costs of each type of capital (debt, preferred stock, and common stock), and $t$ is the firm's *marginal* tax rate.

The proportions used for the three types of capital are target proportions and are calculated using market values. An analyst can use the WACC to compare the after-tax cost of raising capital to the expected after-tax returns on capital investments.

*Cost of equity capital.* There are three methods. You will likely know which to use by the information given in the problem.

1. CAPM approach: $k_{ce} = \text{RFR} + \beta(R_{market} - \text{RFR})$.

©2011 Kaplan, Inc.

2. Discounted cash flow approach: $k_{ce} = (D_1 / P_0) + g$.

3. Bond yield plus risk premium approach: $k_{ce}$ = current market yield on the firm's long-term debt + risk premium.

*Cost of preferred stock* is always calculated as follows:

$$k_{ps} = \frac{D_{ps}}{P}$$

*Cost of debt* is the average market yield on the firm's outstanding debt issues. Since interest is tax deductible, $k_d$ is multiplied by $(1 - t)$.

Firm decisions about which projects to undertake are independent of the decision of how to finance firm assets at minimum cost. The firm will have long-run target weights for the percentages of common equity, preferred stock, and debt used to fund the firm. Investment decisions are based on a WACC that reflects each source of capital at its target weight, regardless of how a particular project will be financed or which capital source was most recently employed.

An analyst calculating a firm's WACC should use the firm's target capital structure if known, or use the firm's current capital structure based on market values as the best indicator of its target capital structure. The analyst can incorporate trends in the company's capital structure into his estimate of the target structure. An alternative would be to apply the industry average capital structure to the firm.

A firm's WACC can increase as it raises larger amounts of capital, which means the firm has an upward sloping *marginal cost of capital curve*. If the firm ranks its potential projects in descending IRR order, the result is a downward sloping *investment opportunity schedule*. The amount of the capital investment required to fund all projects for which the IRR is greater than the marginal cost of capital is the firm's *optimal capital budget*.

A **project beta** can be used to determine the appropriate cost of equity capital for evaluating a project. Using the "pure-play method," the project beta is estimated based on the equity beta of a firm purely engaged in the same business as the project. The pure-play firm's beta must be adjusted for any difference between the capital structure (leverage) of the pure-play firm and the capital structure of the company evaluating the project.

For a developing market, the **country risk premium** (CRP) is calculated as:

$$CRP = [\text{sovereign bond yield} - \text{T-bond yield}] \times \left( \frac{\text{std. dev. of developing country index}}{\text{std. dev. of sovereign bonds in U.S. currency}} \right)$$

The required return on equity securities is then:

$$k_{CE} = RFR + \beta\,[E(R_{MKT}) - RFR + CRP]$$

A **break-point** refers to a level of total investment beyond which the WACC increases because the cost of one component of the capital structure increases. It is calculated by dividing the amount of funding at which the component cost of capital increases by the target capital structure weight for that source of capital.

When new equity is issued, the **flotation costs** (underwriting costs) should be included as an addition to the initial outlay for the project when calculating NPV or IRR.

## MEASURES OF LEVERAGE
Cross-Reference to CFA Institute Assigned Reading #46

### Business Risk vs. Financial Risk

**Business risk** refers to the risk associated with a firm's operating income and is the result of:

- Sales risk (variability of demand).
- Operating risk (proportion of total costs that are fixed costs).

**Financial risk.** Additional risk common stockholders have to bear because the firm uses fixed cost sources of financing.

*Degree of operating leverage* (DOL) is defined as:

$$DOL = \frac{\%\ \text{change in EBIT}}{\%\ \text{change in sales}}$$

The DOL at a particular level of sales, Q, is calculated as:

$$DOL = \frac{Q(P-V)}{Q(P-V)-F}$$

$$= \frac{S-TVC}{S-TVC-F}$$

One way to help remember this formula is to know that if fixed costs are zero, there is no operating leverage (i.e., DOL = 1).

*Degree of financial leverage* (DFL) is defined as:

$$DFL = \frac{\% \text{ change in EPS}}{\% \text{ change in EBIT}}$$

The DFL at a particular level of sales is calculated as:

$$DFL = \frac{EBIT}{EBIT - \text{interest expense}}$$

One way to help remember this formula is to know that if interest costs are zero (no fixed-cost financing), there is no financial leverage (i.e., DFL = 1). In this context, we treat preferred dividends as interest.

*Degree of total leverage* (DTL) is the product of DOL and DFL:

$$DTL = DOL \times DFL$$

$$= \frac{\% \text{ change in EBIT}}{\% \text{ change in sales}} \times \frac{\% \text{ change in EPS}}{\% \text{ change in EBIT}} = \frac{\% \text{ change in EPS}}{\% \text{ change in sales}}$$

$$= \frac{Q(P-V)}{Q(P-V)-F-I} = \frac{S-TVC}{S-TVC-F-I}$$

## Breakeven Quantity of Sales

A firm's *breakeven point* is the quantity of sales a firm must achieve to just cover its fixed and variable costs. The breakeven quantity is calculated as:

$$Q_{BE} = \frac{\text{total fixed costs}}{\text{price} - \text{variable cost per unit}}$$

The *operating breakeven quantity* considers only fixed operating costs:

$$Q_{OBE} = \frac{\text{fixed operating costs}}{\text{price} - \text{variable cost per unit}}$$

## Effects of Operating Leverage and Financial Leverage

A firm with greater operating leverage (greater fixed costs) will have a higher breakeven quantity than an identical firm with less operating leverage. If sales are greater than the breakeven quantity, the firm with greater operating leverage will generate larger profit.

Financial leverage reduces net income by the interest cost, but increases return on equity because the (reduced) net income is generated with less equity (and more debt). A firm with greater financial leverage will have a greater risk of default, but will also offer greater potential returns for its stockholders.

## DIVIDENDS AND SHARE REPURCHASES: BASICS
Cross-Reference to CFA Institute Assigned Reading #47

**Cash dividends** transfer cash from the firm to its shareholders. This reduces the company's assets and the market value of its equity. When the dividend is paid, the stock price should drop by the amount of the per share dividend. Therefore, the dividend does not change the shareholder's wealth.

Types of cash dividends:

*   *Regular dividend.* A company pays out a portion of its earnings on a schedule.
*   *Special dividend.* One-time cash payment to shareholders.
*   *Liquidating dividend.* A company goes out of business and distributes the proceeds to shareholders. These are taxed as a return of capital.

## Dividend Payment Chronology

- *Declaration date:* board of directors approves the dividend payment.
- *Ex-dividend date:* first day the stock trades without the dividend (two business days before the record date).
- *Holder-of-record date:* date on which shareholders must own the shares in order to receive the dividend.
- *Payment date:* dividend is paid by check or electronic transfer.

## Stock Dividends, Stock Splits, and Reverse Stock Splits

These actions change the number of shares outstanding, but the share price changes proportionately, so a shareholder's wealth and ownership stake are not affected.

- *Stock dividend.* Shareholders receive additional shares of stock (e.g., 10% more shares).
- *Stock split.* Each "old" share is replaced by more than one "new" share (e.g., 3:2 or 2:1).
- *Reverse stock split.* Replace "old" shares with a smaller number of "new" shares.

## Share Repurchases

A company can buy back shares of its common stock. Since this uses the company's cash, it can be seen as an alternative to a cash dividend. Taxes aside, neither cash dividends nor share repurchases affect the shareholder's wealth.

Three repurchase methods:

1. Buy in the open market.
2. Make a tender offer for a fixed number of shares at a fixed price.
3. Directly negotiate with a large shareholder.

If a firm borrows funds to repurchase its shares, EPS will rise if the after-tax cost of debt is less than the earnings yield (E/P) of its shares.

For a firm that repurchases its shares with retained earnings, the book value of its shares will increase if the price paid for repurchased shares is less than their book value.

## WORKING CAPITAL MANAGEMENT
Cross-Reference to CFA Institute Assigned Reading #48

**Primary sources of liquidity** are a company's normal sources of short-term cash, such as selling goods and services, collecting receivables, or using trade credit and short-term borrowing. **Secondary sources of liquidity** are the measures a company must take to generate cash when its primary sources are inadequate, such as liquidating assets, renegotiating debt, or filing for bankruptcy.

**Drags and pulls on liquidity** include uncollectable receivables or debts, obsolete inventory, tight short-term credit, and poor payables management.

**Liquidity measures** include:

- Current ratio.
- Quick ratio.
- Cash ratio.

**Measures of working capital effectiveness** include:

- Receivables turnover, number of days receivables.
- Inventory turnover, number of days of inventory.
- Payables turnover, number of days of payables.
- Operating cycle, cash conversion cycle.

> operating cycle = days of inventory + days of receivables
>
> cash conversion cycle = days of inventory + days of receivables − days of payables

## Managing a Company's Net Daily Cash Position

The purpose of managing a firm's daily cash position is to make sure there is sufficient cash (target balance) but to not keep excess cash balances because of the interest foregone by not investing the cash in short-term securities to earn interest. These short-term securities include:

- U.S. Treasury bills.
- Short-term federal agency securities.
- Bank certificates of deposit.
- Banker's acceptances.
- Time deposits.
- Repurchase agreements.
- Commercial paper.
- Money market mutual funds.
- Adjustable-rate preferred stock.

Adjustable-rate preferred stock has a dividend rate that is reset periodically to current market yields (through an auction in the case of auction-rate preferred) and offers corporate holders a tax advantage because a percentage of the dividends received is exempt from federal tax.

Yield measures used to compare different options for investing excess cash balances include:

$$\% \text{ discount from face value} = \left( \frac{\text{face value} - \text{price}}{\text{face value}} \right)$$

$$\text{discount-basis yield} = \left( \frac{\text{face value} - \text{price}}{\text{face value}} \right) \left( \frac{360}{\text{days}} \right)$$

$$= \% \text{ discount} \left( \frac{360}{\text{days}} \right)$$

$$\text{money market yield} = \left( \frac{\text{face value} - \text{price}}{\text{price}} \right) \left( \frac{360}{\text{days to maturity}} \right)$$

$$\text{bond equivalent yield} = \left( \frac{\text{face value} - \text{price}}{\text{price}} \right) \left( \frac{365}{\text{days to maturity}} \right)$$

$$= \text{HPY} \left( \frac{365}{\text{days}} \right)$$

Note that in Quantitative Methods, the bond equivalent yield was defined differently, as two times the effective semiannual holding period yield.

## Cash Management Investment Policy

- An investment policy statement typically begins with a statement of the purpose and objective of the investment portfolio and some general guidelines about the strategy to be employed to achieve those objectives and the types of securities that will be used.
- The investment policy statement will also include specific information about who is allowed to purchase securities, who is responsible for complying with company guidelines, and what steps will be taken if the investment guidelines are not followed.
- Finally, the investment policy statement will include limitations on the specific types of securities permitted for investment of short-term funds, limitations on the credit ratings of portfolio securities, and limitations on the proportions of the total short-term securities portfolio that can be invested in the various types of permitted securities.

An investment policy statement should be evaluated on how well the policy can be expected to satisfy the goals and purpose of short-term investments, generating yield without taking on excessive credit or liquidity risk. The policy should not be overly restrictive in the context of meeting the goals of safety and liquidity.

## Evaluating Firm Performance in Managing Receivables, Inventory, and Payables

### Receivables

The management of accounts receivable begins with calculation of the average days of receivables and comparison of this ratio to a firm's historical performance or to the average ratios for a group of comparable companies.

More detail about accounts receivable performance can be gained by using an aging schedule that shows amounts of receivables by the length of time they have been outstanding.

Presenting the amounts in an aging schedule as percentages of total outstanding receivables can facilitate analysis of how the aging schedule for receivables is changing over time.

Another useful metric for monitoring accounts receivable performance is the *weighted average collection period*, the average days outstanding per dollar of receivables. The weights are the percentages of total receivables in each category of days outstanding, and these are multiplied by the average days to collect accounts within each aging category.

Analysis of the historical trends and significant changes in a firm's aging schedule and weighted average collection days can give a clearer picture of what is driving changes in the simpler metric of average days of receivables.

The company must always evaluate the tradeoff between more strict credit terms and borrower creditworthiness and the ability to make sales. Terms that are too strict will lead to less-than-optimal sales. Terms that are too lenient will increase sales at the cost of longer average days of receivables, which must be funded at some cost and will increase bad accounts, directly affecting profitability.

### Inventory

Inventory management involves a tradeoff as well. Inventory levels that are too low will result in lost sales (stock outs), while inventory that is too large will have costs (carrying costs) because the firm's capital is tied up in inventory.

©2011 Kaplan, Inc.

Reducing inventory will free up cash that can be invested in interest-bearing securities or used to reduce debt or equity funding.

Increasing inventory in terms of average days' inventory or a decreasing inventory turnover ratio can both indicate inventory that is too large. A large inventory can lead to greater losses from obsolete items and can also indicate that items that no longer sell well are included in inventory.

Comparison of average days of inventory and inventory turnover ratios between industries, or even between two firms that have different business strategies, can be misleading.

### *Payables*

Payables must be managed well because they represent a source of working capital to the firm. If the firm pays its payables prior to their due dates, cash is unnecessarily used and interest on it is sacrificed. If a firm pays its payables late, it can damage relationships with suppliers and lead to more restrictive credit terms or even the requirement that purchases be made for cash. Late payment can also result in interest charges that are high compared to those of other sources of short-term financing.

- A company with a short payables period (high payables turnover) may simply be taking advantage of discounts for paying early because it has good low-cost funds available to finance its working capital needs.
- A company with a long payables period may be such an important buyer that it can effectively utilize accounts payable as a source of short-term funding with relatively little cost (suppliers will put up with it).
- Monitoring the changes in days' payables outstanding over time for a single firm will, however, aid the analyst and an extension of days' payables may serve as an early warning of deteriorating short-term liquidity.

A discount is often available for early payment of an invoice (for example, "2/10 net 60" is a 2% discount for paying an invoice within 10 days that is due in full after 60 days). Paying the full invoice later instead of taking the discount is a use of trade credit. The **cost of trade credit** can be calculated as:

$$\text{cost of trade credit} = \left(1 + \frac{PD}{1 - PD}\right)^{\frac{365}{\text{days past discount}}} - 1$$

where:
PD = percent discount (in decimals)
days past discount = the number of days after the end of the discount period

## Sources of Short-Term Funding

### Bank Sources

- *Uncommitted line of credit:* Non-binding offer of credit.
- *Committed (regular) line of credit:* Binding offer of credit to a certain maximum amount for a specific time period. Requires a fee, called an overdraft line of credit outside the United States.
- *Revolving line of credit:* Most reliable line of credit, typically for longer terms than a committed line of credit, can be listed on a firm's financial statements in the footnotes as a source of liquidity.

Lines of credit are used primarily by large, financially sound companies.

- *Banker's acceptances:* Used by firms that export goods and are a guarantee from the bank of the firm that has ordered the goods, stating that a payment will be made upon receipt of the goods. The exporting company can then sell this acceptance at a discount in order to generate funds.
- *Collateralized borrowing:* Firms with weaker credit can borrow at better rates if they pledge specific collateral (receivables, inventory, equipment). A *blanket lein* gives the lender a claim to all current and future firm assets as collateral additional to specific named collateral.

### Non-Bank Sources

- *Factoring:* The actual sale of receivables at a discount from their face value. The factor takes on the responsibility for collecting receivables and the credit risk of the receivables portfolio.
- Smaller firms and firms with poor credit may use *nonbank finance* companies for short-term funding. The cost of such funding is higher than other sources and is used by firms for which normal bank sources of short-term funding are not available.
- Large, creditworthy companies can also issue short-term debt securities called *commercial paper*. Interest costs are typically slightly less than the rate the firm could get from a bank.

## Managing Short-Term Funding

In managing its short-term financing, a firm should focus on the objectives of having sufficient sources of funding for current as well as for future foreseeable cash needs, and should seek the most cost-effective rates available given its needs, assets, and creditworthiness. The firm should have the ability to prepay short-term borrowings when cash flow permits and have the flexibility to structure its short-term financing so that the debt matures without peaks and can be matched to expected cash flows.

For large borrowers, it is important that the firm has alternative sources of short-term funding and even alternative lenders for a particular type of financing. It is often worth having slightly higher overall short-term funding costs in order to have flexibility and redundant sources of financing.

## FINANCIAL STATEMENT ANALYSIS
Cross-Reference to CFA Institute Assigned Reading #49

**Pro forma balance sheets** and **pro forma income statements** are forward-looking financial statements that are constructed based on specific assumptions about future business conditions and firm performance.

One common assumption is that changes in sales drive changes in income statement and balance sheet items (a *sales-driven* forecast).

The steps involved in constructing sales-driven pro forma financial statements are:

1.  Estimate the relation between changes in sales and the changes in sales-driven income statement and balance sheet items.

2.  Estimate future tax rate, interest rate on debt, lease payments, et cetera.

3.  Forecast sales for the period of interest.

4.  Estimate fixed operating costs and fixed financial costs.

5.  Integrate these estimates into pro forma financial statements for the period of interest.

One way to construct pro forma financial statements for the next period would be to estimate sales for the next period and maintain the same percentage of sales for cost of goods sold, SG&A, nonoperating income, current assets, net PPE, and current liabilities. While this would be a somewhat simplistic method of developing financial projections, it will serve as a starting point from which we can then add more realistic assumptions for the change in individual items from period to period.

Initially, assume that long-term debt and common stock remain the same (i.e., no issuance or retirement of debt or common stock, and that the effective tax rate remains constant).

## Estimating Sales

To construct pro forma financial statements under this approach, the first step is to estimate next-period sales. There are several methods, ranging from simple to fairly complex:

1. Calculate the average compound growth rate of sales over a 5- or 10-year period and use that rate of increase for next period's sales.

2. Use regression analysis to estimate the relation between GDP growth and growth in firm sales and use economists' estimates of GDP growth to forecast the change in sales.

3. Economic cycles and seasonality of sales can also be incorporated into more complex sales forecasting models.

4. Specific events, such as new product introductions, changes in regulation, and introduction and acceptance of competing products, can also be incorporated into sales forecasts.

These methods can also be applied to a company's sales in a (business) segment-by-segment analysis, and the forecast sales for each segment can be aggregated into a total revenue forecast.

Specific assumptions can be developed for any of the balance sheet and income statement items in the pro forma statements. A few examples, from many possible items, are:

1. Analysis of the tax reconciliation (between tax expense and actual taxes payable) or information about changes in statutory rates can lead to specific assumptions about changes in tax rates going forward.

2. Information about planned capital expenditures can lead to better estimates of changes in fixed assets for the next period(s), compared to the percentage-of-sales estimate.

3. Trends or anticipated changes in the cost structure, raw materials prices, et cetera, can be used to adjust COGS as a percentage of sales.

## Reconciliation of Pro Forma Statements

Once the pro forma income statement and balance sheet are constructed, they must be *reconciled* to be consistent with each other. Pro forma balance sheet assets will not necessarily equal pro forma liabilities and equity. If pro forma required assets are greater (less) than liabilities plus equity, we have a *financial deficit (surplus)*.

Additional assumptions are necessary to reconcile the income statement and balance sheet. A simple, but not necessarily realistic, assumption that would reconcile the statements is that any surplus is paid out as dividends or that any deficit is funded by reducing dividend payments. Such changes in dividends would change retained earnings and equity so that the balance sheet would balance and be consistent with the income statement.

Other, more realistic, assumptions typically require multiple iterations to reconcile the pro forma income statement and balance sheet. Consider a financial surplus that is assumed to be used to reduce debt. The reduction in debt will balance pro forma assets with liabilities plus equity, but will also reduce interest expense on the income statement, which will increase retained earnings and equity, leading to a (smaller) financial surplus after adjusting the amount of debt. Further reductions in debt (and interest expense) will decrease the surplus until the pro forma income statement and balance sheet are consistent with each other.

Other assumptions about how any surplus is used or how any deficit is funded are possible (such as maintaining the current capital structure and dividend). Increasing or decreasing equity through stock issuance or repurchase will affect pro forma retained earnings for a dividend-paying stock. The process to reconcile the pro forma statements is essentially the same for these alternative assumptions.

## CORPORATE GOVERNANCE OF LISTED COMPANIES
Cross-Reference to CFA Institute Assigned Reading #50

Corporate governance refers to the procedures, policies, and controls within a firm that determine how it is managed. In general, good corporate governance will result in protecting and advancing shareholder interests and in a firm management that acts ethically and legally, and also reports accurate financial information in a timely manner.

Board members should be independent of management, not have other employment with the firm, be qualified/experienced, and be annually elected. The board itself should have the authority to hire outside consultants without management approval and have committees devoted to executive compensation, risk management, legal matters, and governance issues.

Shareholder rights should include proxy voting without attending the meeting, confidential voting, cumulative voting, approval over corporate structure changes, and ability to introduce proposals for board consideration. Shareholder rights are enhanced when there are not different classes of stock that separate economic ownership from voting rights.

A board should have a majority of independent members, which means they do not have other relationships with management or the firm itself, and these members should regularly meet outside the presence of management. The audit committee of the board should be completely made up of independent members, be comprised of financial experts, have the authority to approve or reject any non-audit engagements of the auditor with the firm, and control the audit budget. Shareholders should have approval rights on the acceptance of the external auditor.

Members of the compensation committee should be independent and see that executive compensation is appropriate and is tied to the long-term performance/profitability of the firm. Shareholders should insist that the firm provide them with details regarding compensation, see that the terms and conditions of option grants are reasonable, and be alert to instances of option re-pricing.

In general, anti-takeover defenses benefit entrenched management and harm shareholders by decreasing share values.

# Portfolio Management

| Weight on Exam | 5% |
|---|---|
| SchweserNotes™ Reference | Book 4, Pages 134–202 |

## Portfolio Management: An Overview
Cross-Reference to CFA Institute Assigned Reading #51

### The Portfolio Perspective

The **portfolio perspective** refers to evaluating individual investments by their contribution to the risk and return of an investor's overall portfolio. The alternative is to examine the risk and return of each security in isolation. An investor who holds all his wealth in a single stock because he believes it to be the best stock available is not taking the portfolio perspective—his portfolio is very risky compared to a diversified portfolio.

Modern portfolio theory concludes that the extra risk from holding only a single security is not rewarded with higher expected investment returns. Conversely, diversification allows an investor to reduce portfolio risk without necessarily reducing the portfolio's expected return.

The **diversification ratio** is calculated as the ratio of the risk of an equal-weighted portfolio of $n$ securities (standard deviation of returns) to the risk of a single security selected at random from the portfolio. If the average standard deviation of returns of the $n$ stocks is 25%, and the standard deviation of returns of an equal-weighted portfolio of the $n$ stocks is 18%, the diversification ratio is 18 / 25 = 0.72.

- Portfolio diversification works best when financial markets are operating normally.
- Diversification provides less reduction of risk during market turmoil.
- During periods of financial crisis, correlations tend to increase, which reduces the benefits of diversification.

## Investment Management Clients

**Individual investors** save and invest for a variety of reasons, including purchasing a house or educating their children. In many countries, special accounts allow citizens to invest for retirement and to defer any taxes on investment income and gains until the funds are withdrawn. Defined contribution pension plans are popular vehicles for these investments.

Many types of **institutions** have large investment portfolios. **Defined benefit pension plans** are funded by company contributions and have an obligation to provide specific benefits to retirees, such as a lifetime income based on employee earnings.

An **endowment** is a fund that is dedicated to providing financial support on an ongoing basis for a specific purpose. A **foundation** is a fund established for charitable purposes to support specific types of activities or to fund research related to a particular disease.

The investment objective of a **bank** is to earn more on the bank's loans and investments than the bank pays for deposits of various types. Banks seek to keep risk low and need adequate liquidity to meet investor withdrawals as they occur.

**Insurance companies** invest customer premiums with the objective of funding customer claims as they occur.

**Investment companies** manage the pooled funds of many investors. **Mutual funds** manage these pooled funds in particular styles (e.g., index investing, growth investing, bond investing) and restrict their investments to particular subcategories of investments (e.g., large-firm stocks, energy stocks, speculative bonds) or particular regions (emerging market stocks, international bonds, Asian-firm stocks).

**Sovereign wealth funds** refer to pools of assets owned by a government.

Figure 1 provides a summary of the risk tolerance, investment horizon, liquidity needs, and income objectives for these different types of investors.

## Figure 1: Characteristics of Different Types of Investors

| Investor | Risk Tolerance | Investment Horizon | Liquidity Needs | Income Needs |
|---|---|---|---|---|
| Individuals | Depends on individual | Depends on individual | Depends on individual | Depends on individual |
| DB pensions | High | Long | Low | Depends on age |
| Banks | Low | Short | High | Pay interest |
| Endowments | High | Long | Low | Spending level |
| Insurance | Low | Long—life Short—P&C | High | Low |
| Mutual funds | Depends on fund | Depends on fund | High | Depends on fund |

## Steps in the Portfolio Management Process

**Planning** begins with an analysis of the investor's risk tolerance, return objectives, time horizon, tax exposure, liquidity needs, income needs, and any unique circumstances or investor preferences.

This analysis results in an **investment policy statement (IPS)** that:

- Details the investor's investment objectives and constraints.
- Specifies an objective benchmark (such as an index return).
- Should be updated at least every few years and anytime the investor's objectives or constraints change significantly.

The **execution** step requires an analysis of the risk and return characteristics of various asset classes to determine the asset allocation. In *top-down* analysis, a portfolio manager examines current macroeconomic conditions to identify the asset classes that are most attractive. In *bottom-up* analysis, portfolio managers seek to identify individual securities that are undervalued.

**Feedback** is the final step. Over time, investor circumstances will change, risk and return characteristics of asset classes will change, and the actual weights of the assets in the portfolio will change with asset prices. The portfolio manager must monitor changes, **rebalance** the portfolio periodically, and evaluate performance relative to the benchmark portfolio identified in the IPS.

# PORTFOLIO RISK AND RETURN: PART I
Cross-Reference to CFA Institute Assigned Reading #52

## Risk and Return of Major Asset Classes

Based on U.S. data over the period 1926–2008, Figure 2 indicates that small capitalization stocks have had the greatest average returns and greatest risk over the period. T-bills had the lowest average returns and the lowest standard deviation of returns.

### Figure 2: Risk and Return of Major Asset Classes in the United States (1926–2008)[1]

| Assets Class | Average Annual Return (Geometric Mean) | Standard Deviation (Annualized Monthly) |
|---|---|---|
| Small-cap stocks | 11.7% | 33.0% |
| Large-cap stocks | 9.6% | 20.9% |
| Long-term corporate bonds | 5.9% | 8.4% |
| Long-term Treasury bonds | 5.7% | 9.4% |
| Treasury bills | 3.7% | 3.1% |
| Inflation | 3.0% | 4.2% |

Results for other markets around the world are similar: asset classes with the greatest average returns also have the highest standard deviations of returns.

## Variance and Standard Deviation

Variance of the rate of return for a risky asset calculated from expectational data (a probability model) is the probability-weighted sum of the squared differences between the returns in each state and the unconditional expected return.

$$\text{variance} = \sigma^2 = \sum_{i=1}^{n} \left\{ [R_i - E(R)]^2 \times P_i \right\}$$

$$\text{standard deviation} = \sigma = \sqrt{\sigma^2}$$

1.  2009 Ibbotson SBBI Classic Yearbook

## Covariance and Correlation

Covariance measures the extent to which two variables move together over time. The covariance of returns is an absolute measure of movement and is measured in return units squared.

Using *historical data*, we take the product of the two securities' deviations from their expected returns for each period, sum them, and divide by the number of (paired) observations minus one.

$$cov_{1,2} = \frac{\sum_{t=1}^{n}\left\{ [R_{t,1} - \overline{R}_1][R_{t,2} - \overline{R}_2] \right\}}{n-1}$$

Covariance can be standardized by dividing by the product of the standard deviations of the two securities. This standardized measure of co-movement is called their *correlation coefficient* or *correlation* and is computed as:

$$\text{correlation of assets 1 and 2} = \rho_{1,2} = \frac{cov_{1,2}}{\sigma_1\sigma_2} \quad \text{so that, } cov_{1,2} = \rho_{1,2}\sigma_1\sigma_2$$

## Risk Aversion

A **risk-averse** investor is simply one that dislikes risk (i.e., prefers less risk to more risk). Given two investments that have equal expected returns, a risk-averse investor will choose the one with less risk (standard deviation, $\sigma$).

A **risk-seeking** (risk-loving) investor actually prefers more risk to less and, given equal expected returns, will choose the more risky investment. A **risk-neutral** investor has no preference regarding risk and would be indifferent between two such investments.

A risk-averse investor may select a very risky portfolio despite being risk averse; a risk-averse investor may hold very risky assets if he feels that the extra return he expects to earn is adequate compensation for the additional risk.

## Risk and Return for a Portfolio of Risky Assets

When risky assets are combined into a portfolio, the expected portfolio return is a weighted average of the assets' expected returns, where the weights are the percentages of the total portfolio value invested in each asset.

The standard deviation of returns for a portfolio of risky assets depends on the standard deviations of each asset's return ($\sigma$), the proportion of the portfolio in each asset (w), and, crucially, on the covariance (or correlation) of returns between each asset pair in the portfolio.

Portfolio standard deviation for a two-asset portfolio:

$$\sigma_p = \sqrt{w_1^2\sigma_1^2 + w_2^2\sigma_2^2 + 2w_1w_2\sigma_1\sigma_2\rho_{12}}$$

which is equivalent to:

$$\sigma_p = \sqrt{w_1^2\sigma_1^2 + w_2^2\sigma_2^2 + 2w_1w_2\text{Cov}_{12}}$$

If two risky asset returns are perfectly positively correlated, $\rho_{12} = +1$, then the square root of portfolio variance (the portfolio standard deviation of returns) is equal to:

$$\sigma_{\text{portfolio}} = \sqrt{\text{Var}_{\text{portfolio}}} = \sqrt{w_1^2\sigma_1^2 + w_2^2\sigma_2^2 + 2w_1w_2\sigma_1\sigma_2(1)} = w_1\sigma_1 + w_2\sigma_2$$

In this unique case, with $\rho_{12} = +1$, the portfolio standard deviation is simply the weighted average of the standard deviations of the individual asset returns.

Other things equal, the greatest portfolio risk results when the correlation between asset returns is +1. For any value of correlation less than +1, portfolio variance is reduced. Note that for a correlation of zero, the entire third term in the portfolio variance equation is zero. For negative values of correlation $\rho_{12}$, the third term becomes negative and further reduces portfolio variance and standard deviation.

## Efficient Frontier

The Markowitz efficient frontier represents the set of possible portfolios that have the greatest expected return for each level of risk (standard deviation of returns).

**Figure 3: Minimum Variance and Efficient Frontiers**

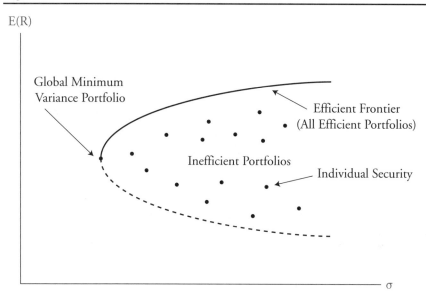

## An Investor's Optimal Portfolio

An investor's **expected utility function** depends on his degree of risk aversion. An **indifference curve** plots combinations of risk (standard deviation) and expected return among which an investor is indifferent, as they all have equal expected utility.

Indifference curves slope upward for risk-averse investors because they will only take on more risk if they are compensated with greater expected return. An investor who is relatively more risk averse requires a relatively greater increase in expected return to compensate for taking on greater risk. In other words, a more risk-averse investor will have steeper indifference curves.

In our previous illustration of efficient portfolios available in the market, we included only risky assets. When we add a risk-free asset to the universe of available assets, the efficient frontier is a straight line. Using the formulas:

$$E(R_{portfolio}) = W_A E(R_A) + W_B E(R_B)$$

$$\sigma_{portfolio} = \sqrt{W_A^2 \sigma_A^2 + W_B^2 \sigma_B^2 + 2 W_A W_B \rho_{AB} \sigma_A \sigma_B}$$

allow Asset B to be the risk-free asset and Asset A to be a risky portfolio of assets.

Because a risk-free asset has zero standard deviation and zero correlation of returns with those of the risky portfolio, this results in the reduced equation:

$$\sigma_{portfolio} = \sqrt{W_A^2\sigma_A^2} = W_A\sigma_A$$

If we put X% of our portfolio into the risky asset portfolio, the resulting portfolio will have standard deviation of returns equal to X% of the standard deviation of the risky asset portfolio. The relationship between portfolio risk and return for various portfolio allocations is linear, as illustrated in Figure 4.

**Figure 4: Capital Allocation Line and Risky Asset Weights**

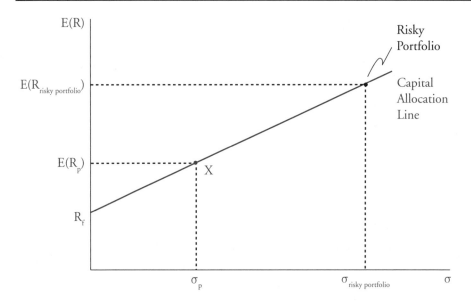

Combining a risky portfolio with a risk-free asset is the process that supports the **two-fund separation theorem**, which states that all investors' optimum portfolios will be made up of some combination of an optimal portfolio of risky assets and the risk-free asset. The line representing these possible combinations of risk-free assets and the optimal risky asset portfolio is referred to as the **capital allocation line**.

Point X on the capital allocation line in Figure 4 represents a portfolio that is 40% invested in the risky asset portfolio and 60% invested in the risk-free asset. Its expected return will be $0.40[E(R_{risky\ asset\ portfolio})] + 0.60(R_f)$ and its standard deviation will be $0.40(\sigma_{risky\ asset\ portfolio})$.

We can combine the capital allocation line with indifference curves to illustrate the logic of selecting an optimal portfolio (i.e., one that maximizes the investor's expected utility). In Figure 5, we can see that an investor with preferences represented by indifference curves $I_1$, $I_2$, and $I_3$ can reach the level of expected utility on $I_2$ by selecting portfolio X. This is the optimal portfolio for this investor, as any portfolio that lies on $I_2$ is preferred to all portfolios that lie on $I_3$ (and in fact to any portfolios that lie between $I_2$ and $I_3$). Portfolios on $I_1$ are preferred to those on $I_2$, but none of the portfolios that lie on $I_1$ are available in the market.

**Figure 5: Risk-Averse Investor's Indifference Curves**

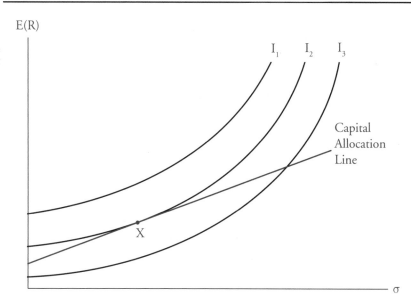

The final result of our analysis here is not surprising; investors who are less risk averse will select portfolios with more risk. As illustrated in Figure 6, the flatter indifference curve for Investor B ($I_B$) results in an optimal (tangency) portfolio that lies to the right of the one that results from a steeper indifference curve, such as that for Investor A ($I_A$). An investor who is less risk averse should optimally choose a portfolio with more invested in the risky asset portfolio and less invested in the risk-free asset.

**Figure 6: Portfolio Choices Based on Investor's Indifference Curves**

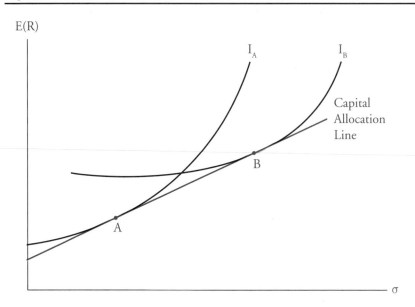

# PORTFOLIO RISK AND RETURN: PART II
Cross-Reference to CFA Institute Assigned Reading #53

The following figure illustrates the possible risk-return combinations from combining a risk-free asset with three different (efficient) risky portfolios, X, Y, and M.

**Figure 7: Combining a Risk-Free Asset With a Risky Portfolio**

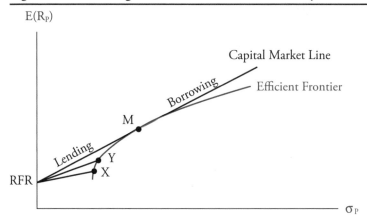

This figure also illustrates the point that combining a risk-free asset with risky Portfolio M (the *tangency* portfolio) results in the best available set of risk and return opportunities. Combining the risk-free asset with either Portfolio X or Portfolio Y results in a less preferred set of possible portfolios.

Since all investors who hold any risky assets will choose to hold Portfolio M, it must contain *all* available risky assets, and we can describe it as the "market portfolio."

Investors at Point M have 100% of their funds invested in Portfolio M. Between $R_f$ and M, investors hold both the risk-free asset and Portfolio M. This means investors are *lending* some of their funds at the risk-free rate and investing the rest in the risky market Portfolio M. To the right of M, investors hold more than 100% of Portfolio M. This means they are *borrowing* funds to buy more of Portfolio M. The *levered positions* represent a 100% investment in Portfolio M and borrowing to invest even more in Portfolio M.

In short, adding a risk-free asset to the set of risky assets considered in the Markowitz portfolio theory results in a new efficient frontier that is now a straight line, the capital market line (CML).

## Security Market Line: Systematic and Unsystematic Risk

Under the assumptions of capital market theory, diversification is costless, and investors will only hold efficient portfolios. The risk that is eliminated by diversification is called *unsystematic risk* (also referred to as unique, diversifiable, or firm-specific risk). Since unsystematic risk is assumed to be eliminated at no cost, investors need not be compensated in equilibrium for bearing unsystematic risk.

The risk that remains in efficient portfolios is termed *systematic risk* (also referred to as non-diversifiable or market risk), which is measured by an asset's or portfolio's beta. This crucial result is the basis for the capital asset pricing model (CAPM). The equilibrium relationship between systematic risk and expected return is illustrated by the security market line (SML) as shown in Figure 8.

The *total risk* (standard deviation of returns) for any asset or portfolio of assets can be separated into systematic and unsystematic risk.

> total risk = systematic risk + unsystematic risk

Well-diversified (efficient) portfolios have no unsystematic risk, and a risk-free asset has no systematic (market) risk either. Systematic risk is measured in units of market risk, referred to as the beta of an asset or portfolio, so that the beta of the market portfolio is equal to one. The market portfolio simply has one "unit" of market risk.

**Figure 8: Security Market Line**

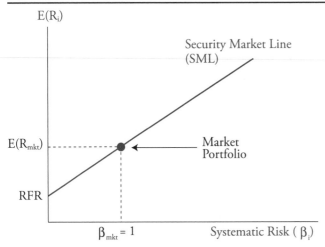

$$\text{CAPM: } E(R_i) = \text{RFR} + (E(R_{MKT}) - \text{RFR}) \times \text{beta}_i$$

Note that required return and expected return are the same in equilibrium.

## Return Generating Models

**Return generating models** are used to estimate the expected returns on risky securities based on specific factors. For each security, we must estimate the sensitivity of its returns to each factor included in the model. Factors that explain security returns can be classified as macroeconomic, fundamental, and statistical factors.

**Multifactor models** most commonly use macroeconomic factors such as GDP growth, inflation, or consumer confidence, along with fundamental factors such as earnings, earnings growth, firm size, and research expenditures.

The general form of a multifactor model with $k$ risk factors is as follows:

$$E(R_i) - R_f = \beta_{i1} \times E(\text{Factor 1}) + \beta_{i2} \times E(\text{Factor 2}) + \ldots + \beta_{ik} \times E(\text{Factor k})$$

This model states that the expected excess return (above the risk-free rate) for Asset $i$ is the sum of each **factor sensitivity** or **factor loading** (the $\beta$s) for Asset $i$ multiplied by the expected value of that factor for the period. The first factor is often the expected excess return on the market, $E(R_m) - R_f$.

One multifactor model that is often used is that of Fama and French. They estimated the sensitivity of security returns to three factors: firm size, firm book value to market value ratio, and the return on the market portfolio minus the risk-free rate (excess return on the market portfolio). Carhart suggests a fourth factor that measures price momentum using prior period returns. Together, these four factors do a relatively good job of explaining returns differences for U.S. equity securities over the period for which the model has been estimated.

The **market model** is a single factor (sometimes termed single index) model. The only factor is the expected excess return on the market portfolio (market index).

The form of the market model is as follows:

$$E(R_i) - R_f = \beta_i[E(R_m) - R_f]$$

In this case, the factor sensitivity or beta for Asset $i$ is a measure of how sensitive the excess return on Asset $i$ is to the excess return on the overall market portfolio.

## Beta

The sensitivity of an asset's return to the return on the market index in the context of the market model is referred to as its **beta**. Beta is a standardized measure of the covariance of the asset's return with the market return. Beta can be calculated as follows:

$$\beta_i = \frac{\text{covariance of Asset } i\text{'s return with the market return}}{\text{variance of the market return}} = \frac{\text{Cov}_{im}}{\sigma_m^2}$$

We can use the definition of the correlation between the returns on Asset $i$ with the returns on the market index:

$$\rho_{im} = \frac{\text{Cov}_{im}}{\sigma_i \sigma_m}$$

to get $\text{Cov}_{im} = \rho_{im}\sigma_i\sigma_m$.

---

Substituting for $\text{Cov}_{im}$ in the equation for $B_i$, we can also calculate beta as:

$$\beta_i = \frac{\rho_{im}\sigma_i\sigma_m}{\sigma_m^2} = \rho_{im}\frac{\sigma_i}{\sigma_m}$$

## SML and Equilibrium

You should be able to compute an asset's expected return using the SML and determine whether the aseet is underpriced or overpriced relative to its equilibrium value. In solving problems, be careful to note whether you are given the expected return on the market, $E(R_M)$, or the market risk premium, $E(R_M) - R_f$.

An analyst may identify assets for which his forecasted returns differ from the expected return based on the asset's beta. Assets for which the forecasted return differs from its equilibrium expected returns will plot either above or below the SML. Consider three stocks, A, B, and C, that are plotted on the SML diagram in Figure 9 based on their forecasted returns.

## Figure 9: Identifying Mispriced Securities

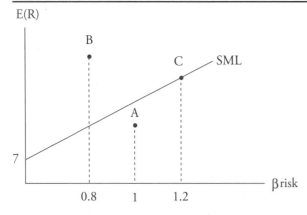

According to the forecasts, Asset B is underpriced, Asset A is overpriced, and Asset C is priced at its equilibrium value.

There are several measures of risk-adjusted returns that are used to evaluate relative portfolio performance.

One such measure is the **Sharpe ratio** $\left(\dfrac{R_P - R_f}{\sigma_P}\right).$

The Sharpe ratio of a portfolio is its *excess returns per unit of total portfolio risk,* and higher Sharpe ratios indicate better risk-adjusted portfolio performance. Note that this is a slope measure and, as illustrated in Figure 10, the Sharpe ratios of all portfolios along the CML are equal. Because the Sharpe ratio uses total risk, rather than systematic risk, it accounts for any unsystematic risk that the portfolio manager has taken.

In Figure 10, we illustrate that the Sharpe ratio is the slope of the CAL for a portfolio and can be compared to the slope of the CML to evaluate risk-adjusted performance.

## Figure 10: Sharpe Ratios as Slopes

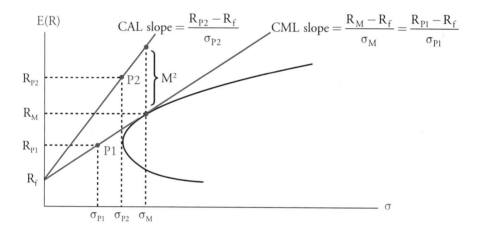

The **M-squared** ($M^2$) measure produces the same portfolio rankings as the Sharpe ratio but is stated in percentage terms (as illustrated in Figure 10). It is calculated for Portfolio 2 as:

$$(R_{P2} - R_f)\frac{\sigma_M}{\sigma_{P2}} - (R_M - R_f)$$

Two measures of risk-adjusted returns based on systematic risk (beta) rather than total risk are the **Treynor measure** and **Jensen's alpha**. They are similar to the Sharpe ratio and $M^2$ measures in that the Treynor measure is a slope and Jensen's alpha is in percentage returns.

The Treynor measure is calculated as $\dfrac{R_P - R_f}{\beta_P}$, interpreted as excess returns per unit of systematic risk, and represented by the slope of a line as illustrated in Figure 11.

Jensen's alpha for Portfolio P is calculated as $\alpha_p = (R_p - R_f) - \beta_p(R_M - R_f)$ and is the percentage portfolio return above that of a portfolio (or security) with the same beta as the portfolio that lies on the SML, as illustrated in Figure 11.

**Figure 11: Treynor Measure and Jensen's Alpha**

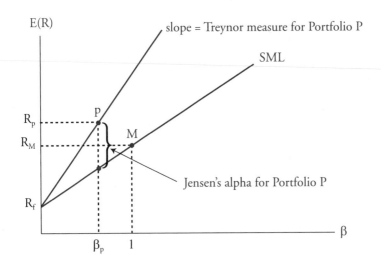

## Basics Of Portfolio Planning And Construction
Cross-Reference to CFA Institute Assigned Reading #54

### Importance of Investment Policy Statement

Understand the basic inputs to an investment policy statement and how these inputs relate to individuals, pensions, and endowments.

- The policy statement requires that risks and costs of investing, as well as the return requirements, all be objectively and realistically articulated.
- The policy statement imposes investment discipline on, and provides guidance for, both the client and the portfolio manager.

The major components of an IPS typically address the following:

- *Description of Client* circumstances, situation, and investment objectives.
- *Statement of the Purpose* of the IPS.
- *Statement of Duties and Responsibilities* of investment manager, custodian of assets, and the client.
- *Procedures* to update IPS and to respond to various possible situations.
- *Investment Objectives* derived from communications with the client.
- *Investment Constraints* that must be considered in the plan.

- *Investment Guidelines* such as how the policy will be executed, asset types permitted, and leverage to be used.
- *Evaluation of Performance,* the benchmark portfolio for evaluating investment performance, and other information on evaluation of investment results.
- *Appendices* containing information on strategic (baseline) asset allocation and permitted deviations from policy portfolio allocations, as well as how and when the portfolio allocations should be rebalanced.

## Risk and Return Objectives

**Absolute risk objectives** can be stated in terms of the probability of specific portfolio results, either percentage losses or dollar losses, or in terms of strict limits on portfolio results. An absolute return objective may be stated in nominal terms, such as "an overall return of at least 6% per annum," or in real returns, such as "a return of 3% more than the annual inflation rate each year."

**Relative risk objectives** relate to a specific benchmark and can also be strict, such as, "Returns will not be less than 12-month euro LIBOR over any 12-month period," or stated in terms of probability, such as, "No greater than a 5% probability of returns more than 4% below the return on the MSCI World Index over any 12-month period."

The account manager must make sure that the stated risk and **return objectives** are compatible, given the reality of expected investment results and uncertainty over time.

## Risk Tolerance

An investor's **ability to bear risk** depends on financial circumstances. Longer investment horizons (20 years rather than 2 years), greater assets versus liabilities (more wealth), more insurance against unexpected occurrences, and a secure job all suggest a greater ability to bear investment risk.

An investor's **willingness to bear risk** is based primarily on the investor's attitudes and beliefs about investments (various asset types).

If the investor's willingness to take on investment risk is high but the investor's ability to take on risk is low, the low ability to take on investment risk will prevail in the advisor's assessment.

In situations where ability is high but willingness is low, the advisor may attempt to educate the investor about investment risk and correct any misconceptions.

# Investment Objectives and Constraints

The investment policy statement should include the following:

*Investment objectives:*

- Return objectives.
- Risk tolerance.

*Constraints:*

- Liquidity needs.
- Time horizon.
- Tax concerns.
- Legal and regulatory factors.
- Unique needs and preferences.

## Asset Allocation

After having determined the investor objectives and constraints, a **strategic asset allocation** is developed which specifies the percentage allocations to the included asset classes. In choosing asset classes for an account, the correlations of returns *within* an asset class should be relatively high, and the correlations of returns *between* asset classes should be relatively low in comparison.

Once the portfolio manager has identified the investable asset classes for the portfolio, an *efficient frontier* can be constructed and the manager can identify that portfolio (the strategic asset allocation) which best meets the risk and return requirements of the investor.

A manager who varies from strategic asset allocation weights in order to take advantage of perceived short-term opportunities is adding **tactical asset allocation** to the portfolio strategy. **Security selection** refers to deviations from index weights on individual securities within an asset class.

# SECURITIES MARKETS AND EQUITY INVESTMENTS

Study Sessions 13 & 14

| | |
|---|---|
| Weight on Exam | 10% |
| SchweserNotes™ Reference | Book 4, Pages 203–329 |

## STUDY SESSION 13: MARKET ORGANIZATION, MARKET INDICES, AND MARKET EFFICIENCY

### MARKET ORGANIZATION AND STRUCTURE
Cross-Reference to CFA Institute Assigned Reading #55

The three main functions of the financial system are to:

1. Allow entities to save and borrow money, raise equity capital, manage risks, trade assets currently or in the future, and trade based on their estimates of asset values.

2. Determine the returns (i.e., interest rates) that equate the total supply of savings with the total demand for borrowing.

3. Allocate capital to its most efficient uses.

### Assets and Markets

**Financial assets** include securities (stocks and bonds), derivative contracts, and currencies. **Real assets** include real estate, equipment, commodities, and other physical assets.

**Debt securities** are promises to repay borrowed funds. **Equity securities** represent ownership positions.

**Public securities** are traded on exchanges or through securities dealers and are subject to regulatory oversight. Securities that are not traded in public markets are referred to as **private securities**. Private securities are often illiquid and not subject to regulation.

**Derivative contracts** have values that are derived from the values of other assets. **Financial derivative contracts** are based on equities, equity indexes, debt, debt indexes, or other financial contracts. **Physical derivative contracts** derive their values from the values of physical assets such as gold, oil, and wheat.

Markets for immediate delivery are referred to as **spot markets**. Contracts for the future delivery of physical and financial assets include forwards, futures, and options.

The **primary market** is the market for newly issued securities. Subsequent sales of securities are said to occur in the **secondary market**.

**Money markets** refer to markets for debt securities with maturities of one year or less. **Capital markets** refer to markets for longer-term debt securities and equity securities that have no specific maturity date.

**Traditional investment markets** refer to those for debt and equity. **Alternative markets** refer to those for hedge funds, commodities, real estate, collectibles, gemstones, leases, and equipment. Alternative assets often are more difficult to value, illiquid, and require investor due diligence.

## Types of Securities

**Fixed income securities** typically refer to debt securities that are promises to repay borrowed money in the future.

*Convertible debt* is debt that an investor can exchange for a specified number of equity shares of the issuing firm.

**Equity securities** represent ownership in a firm and include common stock, preferred stock, and warrants.

- **Common stock** is a residual claim on a firm's assets.
- **Preferred stock** is an equity security with scheduled dividends that typically do not change over the security's life and must be paid before any dividends on common stock may be paid.
- **Warrants** are similar to options in that they give the holder the right to buy a firm's equity shares at a fixed exercise price prior to the warrant's expiration.

**Pooled investment vehicles** include mutual funds, depositories, and hedge funds. The investor's ownership interests are referred to as *shares, units, depository receipts,* or *limited partnership interests*.

- **Mutual funds** are pooled investment vehicles in which investors can purchase shares, either from the fund itself (open-end funds) or in the secondary market (closed-end funds).
- **Exchange-traded funds** (ETFs) and **exchange-traded notes** (ETNs) trade like closed-end funds, but have special provisions for in-kind creation and redemption.
- **Asset-backed securities** represent a claim to a portion of the cash flows from a pool of financial assets such as mortgages, car loans, or credit card debt.
- **Hedge funds** are organized as limited partnerships, and purchase is usually restricted to investors of substantial wealth and investment knowledge.

## Contracts

**Financial contracts** are often based on securities, currencies, commodities, or security indexes (portfolios). They include futures, forwards, options, swaps, and insurance contracts.

**Forward contracts** are agreements to buy or sell an asset in the future at a price specified in the contract at its inception and are not typically traded on exchanges or in dealer markets.

**Futures contracts** are similar to forward contracts except that they are standardized as to amount, asset characteristics, and delivery time, and are traded on an exchange.

In a **swap contract**, two parties make payments that are equivalent to one asset or portfolio being traded for another. In a simple *interest rate swap*, floating rate interest payments are exchanged for fixed rate payments over multiple settlement dates. A *currency swap* involves a loan in one currency for the loan of another currency for a period of time. An *equity swap* involves the exchange of the return on an equity index or portfolio for the interest payment on a debt instrument.

A **call option** gives the option buyer the right (but not the obligation) to buy an asset. A **put option** gives the option buyer the right (but not the obligation) to sell an asset.

An **insurance contract** pays a cash amount if a future event occurs.

**Credit default swaps** are a form of insurance that makes a payment if an issuer defaults on its bonds.

## Currencies, Commodities, and Real Assets

**Currencies** are issued by a government's central bank. Some are referred to as **reserve currencies**, which are those held by governments and central banks worldwide and include the dollar and euro, and secondarily the British pound, Japanese yen, and Swiss franc.

**Commodities** trade in spot, forward, and futures markets. They include precious metals, industrial metals, agricultural products, energy products, and credits for carbon reduction.

Examples of **real assets** are real estate, equipment, and machinery. Although they have been traditionally held by firms for their use in production, real assets are increasingly held by institutional investors both directly and indirectly.

## Brokers, Dealers, and Exchanges

**Brokers** help their clients buy and sell securities by finding counterparties to trades in a cost efficient manner.

**Block brokers** help with the placement of large trades.

**Investment banks** help corporations sell common stock, preferred stock, and debt securities to investors. They also provide advice to firms, notably about mergers, acquisitions, and raising capital.

**Exchanges** provide a venue where traders can meet. Exchanges sometimes act as brokers by providing electronic order matching.

**Alternative trading systems** (ATS), which serve the same trading function as exchanges but have no regulatory function, are also known as **electronic communication networks** or **multilateral trading facilities**. ATS that do not reveal current client orders are known as *dark pools*.

**Dealers** facilitate trading by buying for or selling from their own inventory.

Some dealers also act as brokers. **Broker-dealers** have an inherent conflict of interest. As brokers, they should seek the best prices for their clients, but as dealers, their goal is to profit through prices or spreads. As a result, traders typically place limits on how their orders are filled when they transact with broker-dealers.

Dealers that trade with central banks when the banks buy or sell government securities in order to affect the money supply are referred to as **primary dealers**.

## Investment Positions

An investor who owns an asset, or has the right or obligation under a contract to purchase an asset, is said to have a **long position**. A **short position** can result from borrowing an asset and selling it, with the obligation to replace the asset in the future (a short sale). The party to a contract who must sell or deliver an asset in the future is also said to have a short position. In general, investors who are long benefit from an increase in the price of an asset and those who are short benefit when the asset price declines.

In a **short sale**, the short seller (1) simultaneously borrows and sells securities through a broker, (2) must return the securities at the request of the lender or when the short sale is closed out, and (3) must keep a portion of the proceeds of the short sale on deposit with the broker. Short sellers hope to profit from a fall in the price of the security or asset sold short. The repayment of the borrowed security or other asset is referred to as "covering the short position."

## Margin Transactions

*Margin purchase transactions* involve paying for part of the cost of a security, a loan for the rest from a broker, and leaving the securities on deposit with the broker as collateral. Currently a maximum of 50% of the purchase price can be borrowed. A minimum of 50% of the purchase price must be deposited in cash which is referred to as the *initial margin*.

The *equity* in a margin account for a long position is the market value of the securities minus the loan amount. At any point in time, the *margin percentage* in an account is the equity in the account as a percentage of the market value of the securities held. *Maintenance margin*, or minimum margin, is the minimum percentage of equity permitted; if the margin percentage falls below this minimum, more cash or securities must be deposited in order to maintain the position.

To calculate the rate of return on a margin transaction, divide the gain or loss on the security position by the margin deposit.

The following formula indicates how to calculate the stock price that will trigger a margin call based on the initial price, $P_0$ (for a long position).

$$\text{trigger price (margin purchases)} = P_0 \left( \frac{1 - \text{initial margin}\%}{1 - \text{maintenance margin}\%} \right)$$

## Bid and Ask Prices

Securities dealers provide prices at which they will buy and sell shares. The **bid price** is the price at which a dealer will buy a security. The **ask** or **offer price** is the price at which a dealer will sell a security. The difference between the bid and ask prices is referred to as the **bid-ask spread** and is the source of a dealer's compensation. The bid and ask are quoted for specific trade sizes (**bid size** and **ask size**).

The quotation in the market is the highest dealer bid and lowest dealer ask from among all dealers in a particular security. More liquid securities have market quotations with bid-ask spreads that are lower (as a percentage of share price) and therefore have lower transactions costs for investors. Traders who post bids and offers are said to *make a market*, while those who trade with them at posted prices are said to *take the market*.

## Execution Instructions

The most common orders, in terms of execution instructions, are market or limit orders. A **market order** instructs the broker to execute the trade immediately at the best available price. A **limit order** places a *minimum* execution price on sell orders and a *maximum* execution price on buy orders. The disadvantage of a limit order is that it might not be filled.

## Validity Instructions

Validity instructions specify *when* an order should be executed. Most orders are **day orders**, meaning they expire if unfilled by the end of the trading day. Good-till-cancelled orders remain open until they are filled. **Immediate or cancel** orders (also known as **fill or kill** orders) are cancelled unless they can be filled immediately. **Good-on-close** orders are only filled at the end of the trading day. If they are market orders, they are referred to as **market-on-close** orders. These are often used by mutual funds because their portfolios are valued using closing prices. There are also **good-on-open** orders.

**Stop (stop loss) orders** are not executed unless the stop price has been reached. A **stop sell order** is placed at a "stop" price below the current market price, executes if the stock trades at or below the stop price, and can limit the losses on a long position. A **stop buy order** is placed at a "stop" price above the current market price, executes if the stock trades at or above the stop price, and can limit losses on a short position.

## Primary and Secondary Markets

**Primary capital markets** refers to the markets for newly issued securities, either:

- **Initial public offerings** (IPOs).
- **Seasoned offerings** (secondary issues).

**Secondary financial markets** refers to markets where previously issued securities trade.

## Market Structures

In **call markets**, orders are accumulated and securities trade only at specific times. Call markets are potentially very liquid when in session because all traders are present, but they are obviously illiquid between sessions. In a call market, all trades, bids, and asks are at prices that are set to equate supply and demand.

In **continuous markets**, trades occur at any time the market is open with prices set either by the auction process or by dealer bid-ask quotes.

There are three main categories of securities markets: *quote-driven markets* where investors trade with dealers, *order-driven markets* where rules are used to match buyers and sellers, and *brokered markets* where investors use brokers to locate a counterparty to a trade.

In **quote-driven markets**, traders transact with dealers (market makers) who post bid and ask prices. Dealers maintain an inventory of securities. Quote-driven markets are thus sometimes called **dealer markets**, **price-driven markets**, or **over-the-counter markets**. Most securities other than stocks trade in quote-driven markets. Trading often takes place electronically.

In **order-driven markets**, orders are executed using trading rules, which are necessary because traders are usually anonymous. Exchanges and automated trading systems are examples of order-driven markets.

In **brokered markets**, brokers find the counterparty in order to execute a trade. This service is especially valuable when the trader has a security that is unique or illiquid. Examples are large blocks of stock, real estate, and artwork. Dealers typically do not carry an inventory of these assets and there are too few trades for these assets to trade in order-driven markets.

## Characteristics of a Well-Functioning Financial System

A market is said to be **complete** if:

- Investors can save for the future at fair rates of return.
- Creditworthy borrowers can obtain funds.
- Hedgers can manage their risks.
- Traders can obtain the currencies, commodities, and other assets they need.

If a market can perform these functions at low trading costs (including commissions, bid-ask spreads, and price impacts) it is said to be **operationally efficient**. If security prices reflect all public information associated with fundamental value in a timely fashion, then the financial system is **informationally efficient**. A well-functioning financial system has complete markets that are operationally and informationally efficient, with prices that reflect fundamental values. Furthermore, in informationally efficiently markets, capital is allocated to its most productive uses. That is, markets are also **allocationally efficient**.

## SECURITY MARKET INDICES
Cross-Reference to CFA Institute Assigned Reading #56

A **security market index** is used to represent the performance of an asset class, security market, or segment of a market. Individual securities are referred to as the **constituent securities** of an index.

A price index is based on security prices, and the percentage change in a price index is referred to as its **price return**. The price return on an index plus the return from dividends paid on index stocks is referred to as the **total return** of an index.

## Index Weighting Methods

A **price-weighted index** is the arithmetic average of the prices of its constituent securities. The divisor of a price-weighted index must be adjusted for stock splits and for changes in the composition of the index so that the index value is unaffected by such changes.

$$\text{price-weighted index} = \frac{\text{sum of stock prices}}{\text{number of stocks in index}}$$

A given percentage price change on a high-priced stock will have a greater impact on index returns than it will on a low-priced stock. Weights based on prices are considered somewhat arbitrary, and the weights of all index stocks must be adjusted when an index stock splits. A portfolio with equal numbers of shares of each index stock will match the performance of a price-weighted index.

An **equal-weighted index** is calculated as the arithmetic average of the returns of index stocks and would be matched by the returns on a portfolio that had equal dollar amounts invested in each index stock. When stock prices change, however, portfolio weights change and the portfolio must be rebalanced periodically to restore equal weights to each index security. Compared to a price-weighted index, an equal-weighted index places more (less) weight on the returns of low-priced (high-priced) stocks. Compared to a market capitalization-weighted index, an equal-weighted index places more (less) weight on returns of stocks with small (large) market capitalizations.

In a **market capitalization-weighted index** (or **value-weighted index**), returns are weights based on the market capitalization of each index stock (current stock price times the number of shares outstanding) as a proportion of the total market capitalization of all the stocks in the index. A market capitalization-weighted index does not need to be adjusted when a stock splits or pays a stock dividend.

$$\text{current index value} = \frac{\text{current total market value of index stocks}}{\text{base year total market value of index stocks}} \times \text{base year index value}$$

A **float-adjusted market capitalization-weighted index** is constructed like a market capitalization-weighted index. The weights, however, are based on the proportionate value of each firm's shares that are available to investors to the total market value of the shares of index stocks that are available to investors. Firms with relatively large percentages of their shares held by controlling stockholders will have less weight than they have in an unadjusted market-capitalization index.

The advantage of market capitalization-weighted indexes of either type is that index security weights represent proportions of total market value.

An index that uses **fundamental weighting** uses weights based on firm fundamentals, such as earnings, dividends, or cash flow. An advantage of a fundamental-weighted index is that it avoids the bias of market capitalization-weighted indexes toward the performance of the shares of overvalued firms and away from the performance of the shares of undervalued firms.

## Rebalancing and Reconstitution

**Rebalancing** refers to periodically adjusting the weights of securities in an index or portfolio to their target weights, and it is important for equal-weighted indexes as portfolio weights change as prices change.

Index **reconstitution** occurs when the securities that make up an index are changed. Securities are deleted if they no longer meet the index criteria and are replaced by securities that do.

## Index Types

**Equity indexes** can be classified as follows:

- *Broad market index.* Provides a measure of a market's overall performance and usually contains more than 90% of the market's total value.
- *Multi-market index.* Typically constructed from the indexes of markets in several countries and is used to measure the equity returns of a geographic region, markets based on their stage of economic development, or the entire world.
- *Multi-market index with fundamental weighting.* Uses market capitalization-weighting for the country indexes, but then weights the country index returns in the global index by a fundamental factor (e.g., GDP).
- *Sector index.* Measures the returns for an industry sector such as health care, financial, or consumer goods firms.
- *Style index.* Measures the returns to market capitalization and value or growth strategies. Some indexes reflect a combination of the two (e.g., small-cap value fund).

Many different **fixed income indexes** are available to investors. The fixed income security universe is much broader than the universe of stocks. Also, unlike stocks, bonds mature and must be replaced in fixed income indexes. As a result, turnover is high in fixed income indexes.

Because fixed income securities often trade infrequently, index providers must often estimate the value of index securities from recent prices of securities with similar characteristics.

Illiquidity, transactions costs, and high turnover of constituent securities make it both difficult and expensive for fixed income portfolio managers to replicate a fixed income index.

**Commodity indexes** are based on futures contract prices for commodities such as grains, livestock, metals, and energy. Different indexes have significantly different commodity exposures and risk and return characteristics.

**Real estate indexes** can be constructed using returns based on appraised values, repeat property sales, or the performance of Real Estate Investment Trusts (REITs).

Most **hedge fund indexes** equally weight the returns of the hedge funds included in the index.

Hedge funds are largely unregulated and are not required to report their performance to index providers. It is often the case that those funds that report are the funds that have been successful, as the poorly performing funds do not choose to report their performance. This results in an upward bias in index returns, with hedge funds appearing to be better investments than they actually are.

## MARKET EFFICIENCY
Cross-Reference to CFA Institute Assigned Reading #57

An **informationally efficient capital market** is one in which the current price of a security fully and quickly reflects all available information about that security without bias.

In a perfectly efficient market, investors should use a passive investment strategy (i.e., buying a broad market index of stocks and holding it) because active investment strategies will underperform on average by the amount of transactions costs and management fees. However, to the extent that market prices are inefficient, active investment strategies can generate positive risk-adjusted returns.

Market efficiency increases with:

- Larger numbers of market participants.
- More information available to investors.
- Fewer impediments to trading such as restrictions on short sales.
- Lower transactions costs.

### Forms of the Efficient Markets Hypothesis

1. The *weak form* of the hypothesis states that current stock prices fully reflect all price and trading volume (market) information. If weak-form efficiency holds, purely technical analysis has no value.

2. The *semistrong form* of the hypothesis holds that public information cannot be used to beat the market. If stock prices are semistrong-form efficient, neither technical nor fundamental analysis has any value in stock selection.

3. *Strong-form* efficiency states that stock prices fully reflect all information, both public and private. If markets were strong-form efficient, even private (inside) information would be of no value in selecting securities.

## Identified Market Pricing Anomalies

A **market anomaly** is something that would lead us to reject the hypothesis of market efficiency.

- The **January effect** or **turn-of-the-year effect** is the finding that during the first five days of January, stock returns, especially for small firms, are significantly higher than they are the rest of the year.
- The **overreaction effect** refers to the finding that firms with poor stock returns over the previous three or five years (losers) have better subsequent returns than firms that had high stock returns over the prior period.
- **Momentum effects** have also been found where high short-term returns are followed by continued high returns.
- The **size effect** refers to evidence that small-cap stocks outperform large-cap stocks. This effect could not be confirmed in later studies, suggesting that either investors had traded on, and thereby eliminated, this anomaly or that the initial finding was simply a random result for the time period examined.
- The **value effect** refers to the finding that value stocks have outperformed growth stocks. Some researchers attribute the value effect to greater risk of value stocks that is not captured in the risk adjustment procedure used in the studies.

The majority of the evidence suggests that reported anomalies are not violations of market efficiency but are due to the methodologies used in the tests of market efficiency. Furthermore, both underreaction and overreaction have been found in the markets, meaning that prices are efficient on average. Other explanations for the evidence of anomalies are that they are transient relations, too small to profit from, or simply reflect returns to risk that the researchers have failed to account for.

Portfolio management based on previously identified anomalies will likely be unprofitable. Investment management based solely on anomalies has no sound economic basis.

## Behavioral Finance

**Behavioral finance** examines investor behavior, its effect on financial markets, how cognitive biases may result in anomalies, and whether investors are rational.

- **Loss aversion** refers to the tendency for investors to dislike losses more than they like gains of equal amounts.
- **Investor overconfidence.** Securities will be mispriced if investors overestimate their ability to value securities. However, it appears that this mispricing may be hard to predict, may only be temporary, may not be exploitable for abnormal profits, and may only exist for high-growth firms.

- **Representativeness.** Investors assume good companies or good markets are good investments.
- **Gambler's fallacy.** Recent results affect investor estimates of future probabilities.
- **Mental accounting.** Investors classify different investments into separate mental accounts instead of viewing them as a total portfolio.
- **Conservatism.** Investors react slowly to changes.
- **Disposition effect.** Investors are willing to realize gains but unwilling to realize losses.
- **Narrow framing.** Investors view events in isolation.

Although investor biases may help explain the existence of security mispricing and anomalies, it is not clear that they are predictable enough so that abnormal profits could be earned by exploiting them.

# STUDY SESSION 14: EQUITY ANALYSIS AND VALUATION

## OVERVIEW OF EQUITY SECURITIES
Cross-Reference to CFA Institute Assigned Reading #58

## Types of Equity Securities

- **Common shares** represent a residual claim (after the claims of debt holders and preferred stockholders) on firm assets.
- **Callable common shares** give the firm the right to repurchase the stock at a pre-specified call price.
- **Putable common shares** give the shareholder the right to sell the shares back to the firm at a specific price.
- **Preference shares** (or **preferred stock**) have features of both common stock and debt. As with common stock, preferred stock dividends are not a contractual obligation, the shares usually do not mature, and the shares can have put or call features. Like debt, preferred shares typically make fixed periodic payments to investors and do not usually have voting rights.
- **Cumulative preference shares** require that current period dividends and any dividends that were not paid must be made up before common shareholders can receive dividends. The dividends of **non-cumulative preference shares** do not accumulate over time when they are not paid, but dividends for the current period must be paid before common shareholders can receive dividends.
- Investors in **participating preference shares** receive extra dividends if firm profits exceed a predetermined level and may receive a value greater than the par value of the preferred stock if the firm is liquidated. **Non-participating preference shares** have a claim equal to par value in the event of liquidation and do not share in firm profits.
- **Convertible preference shares** can be exchanged for common stock at a conversion ratio determined when the shares are originally issued.

## Private Equity

**Private equity** is usually issued to institutional investors via private placements. Private equity markets are smaller than public markets but are growing rapidly.

Compared to public equity, private equity has the following characteristics:

- Less liquidity because no public market for the shares exists.
- Share price is negotiated between the firm and its investors, not determined in a market.
- More limited firm financial disclosure because there is no government or exchange requirement to do so.
- Lower reporting costs because of less onerous reporting requirements.
- Potentially weaker corporate governance because of reduced reporting requirements and less public scrutiny.
- Greater ability to focus on long-term prospects because there is no public pressure for short-term results.
- Potentially greater return for investors once the firm goes public.

The three main types of private equity investments are venture capital, leveraged buyouts, and private investments in public equity.

## Voting Rights

In a **statutory voting** system, each share held is assigned one vote in the election of each member of the board of directors. Under **cumulative voting**, shareholders can allocate their votes to one or more candidates as they choose.

A firm may have different classes of common stock (e.g., "Class A" and "Class B" shares). One class may have greater voting power and seniority if the firm's assets are liquidated. The classes may also be treated differently with respect to dividends, stock splits, and other transactions with shareholders.

## Foreign Equity

**Direct investing** in the securities of foreign companies simply refers to buying a foreign firm's securities in foreign markets. Some obstacles to direct foreign investment are that:

- The investment and return are denominated in a foreign currency.
- The foreign stock exchange may be illiquid.
- The reporting requirements of foreign stock exchanges may be less strict, impeding analysis.
- Investors must be familiar with the regulations and procedures of each market in which they invest.

## Methods for Investing in Foreign Companies

**Depository receipts** (DRs) trade like domestic shares but represent an interest in shares of a foreign firm that are held by a bank in the country in which they trade. When the foreign firm is involved with the issue, they are termed **sponsored DRs**, and investors receive the voting rights for the shares their DRs represent. When the foreign firm is not involved, they are termed **unsponsored DRs**, face less strict reporting requirements, and the depository bank retains the voting rights on the shares.

**Global depository receipts** (GDRs) are issued outside the U.S. and the issuer's home country, are traded primarily on the London and Luxembourg exchanges, are usually denominated in U.S. dollars, and can be sold to U.S. institutional investors.

**American depository receipts** (ADRs) are denominated in U.S. dollars and trade in the United States.

**Global registered shares** (GRS) are traded in different currencies on stock exchanges around the world.

A **basket of listed depository receipts** (BLDR) is an exchange-traded fund (ETF) that is a collection of DRs. ETF shares trade in markets just like common stocks.

## Equity Risk and Return Characteristics

The risk of equity securities is most commonly measured as the standard deviation of returns. Preferred shares are less risky than common stock because preferred shares pay a known, fixed dividend. Because they are less risky, preferred shares have lower average returns than common shares.

Cumulative preferred shares have less risk than non-cumulative preferred shares.

For both common and preferred shares, putable shares are less risky and callable shares are more risky compared to shares with neither option.

Callable shares are the most risky because if the market price rises, the firm can call the shares, limiting the upside potential of the shares.

## Market and Book Value of Equity

A firm's **book value of equity** is the value of the firm's assets on the balance sheet minus its liabilities.

The **market value of equity** is the total value of a firm's outstanding equity shares based on market prices and reflects the expectations of investors about the firm's future performance.

A key ratio used to determine management efficiency is the **accounting return on equity**, usually referred to simply as the **return on equity** (ROE):

$$ROE_t = \frac{NI_t}{\text{average } BV_t} = \frac{NI_t}{(BV_t + BV_{t-1})/2}$$

A firm's **cost of equity** is the expected equilibrium total return (including dividends) on its shares in the market.

## INTRODUCTION TO INDUSTRY AND COMPANY ANALYSIS

Cross-Reference to CFA Institute Assigned Reading #59

Industry analysis is important for company analysis because it provides a framework for understanding the firm. Understanding a firm's business environment can provide insight about the firm's potential growth, competition, and risks. For a credit analyst, industry conditions can provide important information about whether a firm will be able to meet its obligations during the next recession.

### Industry Classification Systems

One way to group companies into an industry group is by the *products and services* they offer. For example, the firms that produce automobiles constitute the auto industry. A **sector** is a group of similar industries. Systems that group firms by products and services usually use a firm's **principal business activity** (the largest source of sales or earnings) to classify firms.

Sectors representative of those used by commercial providers include the following:

- Basic materials and processing.
- Consumer discretionary.
- Consumer staples.
- Energy.
- Financial services.
- Health care.
- Industrial and producer durables.
- Technology.
- Telecommunications and utilities.

Several government bodies provide industry classification of firms.

- *International Standard Industrial Classification of All Economic Activities* (ISIC) was produced by the United Nations in 1948 to increase global comparability of data.
- *Statistical Classification of Economic Activities in the European Community* is similar to the ISIC, but is designed for Europe.
- *Australian and New Zealand Standard Industrial Classification* was jointly developed by those countries.
- *North American Industry Classification System* (NAICS) was jointly developed by the U.S., Canada, and Mexico.

## Other Classification Methods

Firms can be classified by their *sensitivity to business cycles*. This system has two main classifications: cyclical and non-cyclical firms.

A **cyclical firm** is one whose earnings are highly dependent on the stage of the business cycle.

A **non-cyclical firm** produces goods and services for which demand is relatively stable over the business cycle. Examples of non-cyclical industries include health care, utilities, and food and beverage.

Cyclical sector examples include energy, financials, technology, materials, and consumer discretionary. Non-cyclical sector examples include health care, utilities, and consumer staples.

Non-cyclical industries can be further separated into defensive (stable) or growth industries. **Defensive industries** are those that are least affected by the stage of the business cycle and include utilities, consumer staples (such as food producers), and basic services (such as drug stores). **Growth industries** have demand so strong they are largely unaffected by the stage of the business cycle.

*Statistical methods*, such as cluster analysis, can also be used. This method groups firms that historically have had highly correlated returns.

This method has several limitations:

- Historical correlations may not be the same as future correlations.
- The groupings of firms may differ over time and across countries.
- The grouping of firms is sometimes non-intuitive.
- The method is susceptible to a central issue in statistics, i.e., firms can be grouped by a relationship that occurs by chance or not grouped together when they should be.

## Peer Groups

A **peer group** is a set of companies with similar business activities, demand drivers, cost structure drivers, and availability of capital.

To form a peer group, an analyst will often start by identifying companies in the same industry classification, using the commercial classification providers previously described. Usually, the analyst will use other information to verify that the firms in an industry are indeed peers. An analyst might include a company in more than one peer group.

## Elements of an Industry Analysis

A thorough industry analysis should include the following elements:

- Evaluate the relationships between macroeconomic variables and industry trends using information from industry groups, firms in the industry, competitors, suppliers, and customers.
- Estimate industry variables using different approaches and scenarios.
- Compare with other analysts' forecasts of industry variables to confirm the validity of the analysis, and potentially find industries that are misvalued as a result of consensus forecasts.
- Determine the relative valuation of different industries.
- Compare the valuations of industries across time to determine the volatility of their performance over the long run and during different phases of the business cycle. This is useful for long-term investing as well as short-term industry rotation based on the current economic environment.
- Analyze industry prospects based on **strategic groups**, which are groups of firms that are distinct from the rest of the industry due to the delivery or complexity of their products or barriers to entry. For example, full-service hotels are a distinct market segment within the hotel industry.
- Classify industries by **life-cycle stage**, whether it is embryonic, growth, shakeout, mature, or declining.
- Position the industry on the **experience curve**, which shows the cost per unit relative to output. The curve declines because of increases in productivity and economies of scale, especially in industries with high fixed costs.
- Consider the forces that affect industries, which include demographic, macroeconomic, governmental, social, and technological influences.
- Examine the forces that determine competition within an industry.

## External Influences on Industries

The external influences on industry growth, profitability, and risk should be a component of an analyst's strategic analysis. These external factors include macroeconomic, technological, demographic, governmental, and social influences.

**Macroeconomic factors** can be cyclical or structural (longer-term) trends, most notably economic output as measured by GDP or some other measure. Interest rates affect financing costs for firms and individuals, as well as financial institution profitability. Credit availability affects consumer and business expenditures and funding. Inflation affects costs, prices, interest rates, and business and consumer confidence.

**Technology** can change an industry dramatically through the introduction of new or improved products. Computer hardware is an example of an industry that has undergone dramatic transformation. Radical improvements in circuitry were assisted by transformations in other industries, including the computer software and telecommunications industries. Another example of an industry that has been changed by technology is photography, which has largely moved from film to digital media.

**Demographic factors** include age distribution and population size, as well as other changes in the composition of the population. As a large segment of the population reaches their twenties, residential construction, furniture, and related industries see increased demand. An aging of the overall population can mean significant growth for the health care industry and developers of retirement communities.

**Governments** have an important effect on businesses through taxes and regulation. Entry into the health care industry, for example, is controlled by governments that license providers. Some industries, such as the U.S. defense industry, depend heavily on government purchases of goods and services.

**Social influences** relate to how people work, play, spend their money, and conduct their lives; these factors can have a large impact on industries. For example, when women entered the U.S. work force, the restaurant industry benefitted because there was less cooking at home. Child care, women's clothing, and other industries were also dramatically affected.

## Industry Life Cycle

**Industry life cycle** analysis should be a component of an analyst's strategic analysis. The five phases of the industry life-cycle model are illustrated in Figure 1.

**Figure 1: Stages of the Industry Life Cycle**

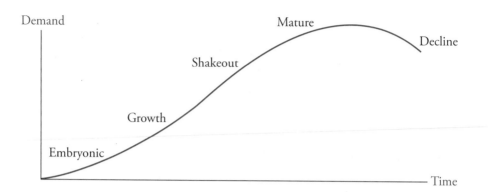

In the **embryonic stage**, the industry has just started. The characteristics of this stage are as follows:

- *Slow growth:* customers are unfamiliar with the product.
- *High prices:* the volume necessary for economies of scale has not been reached.
- *Large investment required:* to develop the product.
- *High risk of failure:* most embryonic firms fail.

In the **growth stage**, industry growth is rapid. The characteristics of this stage are as follows:

- *Rapid growth:* new consumers discover the product.
- *Limited competitive pressures:* The threat of new firms coming into the market peaks during the growth phase, but rapid growth allows firms to grow without competing on price.
- *Falling prices:* economies of scale are reached and distribution channels increase.
- *Increasing profitability:* due to economies of scale.

In the **shakeout stage**, industry growth and profitability are slowing due to strong competition. The characteristics of this stage are as follows:

- *Growth has slowed:* demand reaches saturation level with few new customers to be found.
- *Intense competition:* industry growth has slowed, so firm growth must come at the expense of competitors.
- *Increasing industry overcapacity:* firm investment exceeds increases in demand.
- *Declining profitability:* due to overcapacity.
- *Increased cost cutting:* firms restructure to survive and attempt to build brand loyalty.
- *Increased failures:* weaker firms liquidate or are acquired.

In the **mature stage**, there is little industry growth and firms begin to consolidate. The characteristics of this stage are as follows:

- *Slow growth:* market is saturated and demand is only for replacement.
- *Consolidation:* market evolves to an oligopoly.
- *High barriers to entry:* surviving firms have brand loyalty and low cost structures.
- *Stable pricing:* firms try to avoid price wars, although periodic price wars may occur during recessions.
- *Superior firms gain market share:* the firms with better products may grow faster than the industry average.

In the **decline stage**, industry growth is negative. The characteristics of this stage are as follows:

- *Negative growth:* due to development of substitute products, societal changes, or global competition.
- *Declining prices:* competition is intense and there are price wars due to overcapacity.
- *Consolidation:* failing firms exit or merge.

## Industry Concentration

High industry concentration does not guarantee pricing power.

- Absolute market share may not matter as much as a firm's market share relative to its competitors.
- If industry products are undifferentiated and commodity-like, then consumers will switch to the lowest-priced producer. Firms in industries with greater product differentiation in regard to features, reliability, and service after the sale will have greater pricing power.
- If an industry is capital intensive, and therefore costly to enter or exit, overcapacity can result in intense price competition.

Tobacco, alcohol, and confections are examples of highly concentrated industries in which firms' pricing power is relatively strong. Automobiles, aircraft, and oil refining are examples of highly concentrated industries with relatively weak pricing power.

Although industry concentration does not guarantee pricing power, a fragmented market usually does result in strong price competition.

## Ease of Entry

High barriers to entry benefit existing industry firms because they prevent new competitors from competing for market share. In industries with low barriers to entry, firms have little pricing power. To assess the ease of entry, the analyst should determine how easily a new entrant to the industry could obtain the capital, intellectual property, and customer base needed to be successful. One method of determining the ease of entry is to examine the composition of the industry over time. If the same firms dominate the industry today as ten years ago, entry is probably difficult.

High barriers to entry do not necessarily mean firm pricing power is high. Industries with high barriers to entry may have strong price competition when the products sold are undifferentiated or when high barriers to exit result in overcapacity.

## Capacity

Industry capacity has a clear impact on pricing power. Undercapacity, a situation in which demand exceeds supply at current prices, results in pricing power. Overcapacity, with supply greater than demand at current prices, will result in downward pressure on price.

## Market Share Stability

An analyst should examine whether firms' market shares in an industry have been stable over time. Market shares that are highly variable likely indicate a highly competitive industry in which firms have little pricing power. More stable market shares likely indicate less intense competition in the industry.

Factors that affect market share stability include barriers to entry, introductions of new products and innovations, and the **switching costs** that customers face when changing from one firm's products to another. High switching costs contribute to market share stability and pricing power.

## Five Forces that Determine Industry Competition

The analysis framework developed by Michael Porter[1] delineates five forces that determine industry competition.

1. Rivalry among existing competitors.

2. Threat of new entrants.

3. Threat of substitute products.

4. Bargaining power of buyers.

5. Bargaining power of suppliers.

---

1. Michael Porter, "The Five Competitive Forces That Shape Strategy," *Harvard Business Review,* Volume 86, No. 1: pp. 78–93.

Industry competition and firm profitability are greater when there is (1) less rivalry among existing industry firms, (2) less threat of new entrants, (3) less threat of substitute products, (4) less bargaining power of buyers (customers), and (5) less bargaining power of suppliers.

## Company Analysis

Having gained understanding of an industry's external environment, an analyst can then focus on **company analysis**. This involves analyzing the firm's financial condition, products and services, and **competitive strategy**. Competitive strategy is how a firm responds to the opportunities and threats of the external environment.

Porter has identified two important competitive strategies that can be employed by firms within an industry: a **cost leadership (low-cost) strategy** or a **product or service differentiation strategy**. According to Porter, a firm must decide to focus on one of these two areas to compete effectively.

In a *low-cost strategy*, the firm seeks to have the lowest costs of production in its industry, offer the lowest prices, and generate enough volume to make a superior return. In **predatory pricing**, the firm hopes to drive out competitors and later increase prices. A low-cost strategy firm should have managerial incentives that are geared toward improving operating efficiency.

In a *differentiation strategy*, the firm's products and services should be distinctive in terms of type, quality, or delivery. For success, the firm's cost of differentiation must be less than the price premium buyers place on product differentiation. The price premium should also be sustainable over time. Successful differentiators will have outstanding marketing research teams and creative personnel.

A company analysis should include the following elements:

- Firm overview, including information on operations, governance, and strengths and weaknesses.
- Industry characteristics.
- Product demand.
- Product costs.
- Pricing environment.
- Financial ratios, with comparisons to other firms and over time.
- Projected financial statements and firm valuation.

A firm's return on equity (ROE) should be part of the financial analysis. The ROE is a function of profitability, total asset turnover, and financial leverage (debt).

## EQUITY VALUATION: CONCEPTS AND BASIC TOOLS
Cross-Reference to CFA Institute Assigned Reading #60

### Categories of Equity Valuation Models

In **discounted cash flow models** (or **present value models**), a stock's value is estimated as the present value of cash distributed to shareholders (*dividend discount models*) or the present value of cash available to shareholders after the firm meets its necessary capital expenditures and working capital expenses (*free cash flow to equity models*).

There are two basic types of **multiplier models** (or **market multiple models**) that can be used estimate intrinsic values. In the first type, the ratio of stock price to such fundamentals as earnings, sales, book value, or cash flow per share is used to determine if a stock is fairly valued. For example, the price to earnings (P/E) ratio is frequently used by analysts.

The second type of multiplier model is based on the ratio of **enterprise value** to either earnings before interest, taxes, depreciation, and amortization (EBITDA) or revenue. Enterprise value is the market value of all a firm's outstanding securities minus cash and short-term investments. Common stock value can be estimated by subtracting the value of liabilities and preferred stock from an estimate of enterprise value.

In **asset-based models**, the intrinsic value of common stock is estimated as total asset value minus liabilities and preferred stock. Analysts typically adjust the book values of the firm's assets and liabilities to their fair values when estimating the market value of its equity with an asset-based model.

### Preferred Stock Valuation

The dividend is fixed and the income stream (dividends) theoretically continues forever so we use the formula for the present value of a perpetuity.

$$\text{preferred stock value} = \frac{D_p}{k_p}$$

## Dividend Discount Models (DDM)

All of the valuation models here are based on taking the present value of expected future cash flows.

*One-year holding period:*

For the purposes of this valuation model, we assume that dividends are received annually at the end of the year; so, if you hold the stock one year, you will receive the dividend and the estimated sale price $P_1$. To calculate the present value of these cash flows one year from now:

$$\text{one-period model: } P_0 = \frac{\left(\begin{array}{c}\text{dividend to}\\\text{be received}\end{array}\right)}{(1+k_e)} + \frac{\left(\begin{array}{c}\text{year-}\\\text{end price}\end{array}\right)}{(1+k_e)} \text{ or } P_0 = \frac{D_1 + P_1}{(1+k_e)}$$

Be sure to use the *expected* dividend, $D_1$, in the calculation.

*Multiple-year holding periods:*

With a multiple-year holding period, estimate all the dividends to be received as well as the expected selling price at the end of the holding period.

$$\text{n-period model: } P_0 = \frac{D_1}{(1+k_e)^1} + \frac{D_2}{(1+k_e)^2} + \dots + \frac{D_n}{(1+k_e)^n} + \frac{P_n}{(1+k_e)^n}$$

*Infinite period model (constant growth model):*

We can take the present value of an infinite stream of dividends that grows at a *constant rate* as long as the assumed growth rate, $g_c$, is less than the appropriate discount rate, $k_e$.

$$\text{constant growth model: } P_0 = \frac{D_1}{k_e - g_c}, \text{note that } D_1 = D_0(1+g_c)$$

Other things held constant, the higher the growth rate and the higher the dividend, the greater the present value.

In practice, however, increasing the dividend will decrease retained earnings and the firm's sustainable growth rate, so we cannot assume that a firm that increases its dividend will increase firm value.

*Temporary supernormal growth or multi-stage DDM:*

This model assumes that a company's dividends will grow at a high rate for a period of time before declining to a constant growth rate. To calculate the stock price, discount each of the dividends during the high growth period individually and then use the formula for the infinite growth model to find the terminal stock value at the end of the supernormal growth period. Finally, add together the present values of all dividends and of the terminal stock value.

$$\text{value}_{\text{supernormal growth}} = \frac{D_1}{(1+k_e)} + \frac{D_2}{(1+k_e)^2} + \ldots + \frac{D_n}{(1+k_e)^n} + \frac{P_n}{(1+k_e)^n}$$

$D_n$ is the last dividend of the supernormal growth period.

$$P_n = \frac{D_{n+1}}{k_e - \bar{g}c}, \text{where } D_{n+1} \text{ is expected to grow at the constant/normal rate}$$

*Earnings multiplier model (P/E ratio):*

Understand how the DDM relates to the fundamental P/E ratio.

Start with the DDM and then divide both sides of the equation by next year's projected earnings, $E_1$:

$$\text{If constant growth DDM holds: } P_0 = \frac{D_1}{k-g} \text{ then } \frac{P_0}{E_1} = \frac{D_1/E_1}{k-g}$$

*Other things held constant, the P/E ratio:*

- Increases with $D_1/E_1$, the dividend payout ratio.
- Increases with $g$, the growth rate of dividends.
- Decreases with increases in $k$, the required rate of return.
- Increases with ROE, since $g = \text{ROE} \times \text{retention ratio}$.

  ROE = (net income / sales)(sales / total assets)(total assets / equity)

*Problems with using P/E analysis:*

- Earnings are historical accounting numbers and may be of differing quality.
- Business cycles may affect P/E ratios. Currently reported earnings may be quite different from expected future earnings ($E_1$).
- As with the infinite growth model, when k < g, the P/E implied by the DDM is meaningless.

## Estimating the Growth Rate in Dividends

To estimate the growth rate in dividends, the analyst can use three methods:

1. Use the historical growth in dividends for the firm.

2. Use the median industry dividend growth rate.

3. Estimate the sustainable growth rate.

The **sustainable growth rate** is the rate at which equity, earnings, and dividends can continue to grow indefinitely assuming that ROE is constant, the dividend payout ratio is constant, and no new equity is issued.

$$\text{sustainable growth} = (1 - \text{dividend payout ratio}) \times \text{ROE}$$

The quantity (1 − dividend payout ratio) is referred to as the **retention rate**, the proportion of net income that is not paid out as dividends and goes to retained earnings, thus increasing equity.

Some firms do not currently pay dividends but are expected to begin paying dividends at some point in the future. A firm may not currently pay a dividend because it is in financial distress and cannot afford to pay out cash, or because the return the firm can earn by reinvesting cash is greater than what stockholders could expect to earn by investing dividends elsewhere.

For firms that do not currently pay dividends, an analyst must estimate the amount and timing of the first dividend in order to use the Gordon growth model. Because these parameters are highly uncertain, the analyst should compare the estimated value from the Gordon growth model with value estimates from other models.

## Using Price Multiples to Value Equity

Because the dividend discount model is very sensitive to its inputs, many investors rely on other methods. In a **price multiple** approach, an analyst compares a stock's price multiple to a benchmark value based on an index, industry group of firms, or a peer group of firms within an industry.

Common price multiples used for valuation include price-to earnings, price-to-cash flow, price-to-sales, and price-to-book value ratios. Many of these ratios have been shown to be useful for predicting stock returns, with low multiples associated with higher future returns.

When we compare a price multiple, such as P/E, for a firm to those of other firms based on market prices, we are using price multiples based on comparables. By contrast, price multiples based on fundamentals tell us what a multiple should be based on some valuation models.

One criticism of price multiples is that they reflect only the past because historical (trailing) data are often used in the denominator. For this reason, many practitioners use forward (leading or prospective) values in the denominator (sales, book value, earnings, etc.) The use of projected values can result in much different ratios. An analyst should be sure to use price multiple calculations consistently across firms.

*Trailing P/E* uses earnings over the *most recent* 12 months in the denominator. The *leading P/E ratio* (also known as forward or prospective P/E) uses expected earnings for the next four quarters or fiscal year.

$$\text{trailing P/E} = \frac{\text{market price per share}}{\text{EPS over previous 12 months}}$$

$$\text{leading P/E} = \frac{\text{market price per share}}{\text{forecasted EPS over next 12 months}}$$

The *price-to-book (P/B) ratio* is calculated as:

$$\text{P/B ratio} = \frac{\text{market value of equity}}{\text{book value of equity}} = \frac{\text{market price per share}}{\text{book value per share}}$$

A common adjustment is to use *tangible book value*, which is equal to book value of equity less intangible assets (e.g., goodwill, patents).

Furthermore, balance sheets should be adjusted for significant off-balance-sheet assets and liabilities and for differences between the fair and recorded values of assets and liabilities. Finally, book values often need to be adjusted for differences in accounting methods to ensure comparability.

*Price-to-sales (P/S) ratios* are computed by dividing a stock's price per share by sales or revenue per share or by dividing the market value of the firm's equity by its total sales:

$$P/S \text{ ratio} = \frac{\text{market value of equity}}{\text{total sales}} = \frac{\text{market price per share}}{\text{sales per share}}$$

Given one of the definitions of cash flow, the *price-to-cash-flow (P/CF) ratio* is calculated as:

$$P/CF \text{ ratio} = \frac{\text{market value of equity}}{\text{cash flow}} = \frac{\text{market price per share}}{\text{cash flow per share}}$$

where:
cash flow = CF, adjusted CFO, FCFE, or EBITDA

## Enterprise Value Multiples

**Enterprise value** (EV) is a measure of total company value and can be viewed as what it would cost to acquire the firm.

EV = market value of common stock + market value of debt – cash and short-term investments

Cash and short-term investments are subtracted because an acquirer's cost for a firm would be decreased by the amount of the target's liquid assets. Although an acquirer assumes the firm's debt, it receives the firm's cash and short-term investments. Enterprise value is appropriate when an analyst wants to compare the values of firms that have significant *differences in capital structure.*

EBITDA (earnings before interest, taxes, depreciation, and amortization are subtracted) is probably the most frequently used denominator for EV multiples; operating income can also be used. An advantage of using EBITDA instead of net income is that EBITDA is usually positive even when earnings are not. A disadvantage of using EBITDA is that it often includes non-cash revenues and expenses.

## Asset-Based Valuation Models

**Asset-based models** are appropriate when equity value is the market or fair value of assets minus the market or fair value of liabilities. Because market values of firm assets are usually difficult to obtain, the analyst typically starts with the balance sheet to determine the values of assets and liabilities. In most cases, market values are not equal to book values. Possible approaches to valuing assets are to value them at their depreciated values, inflation-adjusted depreciated values, or estimated replacement values.

Applying asset-based models is especially problematic for firms that have a large amount of intangible assets, on or off the balance sheet. The effect of the loss of the current owners' talents and customer relationships on forward earnings may be quite difficult to measure. Analysts often consider asset-based model values as floor or minimum values when significant intangibles, such as business reputation, are involved.

Asset-based model valuations are most reliable when the firm has primarily tangible short-term assets, assets with ready market values (e.g., financial or natural resource firms), or when the firm will cease to operate and is being liquidated.

## Advantages and Disadvantages of Valuation Models

Advantages of discounted cash flow models:

- They are based on the fundamental concept of discounted present value and are well grounded in finance theory.
- They are widely accepted in the analyst community.

Disadvantages of discounted cash flow models:

- Their inputs must be estimated.
- Value estimates are very sensitive to input values.

Advantages of comparable valuation using price multiples:

- Evidence that some price multiples are useful for predicting stock returns.
- Price multiples are widely used by analysts.
- Price multiples are readily available.
- They can be used in time series and cross-sectional comparisons.
- EV/EBITDA multiples are useful when comparing firm values independent of capital structure or when earnings are negative and the P/E ratio cannot be used.

Disadvantages of comparable valuation using price multiples:

- Lagging price multiples reflect the past.
- Price multiples may not be comparable across firms if the firms have different size, products, and growth.
- Price multiples for cyclical firms may be greatly affected by economic conditions at a given point in time.
- A stock may appear overvalued by the comparable method but undervalued by a fundamental method, or vice versa.
- Different accounting methods can result in price multiples that are not comparable across firms, especially internationally.
- A negative denominator in a price multiple results in a meaningless ratio. The P/E ratio is especially susceptible to this problem.

Advantages of price multiple valuations based on fundamentals:

- They are based on theoretically sound valuation models.
- They correspond to widely accepted value metrics.

Disadvantages of price multiple valuations based on fundamentals:

- Price multiples based on fundamentals will be very sensitive to the inputs (especially the k − g denominator).

Advantages of asset-based models:

- They can provide floor values.
- They are most reliable when the firm has primarily tangible short-term assets, assets with ready market values, or when the firm is being liquidated.
- They are increasingly useful for valuing public firms that report fair values.

Disadvantages of asset-based models:

- Market values are often difficult to obtain.
- Market values are usually different than book values.
- They are inaccurate when a firm has a high proportion of intangible assets or future cash flows not reflected in asset values.
- Assets can be difficult to value during periods of hyperinflation.

# FIXED INCOME

| Weight on Exam | 12% |
|---|---|
| SchweserNotes™ Reference | Book 5, Pages 1–159 |

## STUDY SESSION 15: ANALYSIS OF FIXED INCOME INVESTMENTS—BASIC CONCEPTS

### FEATURES OF DEBT SECURITIES
Cross-Reference to CFA Institute Assigned Reading #61

Understand the basics of the different types of bonds. Various provisions for retiring the debt are discussed, along with different types of embedded options. Pay special attention here to the discussion of call features, sinking funds, and refunding provisions.

### Bond Terminology

- The terms under which money is borrowed are contained in an agreement known as the *indenture*. The indenture defines the obligations of and restrictions on the borrower, and forms the basis for all future transactions between the lender/investor and the issuer. These terms are known as covenants and include both *negative* (prohibitions on the borrower) and *affirmative* (actions that the borrower promises to perform) sections.
- The *term to maturity* (or simply maturity) of a bond is the length of time until the loan contract or agreement expires. It defines the (remaining) life of the bond.
- The *par value* of a bond is the amount that the borrower promises to pay on or before the maturity date of the issue.
- The *coupon rate* is the rate that, when multiplied by the par value of a bond, gives the amount of interest to be paid annually by the borrower.

## Coupon Structures

- *Zero-coupon bonds* are bonds that do not pay periodic interest. Such bonds do not carry coupons, but instead are sold at a deep discount from their par values. Market convention dictates that semiannual compounding should be used when pricing zeros.
- *Accrual bonds* are similar to zero-coupon bonds, but are sold originally at par value. There is a stated coupon rate, but the coupon interest builds up at a compound rate until maturity.
- *Step-up notes* have coupon rates that increase over time at a specified rate.
- *Deferred-coupon bonds* carry coupons, but the initial coupon payments are deferred for some period.

## Floating-Rate Securities

- Floating-rate securities make varying coupon interest payments which are set based on a specified interest rate or index using the specified coupon formula:

> new coupon rate = reference rate ± quoted margin

- Some floating rate securities have limits on the coupon rate. An upper limit, which is called a *cap*, puts a maximum on the interest rate paid by the borrower. A lower limit, called a *floor*, puts a minimum on the interest rate received by the lender. When a bond has both a cap and a floor, the combination is called a *collar*.

## Accrued Interest and the Clean and Full Prices

When a bond is sold between coupon payment dates, part of the next coupon belongs to the seller. Normally, bond prices are quoted without accrued interest, and this is called the *clean price*. A bond price that includes accrued interest is called the *full price*.

## Embedded Options

A *call feature* gives the issuer of a bond the right to retire the issue early by paying the call price which is typically above the face value of the bond at the first call date and declines over time to par. A period of years after issuance for which there is no call allowed is called the period of call protection.

A *prepayment option* is similar to a call feature and gives the issuer of an amortizing (e.g., mortgage) security the right to repay principal ahead of scheduled repayment, in whole or in part.

A *put feature* gives the owner of a bond the right to receive principal repayment prior to maturity.

A *conversion option* gives a bondholder the right to exchange the bond for a specified number of common shares of the issuer. When such an option allows exchange for the common shares of another issuer, it is called an *exchange option*.

An embedded option that benefits the issuer will increase the yield required by bond buyers. An embedded option that benefits the bondholder will decrease the yield required on the bond.

## Repurchase Agreements

A *repurchase (repo) agreement* is an arrangement by which an institution sells a security and commits to buy it back at a later date (*repurchase date*), at a predetermined price. The *repurchase price* is greater than the selling price and accounts for the interest charged by the buyer, who is essentially lending funds to the seller.

Most bond dealers finance inventories with repo agreements rather than with margin loans, which typically have higher rates and more restrictions.

## RISKS ASSOCIATED WITH INVESTING IN BONDS
Cross-Reference to CFA Institute Assigned Reading #62

The most important risks associated with investing in bonds are interest rate risk, reinvestment risk, and credit risk.

*Interest rate risk*. As the rates go up (down), bond prices go down (up). This is the source of interest rate risk, which is approximated by *duration*.

*Call risk*. Call protection reduces call risk. When interest rates are more volatile, callable bonds have more call risk.

*Prepayment risk*. If rates fall, causing prepayments to increase, the investor must reinvest at the new lower rate.

*Yield curve risk*. Changes in the shape of the yield curve mean that yields change by different amounts for bonds with different maturities.

*Reinvestment risk*. Reinvestment risk occurs when interest rates decline and investors are forced to reinvest bond cash flows at lower yields. Reinvestment risk is the

©2011 Kaplan, Inc.

greatest for bonds that have embedded call options, prepayment options, or high coupon rates, and is greater for amortizing securities than for non-amortizing securities.

*Credit risk.* Credit risk comes in three forms—*default risk, credit spread risk,* and *downgrade risk.*

*Liquidity risk.* Since investors prefer more liquidity to less, a decrease in a security's liquidity will decrease its price, and the required yield will be higher.

*Exchange-rate risk.* This is the uncertainty about the value of foreign currency cash flows to an investor in terms of his home country currency.

*Volatility risk.* This risk is present for fixed-income securities that have embedded options—call options, prepayment options, or put options. Changes in interest rate volatility affect the value of these options and thus affect the value of securities with embedded options.

*Inflation risk.* This is the risk of *unexpected* inflation, also called purchasing power risk.

*Event risk.* Risks outside the risks of financial markets (i.e., natural disasters, corporate takeovers).

**Figure 1: Bond Characteristics and Interest Rate Risk**

| Characteristic | Interest Rate Risk | Duration |
|---|---|---|
| Maturity up | Interest rate risk up | Duration up |
| Coupon up | Interest rate risk down | Duration down |
| Add a call | Interest rate risk down | Duration down |
| Add a put | Interest rate risk down | Duration down |

## Duration of a Bond

Duration is a measure of price sensitivity of a security to changes in yield. It can be interpreted as an approximation of the percentage change in the bond price for a 1% change in yield. It is the ratio of the percentage change in bond price to the change in yield in percent.

$$\text{duration} = -\frac{\% \text{ change in bond price}}{\text{yield change in } \%}$$

To get the approximate percentage bond price change, given its duration and a specific change in yield, use the following formula:

percent change in bond price = – duration × yield change in %

**Dollar duration** is simply the approximate price change in dollars (or other currency) in response to a change in yield of 100 basis points (1%). With a duration of 5.2 and a market value of $1.2 million, we can calculate the dollar duration as 5.2% × $1.2 million = $62,400.

## OVERVIEW OF BOND SECTORS AND INSTRUMENTS
Cross-Reference to CFA Institute Assigned Reading #63

### Securities Issued by the U.S. Department of the Treasury

*Treasury securities.* Issued by the U.S. Treasury, thus backed by the full faith and credit of the U.S. government and considered to be credit risk free.

*Treasury bills.* T-bills have maturities of less than one year and do not make explicit interest payments, paying only the face (par) value at the maturity date. They are sold at a discount to par and interest is received when the par value is paid at maturity.

*Treasury notes and Treasury bonds.* Pay semiannual coupon interest at a rate that is fixed at issuance. Notes have original maturities of 2, 3, 5, and 10 years. Bonds have original maturities of 20 or 30 years.

*Treasury inflation protected securities* (TIPS). Coupon rate is fixed, but the face/principal value of the security is adjusted semiannually based on the change in the consumer price index (CPI). This inflation-adjusted principal is multiplied by the fixed coupon rate to determine the interest payments to investors.

coupon payment = inflation adjusted par value × (stated coupon rate / 2)

*Treasury STRIPS.* Since the U.S. Treasury does not issue zero-coupon notes and bonds, investment bankers began stripping the coupons from Treasuries to create zero-coupon bonds to meet investor demand. These stripped securities are of two types:

- *Coupon strips* are the coupon payments, each of which has been stripped from the original security and acts like a fixed-term zero-coupon bond.
- *Principal strips* refer to the principal payments from stripped bonds.

*Federal agency securities.* Agency bonds are debt securities issued by various agencies and organizations of the U.S. government, such as the Federal Home Loan Bank (FHLB). Most agency issues are not obligations of the U.S. Treasury and technically should not be considered to be riskless like Treasury securities. However, they are very high-quality securities that have almost no risk of default.

## Mortgage Passthrough Securities

A *mortgage passthrough security* is created by pooling a large number of mortgages together. Shares are sold in the form of *participation certificates.* Interest, scheduled principal payments, and prepayments are passed through to investors after deducting small administrative and servicing fees. Like the underlying mortgage loans, mortgage passthroughs are *amortizing securities.* Prepayment risk is the risk that homeowners either pay additional principal or pay off the entire loan balance prior to the stated maturity. This typically happens when interest rates are low—so the investor gets more principal back in a low-interest-rate environment.

*Collateralized mortgage obligations* (CMOs) are created from mortgage passthrough securities. Different tranches (slices) represent claims to different cash flows from the passthrough securities and can have different maturities or different prepayment risk than the original passthrough.

## Securities Issued by Municipalities in the United States

The coupon interest on *municipal bonds* is typically exempt from federal taxation in the United States and from state income tax in the state of issuance. Two types of municipal bonds (munis) are:

- *Tax-backed debt* (general obligation bonds) is secured by the full faith and credit of the borrower and is backed by its unlimited taxing authority, which includes the ability to impose individual income tax, sales tax, property tax, or corporate tax.
- *Revenue bonds* are supported only by the revenues generated from projects that are funded with the help of the original bond issue.

To compare tax exempt with taxable bonds (like corporates), you must convert the tax exempt yield to a taxable equivalent yield.

$$\text{taxable equivalent yield} = \frac{\text{tax exempt municipal yield}}{1 - \text{marginal tax rate}}$$

*Insured bonds* are guaranteed for the life of the issue by a third party.

*Pre-refunded bonds* have been collateralized with Treasury securities in an amount sufficient to make scheduled interest and principal payments and are considered of the highest quality.

## Corporate Bonds

*Secured bonds* have first claim to specific assets in the event of default.

*Unsecured bonds* are called *debentures*. Those with first claim to cash flows and to proceeds of asset sales in the event of liquidation are called *senior bonds*.

*Junior bonds* have a claim after those of senior bonds and are sometimes called *subordinated* bonds or notes. All bonds have priority to cash flows before those of preferred stock and common stock.

## Asset-Backed Securities

Asset-backed securities (ABS) are collateralized by financial assets that the corporation has sold to a separate legal entity. They lower borrowing costs when the separate entity (special purpose vehicle) can attain a higher credit rating than the corporation.

With this structure, financial difficulties of the corporation should not affect the ABS credit. Often, credit enhancements in the form of guarantees of another corporation, a bank letter of credit, or bond insurance are employed to further reduce borrowing costs.

## Other Debt Instruments

*Negotiable CDs* are issued in a wide range of maturities by banks, traded in a secondary market, backed by bank assets, and termed Eurodollar CDs when denominated in US$ and issued outside the United States.

*Bankers acceptances* are issued by banks to guarantee a future payment for goods shipped, sold at a discount to the future payment they promise, short-term, and have limited liquidity.

*Collateralized debt obligations* (CDOs) are backed by an underlying pool of debt securities which may be any one of a number of types: corporate bonds, bank loans, emerging markets debt, mortgage-backed securities, or other CDOs.

The primary market in bonds includes underwritten and best-efforts public offerings, as well as private placements. The secondary market in bonds includes some trading on exchanges and a much larger volume of trading in the dealer (OTC) market. Electronic trading networks continue to be an increasingly important part of the secondary market for bonds.

## UNDERSTANDING YIELD SPREADS
Cross-Reference to CFA Institute Assigned Reading #64

### Central Bank Interest Rate Policy Tools

In the United States, the Fed manages short-term rates through *monetary policy tools*:

- *Discount rate.* Rate at which banks can borrow reserves from the Fed.
- *Open market operations.* Buying/selling of Treasury securities by the Fed in the open market. When the Fed buys securities, cash replaces securities in investor accounts, more funds are available for lending, and rates decrease. Sales of securities by the Fed have the opposite effect.
- *Bank reserve requirements.* By increasing the percentage of deposits that banks are required to retain as reserves, the Fed effectively decreases the funds that are available for lending, which tends to increase rates.
- *Persuading banks to tighten or loosen their credit policies.*

### Theories of the Term Structure of Interest Rates

*Pure expectations theory:*

Under this theory, the yield curve only reflects expectations about future short-term interest rates.

> short-term rates expected to rise in the future ⇒ upward-sloping yield curve
> short-term rates expected to fall in the future ⇒ downward-sloping yield curve
> short-term rates expected to rise then fall ⇒ humped yield curve
> short-term rates expected to remain constant ⇒ flat yield curve

*Liquidity preference theory:*

Under this theory, the yield curve is upward sloping to reflect the fact that investors require a term premium that increases at longer maturities.

*Market segmentation theory:*

Under this theory, lenders and borrowers have preferred maturity ranges, and the shape of the yield curve is determined by the supply and demand for securities within each maturity range.

## Yield Spreads

*Nominal yield spreads* measure the difference between the market yields on two bonds. Yield spreads can be caused by differences in credit quality, call features, tax treatment, or maturity.

- *Absolute yield spread.* Quantifies the difference between nominal yields on two bonds or two types of bonds. Calculated by:

$$\text{absolute yield spread} = \text{higher yield} - \text{lower yield}$$

  Typically, the yield spread is calculated between a non-Treasury security and a benchmark Treasury security.

- *Relative spread.* Quantifies the absolute spread as a percentage of the lower yield.

$$\text{relative yield spread} = \frac{\text{higher yield}}{\text{lower yield}} - 1$$

- *Yield ratio.* Calculated as:

$$\text{yield ratio} = \frac{\text{higher yield}}{\text{lower yield}}$$

## Credit Spreads

*Credit spread* refers to the *difference in yield between two issues that are identical in all respects except their credit ratings.* Credit spreads are a function of the state of the economy. During economic expansion, credit spreads decline as corporations are expected to have stronger cash flows. During economic contractions, cash flows are pressured, which leads to a greater probability of default and increasing credit spreads.

# Study Session 16: Analysis of Fixed Income Investments—Analysis and Valuation

## Introduction to the Valuation of Debt Securities
Cross-Reference to CFA Institute Assigned Reading #65

### Bond Valuation Process

- Estimate the cash flows over the life of the security—coupon payments and return of principal.
- Determine the appropriate discount rate based on risk associated with the estimated cash flows.
- Calculate the present value of the estimated cash flows.

### Difficulties in Estimating the Expected Cash Flows

- Timing of principal repayments is not known with certainty.
- Coupon payments are not known with certainty.
- The bond is convertible or exchangeable into another security.

### Bond Valuation

Bond prices, established in the market, can be expressed either as a percentage of par value or as a yield. Yield to maturity (YTM) is the single discount rate that will make the present value of a bond's promised semiannual cash flows equal to the market price.

In the United States, bonds typically make coupon payments (equal to one-half the stated coupon rate times the face value) twice a year, and the yield to maturity is expressed as twice the semiannual discount rate that will make the present value of the semiannual coupon payments equal to the market price. This yield to maturity, calculated for a semiannual-pay bond, is also referred to as a *bond equivalent yield*.

For bonds that make annual payments, the YTM is the annual discount rate that makes the present value of the annual coupon payments equal to the market price. Thus, the relation between an annual and semiannual YTM is:

$$YTM_{annual\text{-}pay} = \left(1 + \frac{YTM_{semiannual\text{-}pay}}{2}\right)^2 - 1$$

$$YTM_{semiannual\text{-}pay} = \left[(1 + YTM_{annual\text{-}pay})^{\frac{1}{2}} - 1\right] \times 2$$

The relation between the semiannual YTM (the bond equivalent yield) and price for a bond with $N$ years to maturity can be represented as:

$$\text{bond price} = \frac{CPN_1}{(1 + YTM/2)} + \frac{CPN_2}{(1 + YTM/2)^2} + \ldots + \frac{CPN_{2N} + Par}{(1 + YTM/2)^{2N}}$$

The price-yield relationship for a zero-coupon bond with $N$ years to maturity is based on a semiannual yield or bond equivalent yield by convention, so we have:

$$\text{zero-coupon bond price} = \frac{\text{face value}}{\left(1 + \dfrac{YTM}{2}\right)^{2N}}$$

$$\text{zero-coupon YTM} = \left[\left(\frac{\text{face value}}{\text{price}}\right)^{\frac{1}{2N}} - 1\right] \times 2$$

A bondholder will actually realize the YTM on his initial investment only if all payments are made as scheduled, the bond is held to maturity, and, importantly, all interim cash flows are reinvested at the YTM.

*Spot rates and no-arbitrage bond values:*

Earlier we discussed a yield curve that plotted YTM versus bond maturity. We can call that the "par yield curve" if it is constructed with the YTMs for bonds trading at par.

*Spot rates* are market discount rates for single payments to be received in the future and can be thought of, theoretically, as equivalent to the market yields on zero-coupon bonds. Given the spot-rate yield curve, we can discount each of a bond's promised cash flows at its appropriate spot rate and sum the resulting present values to get the market value of the bond.

Values calculated in this way are called *no-arbitrage values* and we will present the reason for this terminology shortly. With $C_N$ and $S_N$ being the *N*-period coupon payments and spot rates respectively, we can write:

$$\text{bond value} = \frac{C_1}{(1+S_1)^1} + \frac{C_2}{(1+S_2)^2} + \text{........} \frac{C_N + \text{face}}{(1+S_N)^N}$$

Government bond dealers can separate Treasury bonds into their "pieces," the individual coupon and principal cash flows, a process known as *stripping the bond*. These individual pieces are a series of zero-coupon bonds with different maturity dates, and each can be valued by discounting at the spot rate for the appropriate maturity. Since bond dealers can also recombine a bond's individual cash flows into a bond, arbitrage prevents the market price of the bond from being more or less than the value of the individual cash flows discounted at spot rates.

If the spot-rate or no-arbitrage value is greater than the market price, a bond dealer can buy the bond, strip it, and sell the "pieces" for the greater amount to earn an arbitrage profit. If the market price of the bond is greater than the no-arbitrage value, a dealer can buy the pieces, combine them into a bond, and sell the bond to make a profit.

## YIELD MEASURES, SPOT RATES, AND FORWARD RATES
Cross-Reference to CFA Institute Assigned Reading #66

This chapter includes information on many different types of yield measures. You must be ready to calculate any of them quickly and accurately.

### Sources of Bond Return

- Periodic coupon interest payments.
- Recovery of principal, along with any capital gain or loss.
- Reinvestment income.

### Traditional Measures of Yield

*Current yield:*

$$\text{current yield} = \frac{\text{annual coupon payment}}{\text{bond price}}$$

This measure looks at just one source of return: *a bond's annual interest income*—it does not consider capital gains/losses or reinvestment income.

The relationships between different yield measures are displayed in the following table:

| Bond selling at | Relationship |
|---|---|
| Par | coupon rate = current yield = yield to maturity |
| Discount | coupon rate < current yield < yield to maturity |
| Premium | coupon rate > current yield > yield to maturity |

*Yield to maturity, call, put, refunding:*

Yields to other events besides maturity are calculated in the same way as YTM and are essentially internal rate of return measures. For example, to calculate the yield to call (YTC), we need to use the number of semiannual periods until the call date under consideration (for N) and the call price in place of the maturity value (for FV).

The key to YTC computations is using the right number of periods (to first call) and the appropriate terminal value (the call price).

### Bootstrapping Spot Rates

Understand the concept of bootstrapping spot rates from coupon bond prices using known short-term spot rates.

**Example:**

A 2-year bond with an 8% annual coupon is priced at 100 and the 1-year spot rate is 4%. Use the bootstrapping method to find the 2-year spot rate.

**Answer:**

The arbitrage-free pricing relationship is $100 = \dfrac{8}{1.04} + \dfrac{108}{(1+Z_2)^2}$, so

we can write $100 - 7.6923 = \dfrac{108}{(1+Z_2)^2}$ and solve for $Z_2$ as

$$Z_2 = \left[\frac{108}{92.3077}\right]^{\frac{1}{2}} - 1 = 8.167\%.$$

The idea of bootstrapping is that we can repeat this process sequentially. Given $Z_1$, $Z_2$, and the price of a 3-year bond, we could calculate $Z_3$ in the same manner.

## Forward Rates

A forward rate is a rate for borrowing/lending at some date in the future. The key here is that investors should receive the same total return from investing in a 2-year bond as they would if they invested in a 1-year bond and then rolled the proceeds into a second 1-year bond at maturity of the first bond, one year from today.

This idea is shown in the relation between an N-period spot rate and a series of forward 1-year rates. Letting $_1f_0$ be the current 1-year rate and $_1f_N$ be the 1-year rate $N$ years from now, we can write:

$$\text{N-period spot rate } (S_N) = \left[(1+{_1f_0})(1+{_1f_1})\ldots\ldots(1+{_1f_N})\right]^{\frac{1}{N+1}} - 1$$

The formula for computing the 1-period forward rate $n$ periods from today using spot rates is:

$$_1f_n = \frac{(1+\text{spot}_{n+1})^{n+1}}{(1+\text{spot}_n)^n} - 1$$

## The Option-Adjusted Spread (OAS) and Zero-Volatility (Z) Spreads

The *nominal spread* is simply an issue's YTM minus the YTM of a Treasury security of similar maturity. Therefore, the use of the nominal spread suffers from the same limitations as the YTM.

The *static spread* (or *zero-volatility spread*) is not the spread over a single Treasury's YTM, but the spread over each of the spot rates on the spot rate yield curve. In other words, *the same spread is added to all risk-free spot rates* to make the PV of the bond's promised cash flows equal to its market price. The Z-spread is inherently more accurate than (and will usually differ from) the nominal spread, since it is based upon the arbitrage-free spot rates, rather than a given YTM. The Z-spread will equal the nominal spread if the term structure of interest rates (the yield curve) is perfectly flat.

The *option-adjusted spread* is used when a bond has embedded options. It can be thought of as the difference between the static or Z-spread and the option cost.

> Z-spread – option adjusted spread = option cost in %

For a bond with a call feature, the option cost will be positive (you require a higher yield). For a bond with a put feature, the option cost will be negative since a bond with a put feature will have a lower required yield than an identical option-free bond.

The intuition of the OAS is that it is the spread once any differences in yield due to the embedded option are removed. Thus, it is a spread that reflects differences in yield for differences in credit risk and liquidity. That's why it must be used for bonds with embedded options and will be the same as the Z-spread for option-free bonds.

## INTRODUCTION TO THE MEASUREMENT OF INTEREST RATE RISK
Cross-Reference to CFA Institute Assigned Reading #67

Duration is a measure of the *slope* of the price-yield function, which is steeper at low interest rates and flatter at high interest rates. Hence, duration (interest rate sensitivity) is higher at low rates and lower at high rates. This concept holds for non-callable bonds. Convexity is a measure of the degree of curvature of the price/yield relationship. Convexity accounts for the error in the estimated change in a bond's price based on duration.

©2011 Kaplan, Inc.

## Figure 2: Price-Yield Function of an Option-Free Bond

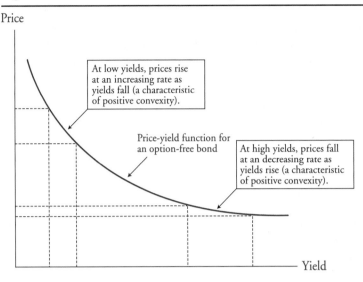

## Figure 2: Price-Yield Function of an Option-Free Bond

If the bond is callable and the bond is likely to be called, as yields fall, no one will pay a price higher than the call price. The price will not rise significantly as yields fall and you will see *negative convexity* at work. Remember, the verbal description of negative convexity is, "as yields fall, prices rise at a decreasing rate." For a positively convex bond, as yields fall, prices rise at an *increasing* rate.

## Figure 3: Price-Yield Function of a Callable Bond

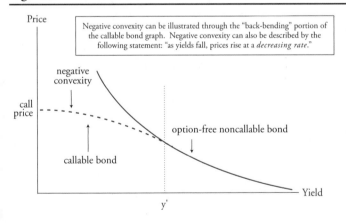

## Measuring Interest Rate Risk

There are two approaches to measuring interest rate risk: the full valuation approach (scenario analysis approach) and the duration/convexity approach.

*Full valuation or scenario analysis approach:*

This approach revalues all bonds in a portfolio under a given interest rate change (yield curve) scenario. It is theoretically preferred and gives a good idea of the change in portfolio value. This method requires accurate valuation models and consists of these steps:

1. Start with current market yield and price.
2. Estimate changes in yields.
3. Revalue bonds.
4. Compare new value to current value.

*Duration/convexity approach:*

This approach provides an approximation of the actual interest rate sensitivity of a bond or bond portfolio. It has an advantage due to its simplicity compared to the full valuation approach.

The most concise, useful description of duration is that it represents *the sensitivity of a bond's (or portfolio's) price to a 1% change in yield to maturity.*

Know this formula for effective duration and be able to make computations with this formula, entering Δy as a decimal (e.g., 0.005 for one-half percent).

$$\text{effective duration} = \frac{\text{value when yield falls by } \Delta y - \text{value when yield rises by } \Delta y}{2 \times \text{beginning value} \times (\Delta y)}$$

The preceding equation provides a measure which allows us to approximate the percentage change in the price of a bond for a 100 basis point (1.00%) change in yield to maturity.

*Modified duration* assumes that the cash flows on the bond will not change (i.e., that we are dealing with a noncallable bond). This differs from *effective duration*, which considers expected changes in cash flows that may occur for bonds with embedded options. Effective duration must be used for bonds with embedded options.

*Modified duration* and *effective duration* are good approximations of potential bond price behavior only for relatively small changes in interest rates. As rate changes grow larger, the curvature of the bond price/yield relationship becomes more important. The widening error in the estimated price is due to the curvature of the actual price path, a bond's *convexity*.

Finally, it is critical that you know how to compute the approximate percentage price change of a bond. Use the decimal change in yield here, too.

$$\text{percentage change in price} = \text{duration effect} + \text{convexity effect}$$
$$= [-\text{duration} \times (\Delta y)] + [\text{convexity} \times (\Delta y)^2] \times 100$$

The *price value of a basis point* (PVBP) is the dollar change in a portfolio or asset value for one basis point change in yield.

$$\text{PVBP} = \text{duration} \times 0.0001 \times \text{value}$$

# DERIVATIVES

| | |
|---|---|
| Weight on Exam | 5% |
| SchweserNotes™ Reference | Book 5, Pages 160–244 |

## DERIVATIVE MARKETS AND INSTRUMENTS
Cross-Reference to CFA Institute Assigned Reading #68

A *derivative* is a security that *derives* its value from the value of or return on another asset or security.

A *contingent claim* has a payoff in the future only if certain events happen. Option contracts are contingent claims and also derivative securities.

A *forward commitment* is just that, a contractual commitment to buy or sell an asset in the future or take or make a loan in the future. Futures, swaps, and forward contracts are forward commitments and also are derivative securities.

Forwards and swaps are typically originated by dealers and have no active secondary market. Futures contracts are originated by and traded in a futures exchange. Some options contracts are traded on an organized options exchange and others are originated by dealers and do not trade in a secondary market.

### Overview of Derivative Contracts

- In a *forward contract* one party agrees to buy, and the counterparty to sell, a physical asset or a security at a specific price on a specific date in the future. If the future price of the asset increases, the buyer (at the older, lower price) has a gain, and the seller a loss.
- A *futures contract* is a forward contract that is standardized and exchange-traded. Futures contracts differ from forward contracts in that futures are traded in an active secondary market, are regulated, are backed by the clearinghouse, and require a daily settlement of gains and losses.
- A *swap* is equivalent to a series of forward contracts. In the simplest swap, one party agrees to pay the short-term (floating) rate of interest on some principal amount, and the counterparty agrees to pay a certain (fixed) rate of interest in return. Swaps of different currencies and equity returns are also common.

- An option to buy an asset at a particular price is termed a *call option*. The seller of the option has an *obligation* to sell the asset at the agreed-upon price, if the call buyer chooses to exercise the right to buy the asset.
- An option to sell an asset at a particular price is termed a *put option*. The seller of the option has an *obligation* to purchase the asset at the agreed-upon price if the put buyer chooses to exercise the right to sell the asset.

## Arbitrage

Arbitrage opportunities arise when assets are mispriced. Trading by arbitrageurs will continue until they affect supply and demand enough to bring asset prices to efficient (no-arbitrage) levels.

There are two arbitrage arguments that are particularly useful in the study and use of derivatives:

1. The first is based on the "law of one price." Two securities or portfolios that have identical cash flows in the future, regardless of future events, should have the same price. If A and B have identical future payoffs and A is priced lower than B, buy A and sell B.
2. The second type of arbitrage is used when two securities with uncertain returns can be combined in a portfolio that will have a certain payoff. If a portfolio consisting of A and B has a certain payoff, the portfolio should yield the risk-free rate.

## FORWARD MARKETS AND CONTRACTS
Cross-Reference to CFA Institute Assigned Reading #69

## Forward Contracts

A *deliverable* forward contract for an asset specifies that the long will pay a certain amount at a specific future date to the short, who will deliver the underlying asset. Neither party pays at contract initiation.

A *cash settlement* forward contract does not require actual delivery of the underlying asset, but instead requires a cash payment to the party that is disadvantaged by the difference between the market price of the asset and the contract price at the settlement date.

Early termination of a forward contract can be accomplished by entering into a new forward contract with the opposite position, at the then-current forward price. This early termination will fix the amount of the gains or losses on the forward contract as of the termination date.

Forward contracts are described by the type of asset that must be purchased or sold under the terms of the contract. Equity forwards require delivery or cash settlement based on the value of a stock, a specific portfolio of stocks, or a stock index.

Currency forwards are widely used to hedge exchange rate risk and require delivery of a specified amount of a particular currency with a contract price in another currency.

Bond forwards are often written on zero-coupon bonds with payoffs to the long that increase if rates decrease. A related type of forward contract is a forward rate agreement where increasing rates increase the payoff to the long position.

## Forward Rate Agreements

A *forward rate agreement* (FRA) can be viewed as a forward contract to borrow or lend money at a certain rate at some future date, although it is a cash settlement contract. The long position in an FRA is the party that would borrow the money (long the loan with the contract "price" being the interest rate on the loan). If the floating rate at contract expiration is above the rate specified in the forward agreement, the long position will profit; the contract can be viewed as the right to borrow at below-market rates.

The London Interbank Offered Rate (LIBOR) is a short-term rate based on the rates at which large London banks will lend U.S. dollars to each other. *Euribor* is a similar rate for borrowing and lending in euros.

The payment at settlement on an FRA is the present value of the difference in interest costs between a riskless loan at the market rate and one made at the rate specified in the contract. The difference in rates is multiplied by the notional amount of the contract to get the difference in interest due at the end of the loan term. Since this hypothetical loan would be made at contract settlement, the interest savings or excess interest costs would be paid later, at the end of the loan term. For this reason, the payment at settlement is the present value of the interest difference, discounted at the rate prevailing at settlement.

The general formula for the payment to the long at settlement is:

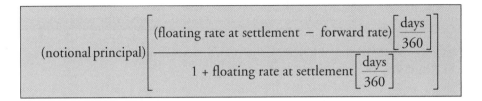

$$(\text{notional principal}) \left[ \frac{(\text{floating rate at settlement} - \text{forward rate})\left[\frac{\text{days}}{360}\right]}{1 + \text{floating rate at settlement}\left[\frac{\text{days}}{360}\right]} \right]$$

## FUTURES MARKETS AND CONTRACTS
Cross-Reference to CFA Institute Assigned Reading #70

## Key Differences Between Futures and Forwards

| Forwards | Futures |
|---|---|
| Private contracts | Exchange-traded |
| Unique customized contracts | Standardized contracts |
| Default risk is present | Guaranteed by clearinghouse |
| Little or no regulation | Regulated |
| No margin deposit required | Margin required and adjusted |

## Margin

There are three types of futures margin (initial, maintenance, and variation).

The first deposit is called the *initial margin*. Initial margin must be posted before any trading takes place. Initial margin is fairly low and equals about one day's maximum fluctuation in the contract value. The margin requirement is low because at the end of every day there is a *daily settlement* process called marking to market.

In *marking to market*, any losses for the day are removed from the trader's account, and any gains are added to the trader's account. Thus, any gains or losses in the value of the futures position (futures contract) are realized each day.

If the margin balance in the trader's account falls below a certain level (called the *maintenance margin*), the trader will get a *margin call* and must deposit more cash or securities (called the *variation margin*) into the account to bring the margin balance back up to the initial level. If the margin balance increases above the initial margin amount, the investor can withdraw funds from the account in the amount of the excess above the initial margin requirement.

## Futures Contract Basics

Futures contracts specify the quality and quantity of the underlying asset, the delivery or settlement date in the future, and the place of delivery. The futures exchange decides which contracts will be traded, determines the minimum price change, and sets limits on daily price moves.

The Futures Clearing Corporation specifies margin requirements and acts as the counterparty to every trade. Standardization makes the futures contracts quite liquid, so to close out a futures position prior to settlement, a trader can just enter into an opposite futures position. The cumulative mark to market in the futures account will have already accounted for any gains or losses on the position prior to the date of the *offsetting* or *closing trade*.

Most futures contracts are terminated by offsetting trades. Delivery of the asset, cash settlement at contract expiration, or an off-exchange delivery called *exchange for physicals* are the other methods of terminating a futures position.

Some bond futures contracts provide valuable delivery options to the short which include what bond to deliver and when during the expiration month to deliver.

## OPTION MARKETS AND CONTRACTS
Cross-Reference to CFA Institute Assigned Reading #71

## Option Terminology and Basics

*Call option:*

- Long position: *right to buy* the underlying stock at a specific price on a future date.
- Short position: *obligation to sell* the stock to the buyer of the call option.

*Put option:*

- Long position: *right to sell* the underlying stock at a specific price on a future date.
- Short position: *obligation to buy* the stock from the buyer of the put option.

The *strike price (X)* represents the exercise price specified in the contract.

The seller or short position in an options contract is sometimes referred to as the *writer* of the option.

*Stock options* are typically on 100 shares of stock.

*American options* allow the owner to exercise the option at any time before or at expiration.

*European options* can only be exercised at expiration. For two otherwise identical options, an American option has more flexibility than the European option, so it is worth at least as much and typically more.

## Moneyness and Intrinsic Value

An option that would provide a positive payoff if exercised is said to be *in the money*. The *intrinsic value* of an option is the amount that it is in the money, and zero otherwise. The difference between the price of an option (called its premium) and its intrinsic value is termed its *time value*.

The following table summarizes the moneyness of options based on the stock's current price, $S$, and the option's exercise strike price, $X$.

| Moneyness | Call Option | Put Option |
|---|---|---|
| In-the-money | $S > X$ | $S < X$ |
| At-the-money | $S = X$ | $S = X$ |
| Out-of-the-money | $S < X$ | $S > X$ |

- In general, an option is more valuable when its time to expiration is longer and when the price of the underlying asset is more volatile.
- Call options increase in value when the asset price increases, the exercise price is lower, or when the risk-free rate is higher.
- Put options increase in value when the asset price is lower, the exercise price is higher, or when the risk-free rate is lower.
- Both put and call options have greater value when the volatility of the price of the underlying asset is greater.

## Interest Rate Options vs. Forward Rate Agreements (FRAs)

For interest rate options, the exercise price is an interest rate, and payoffs depend on a reference rate such as LIBOR. Interest rate options are similar to FRAs because there is no deliverable asset and they are settled in cash, in an amount based on a notional amount and the difference between the strike rate and the reference rate.

The combination of a long interest rate call option plus a short interest rate put option has the same payoff as an FRA. One difference is that interest rate option payoffs are made after the option expiration date at a date corresponding to the end of the loan period specified in the contract (30-day, 60-day, 90-day LIBOR, etc.). Recall that FRAs pay the present value of this interest difference at settlement.

## Other Types of Options

*Commodity options* are on physical underlying assets, such as gold.

*Index option* payoffs are based on the difference between the strike price and the index, times a specified multiplier.

*Options on futures* give the long the right to enter into a futures position at the futures price specified in the option contract.

## Minimum and Maximum Option Values

| Option | Minimum Value | Maximum Value |
|---|---|---|
| European call | $c_t \geq \text{Max}[0, S_t - X / (1 + RFR)^{T-t}]$ | St |
| American call | $C_t \geq \text{Max}[0, S_t - X / (1 + RFR)^{T-t}]$ | St |
| European put | $p_t \geq \text{Max}[0, X / (1 + RFR)^{T-t} - S_t]$ | $X / (1 + RFR)^{T-t}$ |
| American put | $P_t \geq \text{Max}[0, X - S_t]$ | X |

## Put-Call Parity

*Put-call parity* means that portfolios with identical payoffs must sell for the same price to prevent arbitrage. A fiduciary call (composed of a call option and a risk-free bond that will pay *X* at expiration) and a protective put (composed of a share of stock and a long put) both have identical payoffs at maturity. Based on this fact and the law of one price, we can state that, for European options:

$$C + X / (1 + RFR)^T = S + P$$

Each of the individual securities in the put-call parity relationship can be expressed as:

$$S = C - P + X / (1 + RFR)^T$$
$$P = C - S + X / (1 + RFR)^T$$
$$C = S + P - X / (1 + RFR)^T$$
$$X / (1 + RFR)^T = S + P - C$$

The single securities on the left-hand side of the equations all have exactly the same payoffs at expiration as the portfolios on the right-hand side. The portfolios on the right-hand side are the "synthetic" equivalents of the securities on the left. Note that the options must be European-style and the puts and calls must have the same exercise prices for these relations to hold.

The four relations all must hold to prevent arbitrage; if there is a profitable arbitrage opportunity, *all of these relations* will be violated. If the equality does not hold, buy the "cheap" side of the equation and sell the other "expensive" side. This will produce an immediate *arbitrage profit*.

## SWAP MARKETS AND CONTRACTS
Cross-Reference to CFA Institute Assigned Reading #72

One way to view a swap contract is as an exchange of loans. A simple fixed-for-floating rate swap is equivalent to one party borrowing from another at a fixed rate and the other party borrowing the same amount from the first party and paying a floating rate of interest on the loan. If the loans are in different currencies, it's a currency swap; if one of the loans requires the payment of a rate determined by the return on a stock, portfolio, or index, it is termed an equity swap.

## Characteristics of Swap Contracts

* No payment required by either party at initiation except the principal values exchanged in currency swaps.
* Custom instruments.
* Not traded in any organized secondary market.
* Largely unregulated.
* Default risk is a critical aspect of the contracts.
* Institutions dominate.

## Methods of Terminating a Swap

- Mutual termination.
- Offsetting swap contract.
- Resale to a third party.
- Exercising a swaption—an option to enter into an offsetting swap.

## Currency Swaps

In a currency swap, one party makes payments denominated in one currency, while the payments from the counterparty are made in a second currency. Typically, the notional amounts of the contract, expressed in both currencies, are exchanged at contract initiation and returned at the contract termination date in the same amounts. The periodic interest payments in each of the two currencies can be based on fixed or floating rates.

The cash flows that would occur in a currency swap are as follows:

- Unlike an interest rate swap, the notional principal actually changes hands at the beginning of the swap.
- Interest payments are made without netting. *Full interest payments in two different currencies are exchanged at each settlement date.*
- At the termination of the swap agreement (maturity), the counterparties return the notional amounts. *Notional principal is swapped again at the termination of the agreement.*

## Plain Vanilla Interest Rate Swaps

The *plain vanilla interest rate swap* involves trading fixed interest rate payments for floating-rate payments (paying fixed and receiving floating).

The parties involved in any swap agreement are called the *counterparties*.

- The counterparty that wants variable-rate interest agrees to pay fixed-rate interest and is thus called the pay-fixed side of the swap.
- The counterparty that receives the fixed payment and agrees to pay variable-rate interest is called the receive-fixed or pay-floating side of the swap.

Let's look at the cash flows that occur in a plain vanilla interest rate swap.

- Since the notional principal swapped is the same for both counterparties and is denominated in the same currency units, there is no need to actually exchange the cash.

- The determination of the variable interest rate is at the beginning of the settlement period, and the cash interest payment is made at the end of the settlement period. This is called payment in *arrears*. Since the interest payments are in the same currency, there is no need for both counterparties to actually transfer the cash. The difference between the fixed-rate payment and the variable-rate payment is calculated and paid to the appropriate counterparty. *Net interest is paid by the party who owes it.*
- At the conclusion of the swap, only the final net payment is made, since the notional principal was not swapped.

Swaps are a zero-sum game. What one party gains, the other party loses.

### Interest Rate Swap Terminology

- The time frame covered by the swap is called the *tenor* of the swap.
- The *settlement dates* are when the interest payments are to be made.
- The amount used to calculate the payment streams to be exchanged is called the *notional principal.*
- The floating rate quoted is *generally LIBOR flat* or LIBOR plus a spread.

### Swap Interest Payments

The basic formula for the net fixed-rate payment in an interest rate swap is:

$$\begin{pmatrix} \text{net fixed-rate} \\ \text{payment} \end{pmatrix}_t = \begin{pmatrix} \text{swap fixed} \\ \text{rate} - \text{LIBOR}_{t-1} \end{pmatrix} \begin{pmatrix} \dfrac{\text{number of days}}{360} \end{pmatrix} \begin{pmatrix} \text{notional} \\ \text{principal} \end{pmatrix}$$

- If this number is positive, the fixed-rate payer *owes* a net payment to the floating-rate party.
- If this number is negative, then the fixed-rate payer *receives* a net payment from the floating-rate party.

In a swap, the floating-rate payment is made based on what the floating rate was at the *beginning* of the settlement period. Hence, when a swap is negotiated (beginning of first period), the net cash payment at the end of the first period is already known. However, the cash flows for all other periods are indeterminate as of the start of the swap and are based on future values of the floating rate.

### Equity Swaps

In an equity swap, the return on a stock, a portfolio, or a stock index is paid each period by one party in return for a fixed payment. The return can be the capital appreciation or the total return including dividends on the stock or portfolio. The

---

payment is calculated as the percentage return on the equity over the period times the notional amount of the swap.

In an equity swap, the first payment (and the others) are unknown and the fixed-rate payer may actually pay more than the fixed rate if the equity return is negative over the period. It may help to remember that the party that pays equity returns would receive a fixed return on the equity portfolio combined with the swap, regardless of the equity portfolio performance.

## RISK MANAGEMENT APPLICATIONS OF OPTION STRATEGIES
Cross-Reference to CFA Institute Assigned Reading #73

The key here is your ability to interpret option payoff diagrams. It is absolutely critical that you understand each option payoff diagram and be able to make the appropriate computations for option payoffs and the payoffs for the included option strategies (e.g., a covered call).

- Buyer of a call option—long position.
- Writer (seller) of a call option—short position.
- Buyer of a put option—long position.
- Writer (seller) of a put option—short position.

### Call Option Payoff Diagrams

The following graph illustrates the payoff at expiration for a call option as a function of the stock price, for both buyers and writers. Note that this differs from the *profit diagram* that follows in that the profit diagram reflects the initial cost of the option (the *premium*). Remember that the option buyer pays the premium to the option seller and if the option finishes out of the money, the writer keeps the premium and the buyer loses the premium. Options are considered a *zero-sum game* because whatever amount the buyer gains, the seller loses, and vice versa.

$$\text{intrinsic value of a call option} = \max[0, S - X]$$
$$\text{intrinsic value of a put option} = \max[0, X - S]$$

## Figure 1: Call Option Payoff Diagram

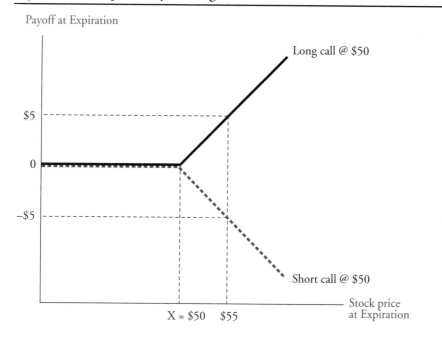

## Figure 2: Profit/Loss Diagram for a Call Option

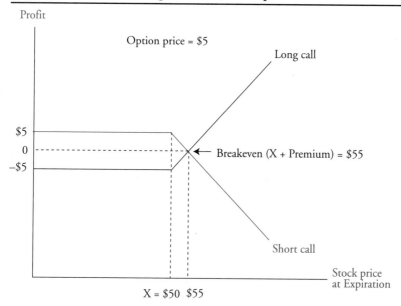

For a *call option:*

$$\text{breakeven}_{call} = \text{strike price} + \text{premium}$$

| | Call Option | |
|---|---|---|
| | *Maximum Loss* | *Maximum Gain* |
| Buyer (long) | Premium | Unlimited |
| Seller (short) | Unlimited | Premium |
| Breakeven | X + premium | |

## Put Option Diagrams

The following graph illustrates the payoff at expiration for a put option as a function of stock price, for both buyers and writers.

### Figure 3: Put Option Payoff Diagram

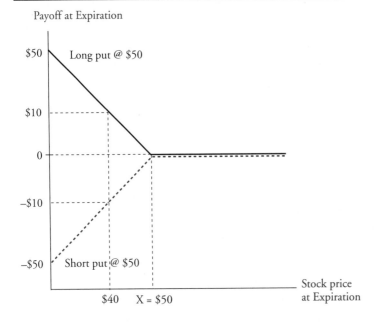

Note that in the *profit diagram* that follows, the cost of the option (the *premium*) is included.

**Figure 4: Profit/Loss Diagram for a Put Option**

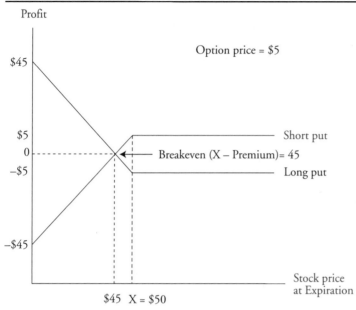

For a *put option:*

|  | Put Option | |
|---|---|---|
|  | *Maximum Loss* | *Maximum Gain* |
| Buyer (long) | Premium | X – premium |
| Seller (short) | X – premium | Premium |
| Breakeven | X – premium | |

## Covered Calls, Protective Puts

A *covered call* is the combination of a long stock and a short call. The term *covered* means that the stock covers the inherent obligation assumed in writing the call. Why would you write a covered call? You feel the stock's price will not go up any time soon, and you want to increase your income by collecting some call option premiums. This strategy for enhancing income is not without risk. The call writer is trading the stock's upside potential above the strike price for the call premium.

A *protective put* is an investment management technique designed to protect a stock from a decline in value. It is constructed by buying a stock and put option on that stock. Any gain on the stock at option expiration is reduced by the put premium paid. The combined (protective put) position will produce profits at option expiration only if the stock price exceeds the sum of the purchase prices of the stock and the put. If the stock price at option expiration is below the put's strike price, the put payoff will limit the maximum loss to the difference between the cost of the position and the strike price of the put.

# ALTERNATIVE INVESTMENTS

| | |
|---|---|
| Weight on Exam | 3% |
| SchweserNotes™ Reference | Book 5, Pages 245–287 |

## ALTERNATIVE INVESTMENTS
Cross-Reference to CFA Institute Assigned Reading #74

You should be aware of the different risk/return profiles, tax issues, legal issues, and other advantages and disadvantages associated with each of the alternative investments discussed here.

## Alternative Investment Features and Characteristics

In the alternative investments material, you should become familiar with the basic characteristics of:

- Open-end and closed-end mutual funds.
- Exchange traded funds (ETFs).
- Real estate.
- Venture capital.
- Hedge funds.
- Closely held companies.
- Commodities.

## Open-End and Closed-End Funds

The *net asset value* (NAV) of an investment company (mutual fund) is the investment company's assets minus its liabilities, stated on a per-share basis.

An open-end investment company, or *open-end fund*, stands ready to redeem shares at any time during regular market hours, typically at the end-of-day NAV. Shares of a closed-end company, or *closed-end fund*, are traded after issuance in the secondary markets. Thus, the liquidity of an open-end fund is provided by the investment company that manages it, whereas the liquidity of a closed-end fund is provided by securities markets.

©2011 Kaplan, Inc.                                                          Page 243

The managers of an *open-end fund* may charge a fee, or "load," to the investors upon purchase (a front-end load) or at redemption (a back-end load). A fund that charges no fee at purchase or redemption is called a "no-load" fund. All funds, regardless of whether it is a load or no-load fund, will charge ongoing fees on an annual basis, which may include management fees, administrative fees, and marketing fees.

The shares of a *closed-end fund* will be issued at a small premium to the value of the underlying assets, the premium serving as compensation for issuance costs. The investment company will also charge an ongoing management fee. Since a closed-end fund is traded in the secondary market subsequent to issuance, the redemption cost for the investor is simply the bid/ask spread of the shares and the commission on the trade. Closed-end funds may trade at significant discounts or premiums to NAV.

## Exchange Traded Funds

An *exchange traded fund* (ETF) is a special type of fund that invests in a portfolio of stocks or bonds and is typically designed to mimic the performance of a specified index.

A feature unique to ETFs is their use of "in-kind" creation and redemption of shares. *Authorized participants* can exchange portfolios of stocks matching the ETF composition for newly created ETF shares or exchange ETF shares for an equivalent portfolio of the underlying stocks. This mechanism prevents the types of market discounts and premiums to NAV common with closed-end funds.

*Advantages of ETFs:*

- ETFs provide an efficient method of diversification.
- ETFs trade like stocks—they can be margined and shorted.
- Some ETFs may be patterned after indexes that have active futures and option markets, allowing for better risk management.
- ETF investors know the exact composition of the fund at all times.
- ETFs typically have very efficient operating expense ratios, as well as no loads to purchase or redeem shares.
- Decreased capital gains tax liability.

*Disadvantages of ETFs:*

- In some countries outside of the United States, there are fewer indexes for ETFs to track, resulting in mid- or low-cap stocks not being well represented in the portfolio.
- The ability to trade ETFs intraday may not be significant to those investors with longer time horizons.

- Investors may encounter inefficient markets (large bid-ask spreads) in ETFs with low trading volume.
- Larger investors may choose to directly invest in an index portfolio, resulting in lower expenses and lower tax consequences.

## Types of Real Estate Investments

- *Outright ownership.*
- *Leveraged equity position.*
- *Mortgages.*
- *Aggregation vehicles.* Common forms include real estate limited partnerships, commingled funds, and real estate investment trusts (REITs).

## Characteristics of Real Estate Investments

Since each property is unique, it is impossible to directly compare to other properties, making it difficult to determine true market value. Real estate as an asset class is somewhat illiquid, because it is immobile, indivisible, and difficult to value.

*Common methods to value real estate:*

- The *cost method* is determined by the replacement cost of improvements, plus an estimate for the value of the land. The market value of an existing property may differ significantly from its replacement cost.
- The *sales comparison method* uses the price of a similar property or properties from recent transactions. Prices from other properties must be adjusted for changes in market conditions and for characteristics unique to each property. In *hedonic* price estimation, sales prices are modeled as a linear function of key property characteristics related to value, and then the model coefficients are used with characteristic values for the subject property to estimate its value.
- The *income method* uses the discounted annual cash flow as if it were a perpetuity, to calculate the present value of the future income stream produced by the property. The net operating income (NOI) is a simplified estimate of annual cash flow equal to annual potential gross rental income minus operating expenses, which include an estimate of the percentage losses from vacancy and collection losses. The NOI is then divided by an estimate of the market required rate of return on similar properties, resulting in an appraisal price.

This simplified model is used quite frequently.

$$\text{NOI} = \text{potential income } (1 - \text{vacancy and bad debt \%})$$
$$- \text{RE taxes} - \text{maintenance} - \text{other expenses}$$

$$\text{real estate value (income method)} = \frac{\text{NOI}}{\text{required return}}$$

- The *discounted after-tax cash flow model* is based on the cash flows to a specific investor and, therefore, depends on the investor's marginal tax rate and the assumed financing for the transaction. The net present value of the property is calculated as the present value of the annual after-tax cash flows, discounted at the investor's required rate of return, minus the initial cash investment. In calculating the annual after-tax operating cash flows, note that interest is tax-deductible and principal repayments are not.

> annual after-tax operating cash flow =
> (NOI – depreciation – interest) × (1 – tax rate) – principal repayment + depreciation

In the year of sale, the after-tax proceeds of the sale are added to that year's after-tax operating cash flows. Taxes (at the capital gains tax rate, on the difference between the depreciated property value and the sales price) and the remaining principal mortgage balance are subtracted from the sales price.

> after-tax sale proceeds = sales price – mortgage balance – tax on gain
>
> tax on gain = capital gains tax rate [sales price – (purchase price – depreciation)]

## Venture Capital

*Stages in venture capital investing:*

- *Seed stage.* Investors are providing capital in the earliest stage of the business and may help fund research and development of product ideas.
- *Early stage.* Companies are entering operation phase but have yet to produce a market-ready product.
- *Formative stage.* Broad category which encompasses the seed stage and early stage.
- *Later stage.* Marketable goods are in production and sales efforts are underway, but the company is still privately held.

Within the *later stage*:

- *Second-stage investing* describes investments in a company that is producing and selling a product, but is not yet generating income.
- *Third-stage financing* would fund a major expansion of the company.
- *Mezzanine* or *bridge financing* would enable a company to take the steps necessary to go public.

The *conditional failure probability* is the probability that a venture investment will fail in any one year, given that it has survived until then. Letting the conditional failure probability in any year be $FP_n$, we can calculate the probability of success for an $N$-year project as:

$$\text{probability of success}_N = [(1 - FP_1)(1 - FP_2)...(1 - FP_N)]$$

Using this result, we can calculate the NPV of a venture capital investment as:

$$NPV = \frac{\text{expected payoff}_N \times \text{probability of success}_N}{(1 + \text{discount rate})^N} - \text{initial investment}$$

## Hedge Funds: Leverage, Risk, and Survivorship Bias

Historically, hedge funds actually hedged risk. Currently, the term is used for many investment strategies that have the form of a private partnership, are largely unregulated, and have an incentive performance fee structure. Many hedge funds have concentrated investments (low diversification) and utilize some type of leverage.

The net return of a hedge fund is calculated by subtracting all manager fees from its gross performance.

Risks associated with hedge funds include the following:

- Illiquidity.
- Potential for mispricing.
- Counterparty credit risk.
- Settlement errors.
- Short covering.
- Margin calls.

Compared to other asset classes, hedge funds tend to have higher returns, lower standard deviation of returns, and higher Sharpe ratios. There are, however, certain biases in reported performance and a smoothing due to value estimation of non-traded assets.

The effect of *survivorship bias* from not reporting the results of failed funds is greater for a hedge fund database than for other asset classes because of the lack of required reporting standards in the industry.

Fund managers tend to "cherry pick" the information they choose to release, reporting on their more successful funds while not providing information on poorly performing funds (self-selection bias). Reported returns for a hedge fund database are therefore overstating performance because of both survivorship bias and self-selection bias.

Survivorship bias has the opposite effect on the risk measures of a hedge fund database. Hedge funds with highly volatile returns tend to fail more frequently, and defunct funds are not generally included in the database. Because the database would only include the more stable funds that have survived, the risk measure of hedge funds as an asset class would be understated.

In a *fund of funds* hedge fund, a manager selects a number of hedge funds and investors purchase interests in the overall fund.

*Advantages* include diversification and risk reduction, professional selection of included funds, and possible access to closed funds.

*Disadvantages* are higher fees and the possibility that fund selection will be poor.

## Closely Held Company Valuation

There are three primary valuation methods:

1. The *cost approach*. The cost to replace the firm's assets.
2. The *comparables approach*. Value relative to that of a benchmark company.
3. The *income approach*. The present value of the expected future cash flows.

Valuation discounts to the valuations of publicly-traded companies are used to adjust for lack of liquidity and lack of marketability, and for lack of control when valuing a minority interest.

A control premium is appropriate when valuing a controlling interest in a privately held company.

## Commodity Investing

Investing in commodities tends to hedge investments in companies that use those same commodities in production. Most investors do not choose to invest in commodities directly, but rather through the purchase of futures contracts, bonds indexed to a commodity price, or the equity of commodity-producing companies.

Futures contracts are usually the most efficient way to participate in the commodities market, but the common stock of commodity producers can also be an effective way to gain exposure to increasing production and consumption in the economy.

Establishing a collateralized commodity futures position involves simultaneously purchasing futures contracts and an amount of government securities equal to the value of the entire futures position. The total return on this strategy will equal the change in price of the futures contract plus the interest earned on the government securities.

## INVESTING IN COMMODITIES
Cross-Reference to CFA Institute Assigned Reading #75

A commodity futures market is in *contango* if the futures price is greater than the spot price. The market is in *backwardation* if the futures price is less than the spot price.

Futures markets that are dominated by long hedgers (users of the commodity who buy futures to protect against price increases) tend to be in contango.

Futures markets that are dominated by short hedgers (producers of the commodity who sell futures to protect against price decreases) tend to be in backwardation.

The return on a commodity investment includes:

- *Collateral yield:* the return on the collateral posted to satisfy margin requirements.
- *Price return:* the gain or loss due to changes in the spot price.
- *Roll yield:* the gain or loss resulting from re-establishing positions as contracts expire.

Note that *roll yield* is positive if the futures market is in backwardation and negative if the market is in contango.

A commodity index strategy is *considered an active investment* because the manager must:

- Decide what maturities to use for the forward or futures contracts.
- Decide when to roll them over into new contracts.
- Manage portfolio weights to match those of the benchmark index selected.
- Determine the best choice of securities to post as collateral and how these should be rolled over as they mature.

# Essential Exam Strategies

The level of review contained in this section is different from our other CFA review materials. As always, our objective is to enhance your chances of passing the CFA exam. Unlike the previous part of this book, which covers *what* you need to know to pass the Level I CFA exam, this section provides you important guidance on *how* to pass the exam. By this time, you have likely studied the entire Level I curriculum and have a solid grasp on the content, so we won't spend any time here reviewing or quizzing you on material you already know. Instead, we provide insights about how to successfully apply your hard-earned knowledge on exam day.

First, we provide some proven approaches to mastering the Level I CFA curriculum. Next, we present a structured plan for the last week before the exam. Following this plan assures that you will be sharp on exam day, and your performance will not be adversely affected by your nerves. We will also spend some time discussing general exam-taking strategies and how to approach individual questions.

## A Formidable Task

Over the past few months, you have studied an enormous amount of material. CFA Institute's assigned readings for the Level I curriculum include more than 3,000 pages. There are more than 540 learning outcome statements. This is a huge amount of material. Realistically speaking, it is virtually impossible to remember every detail within the curriculum. The good news is you don't have to know every detail. From this guide, you will learn how to get the most benefit from the short time remaining until the exam.

As you prepare for the CFA exam, try to focus on the exam itself. Don't add to your stress level by worrying about whether you'll pass or what might happen if you don't. If you must, you can worry about all of that after the exam. If you worry about it before the exam, or especially during the exam, your performance will likely suffer. There is ample stress in remembering the material, let alone worrying whether you'll pass. Many of the tips we provide are proven stress reducers on exam day. Your grasp of the content, combined with the tips we provide, will have you well prepared for the exam experience.

All of the faculty at Kaplan Schweser have earned CFA charters and have extensive experience in teaching the topics covered in the CFA curriculum. As such, we know what you are going through from our own personal experiences, and we have helped tens of thousands of candidates earn the right to use the CFA designation. We've been there and done that! We know the agony and anxiety you are experiencing. Now, we want to share with you the time-honored strategies that we have personally seen lead to success on the Level I CFA exam.

Let's start with some overall thoughts. There are two basic strategies you should follow in learning the CFA curriculum: Focus on the big picture, and know the main concepts.

## The Big Picture

Focusing on the big picture means you should know at least a little about every concept. When we took the exam, some of us were not overly comfortable with debt securities. We just didn't deal with bonds on a regular basis. Still, we knew that we had to learn some of the basics for the exam. For example, even if you don't know the formula for effective duration, at least know that effective duration is a measure of interest rate risk. By remembering some basic information on exam day, you will be able to narrow your answer choices. You probably won't answer many questions correctly with only a basic grasp of the concept, but you can improve your odds on a multiple choice question from 33% to 50%. You also will be able to better distinguish between the relevant and irrelevant information in a question. Continuing with our duration theme, you would know that bond rating information provided in a duration question is not relevant, since bond ratings reflect credit risk, not interest rate risk.

Even if you don't currently work with, for example, futures, and you know you never will, try to at least get a basic grasp of the important concepts within the topic. It is simply a poor exam strategy to completely blow off significant pieces of the curriculum. We have known people in the CFA program who thought that as long as they knew a few of the assigned topics really well, they could bluff their way through the rest of the exam. These were smart individuals, but they had poor exam strategies. So far, none of them have earned their charters.

## Know the Main Concepts

It is important to identify those concepts that are most likely to be covered on the exam. In any given year, some concepts might be omitted, but if you can answer most of the questions concerning these main concepts, you will dramatically increase your chance of passing. Generally, the idea is to be correct on most of the questions dealing with the important concepts, and then rely on your "big picture" knowledge to get points on the remaining material.

## Topic Weighting

In preparing for the exam, you must pay attention to the weights assigned to each topic within the curriculum. The Level I topic weights are as follows:

| Topic | Exam Weight | Number of LOS | Points per LOS |
|---|---|---|---|
| Ethical and Professional Standards | 15% | 13 | 4.15 |
| Quantitative Methods | 12% | 84 | 0.51 |
| Economics | 10% | 81 | 0.44 |
| Financial Reporting and Analysis | 20% | 110 | 0.65 |
| Corporate Finance | 8% | 44 | 0.65 |
| Portfolio Management | 5% | 27 | 0.67 |
| Equity Investments | 10% | 61 | 0.59 |
| Fixed Income Investments | 12% | 67 | 0.64 |
| Derivatives | 5% | 39 | 0.46 |
| Alternative Investments | 3% | 21 | 0.51 |
| Totals | 100% | 547 | 0.66 |

Notice how the LOS counts are not consistent with the exam weights. In fact, some topic areas with a relatively high number of LOS are frequently not covered very heavily on the exam, so allocating your preparation time based on the number of LOS will most likely lead to over-preparation in some areas (e.g., Derivatives) and under-preparation in others (especially Ethics).

## Formulas

You may be surprised to know that the Level I CFA examination is quite conceptual and is not heavily weighted toward computations based on memorized formulas. It is nothing like what my undergraduate students used to refer to as "plug and chug" problems. Certainly, some formulas are required, but you will find that you need to use your calculator much less often than you might imagine after reading the required material. Examples of the types of formulas that you need to commit to memory are the constant growth dividend discount model, the security market line, the correlation coefficient, and both the traditional and expanded DuPont formulas for decomposing ROE.

Many times you will be given questions where the answer can be obtained by using a formula and a fairly lengthy calculation but where you can also identify the correct answer without calculation, if you truly understand the concept or relationship being tested. With any formula you encounter in the required readings,

©2011 Kaplan, Inc.

you should try to gain a clear understanding of what it is telling you (when it is appropriate to use it) and of the relationship among the various input variables.

One example of this sort of understanding is the holding period return or holding period yield. It is simply the percentage increase in the value of an investment over the holding period. If you buy a stock for $100, receive a $5 dividend, and sell it for $103 at the end of the period, the value increased from $100 to $108, an increase of 8% (which is the holding period return or yield). If you understand that the harmonic mean is used to get the average price per share when the same amount is invested over multiple periods, you can easily calculate the harmonic mean of $1, $2, and $3. If you invested a total of $6 at each of these three prices, you would buy 6/1 + 6/2 + 6/3 = 11 shares and spend a total of $6 × 3 = $18. The average price per share (and the harmonic mean) is 18/11 = $1.636.

Think of the formula as just a shorthand way of expressing a relation or concept you need to understand. For example, the formula tells you that the population variance is the average squared deviation from the mean. Approaching formulas in this way will reduce your chances of missing a problem because your memory fails you under the stress of the exam. I can never remember the formula for an updated probability using Bayes' Theorem, but ever since I understood it as presented in a tree diagram (Book 1, pp 219–220), I can calculate updated probabilities without a problem and without worrying whether I "remembered" the precise formula correctly.

## "Characteristic" Lists

Another common source of specific questions is identifying the characteristics of various securities, models, and valuation methods. A typical question format would be "Which of the following most accurately describes…?" Here, the big-picture approach can help you weed out wrong answers. Also, some candidates use mnemonics to help them remember lists of characteristics or lists of pros and cons.

## Know Your Strengths

We each have our own style of learning. Some of us can sit down and study for hours at a time, while some of us learn better in small doses each day. Be aware of your study habits, and do not place unrealistic burdens on yourself. Be especially aware of problems with certain topics. For example, if you have always struggled with accounting, look at ways to improve your grasp of the accounting material—spend more time with it, attend a review course, or join a study group. *Do not* expect that you can ignore a topic and make up for the lost points by excelling in another area. Similarly, do not skip an area just because you think you already know it. There are CPAs who fail the accounting section and PhDs in

Economics who fail the economics section. You need to review the specific material in the assigned CFA curriculum to pass the CFA exam.

## The Rules

At some point in your studies, it would be a good idea to review the Testing Policies section of the CFA Institute web site. Believe it or not, you will probably find this to be a nice break from accounting or derivatives! Be sure that you are able to comply with the requirements for an unexpired, government-issued photo ID (beginning with the December 2011 exam, that ID *must* be a passport). Select an approved calculator and learn how to use it proficiently. You should also read the CFA Program Errata that are issued in the months before the exam.

Be aware of items you can and cannot take to the exam. CFA Institute strictly prohibits taking any of the following into the testing room:

- Backpacks, briefcases, luggage of any kind.
- *Any* study materials.
- Scratch paper, calculator manuals.
- Highlighters, rulers, correction fluid (white-out).
- Cell phones, any personal electronics.

*Do not* expect that these policies do not apply to you. Every year numerous candidates have problems on exam day because they assumed their cases would be legitimate exceptions. There is no such thing. We have stories of people sprinting back to their cars to put stuff away and get back in time to start the exam. If you read the rules and follow them, you reduce the potential for unexpected stress on the day of the exam. That's a good thing!

## Final Preparation

Have a well-defined strategy for the last week before the exam. If at all possible, it is best to take at least some leave from your job. You should save at least one practice exam for the last week. To simulate the real exam, you should avoid looking at this exam or studying questions from it until you are ready to sit down and take it for the first time. Take this exam early in the final week. Take the first half of the exam in a 3-hour period, take a 90-minute break, then take the other half in a second 3-hour period. Time yourself so you can get a feel for the time constraints and pressure of exam day. Remember, you have an average of 90 seconds per question. When you have completed the entire exam, grade your answers and use these results to identify areas where you need to focus your study efforts over the last few days. You should devote most of your time to areas where you performed poorly, but you should also spend enough time keeping your stronger topics fresh in your mind.

At some point during the week before the exam, it is a good idea to visit the actual exam center. Figure out how long it will take to get to your test center and where you can park. It might even be helpful to locate a lunch destination in the area. The fewer surprises and distractions on exam day, the better.

*Expect* problems on exam day. Not major ones, but be prepared for things like cold/hot rooms, noise, lines, etc. Some of these problems you cannot control, but if you are prepared for them, they are less likely to affect your exam performance.

The evening before the exam, it is best to avoid studying. Try to relax and make a concerted effort to get a good night's sleep. Tired candidates make silly mistakes on the exam. If you are not rested, you will more than likely miss easy points. This seems like an obvious and trite point, but it is difficult to overemphasize the importance of going into the exam well rested. If for some unfortunate reason you do not sleep well the night before, do not panic! It happens to the best of us. Sometimes your brain cannot stop thinking about the pressure of the upcoming day. Keep in mind that you can still function and you can still give a solid effort on exam day with just a little sleep (even though it is not recommended). If you're one of those candidates who has difficulty sleeping before an important event, plan accordingly and go to bed early.

## Exam Day

### Answering Level I Multiple-Choice Questions

Read the question carefully! Watch for double negatives like "Which of the following is least likely a disadvantage..." It is very important not to miss words, or parts of words, by reading too quickly (e.g., reading "most likely" instead of "least likely," or "advantages" instead of "disadvantages").

For non-numerical questions, read *all* answer choices. Don't just stop when you get to one that sounds right. There may be a better choice.

For long questions, dissect the bits of information that are provided. What information is relevant? What is most specifically related to the question? Often a wrong answer looks good because it is consistent with information in the question that is actually irrelevant.

After you read the question, determine what you think the question is asking. This can help you filter out extraneous information and focus quickly on appropriate answer choices.

Similarly, after you read the question, it is a good idea to formulate your own answer before reading the answer choices. Develop an expectation of what the answer should be. This may make the correct answer sound better to you when you read it.

On calculation problems, after you have selected an answer choice, pause for a moment and think about whether the answer makes sense. Is the sign of the result correct, or does the direction of change make sense?

Do not look for patterns in answers. Just because the last three questions all had "C" for an answer, do not expect the next answer not to be "C." There is no reason to expect that CFA Institute has a preference for how many questions are answered with the same letter.

Be *very* sure that you are marking your answer in the right place on the answer sheet. If you skip questions or do the topics out of order, be especially careful to check yourself. Obviously, mis-marking can be devastating if you do not catch it right away.

Trust your first impressions. You will find that you are often correct. It is okay to change an answer, but only do so if you have a *good* reason. Over the years, we have heard many stories of how candidates talk themselves out of the correct answer. We have all done this. When you come back to a question, be sure you can justify any change before you make it.

Finally, and probably *most* importantly, *do not lose confidence*. No one has ever received a perfect score on the CFA exam. It just does not happen. Remember, historically 70% has always been a passing score. This means you can miss 30% (roughly 72 questions) and still pass. Even if you have struggled on a few questions, maybe even five or six in a row, do not lose confidence. The worst thing you can do is second-guess yourself—you will take longer on every question and start changing correct answers.

# What To Do With a Difficult Question

There will undoubtedly be questions that give you trouble. You might not understand the question, may think that none of the answers make sense, or simply may not know the concept being tested. The following tips will likely prove to be useful if you find yourself facing a difficult question.

- If the question does not make sense or if none of the answers look remotely correct, reread the question to see if you missed something. If you are still unsure, mark an answer choice and move on. Don't agonize over it and waste precious time that can be allocated to questions you can nail.
- *Never leave an answer blank.* A blank answer has a maximum point value of zero. A randomly marked answer has an expected value of $0.33 \times 1.5 = 0.5$ points, and if you can eliminate one bad answer, this value increases to $0.5 \times 1.5 = 0.75$. You are not penalized for wrong answers.
- If you are unable to determine the "best" answer, you still should be able to help your odds. Try to eliminate one answer choice and then just guess.
- Take some comfort in the fact that the CFA exams are graded on a curve. If the question gave you trouble, it is quite possible that it was troublesome for many other candidates as well.
- Do not lose your confidence over one, or even several, tough questions. You can miss 72 questions (or a few more) and still pass.

# Time Management

Candidates who fail to pass CFA exams cite time management as their biggest downfall. Do not let poor time management determine your exam results. The following are some tips to help you manage your time wisely.

Take at least one practice exam where you time yourself. This will give you some indication of whether you will have problems on exam day. However, do not let your positive results on practice exams lull you into overconfidence. The stress of exam day, plus possible distractions like noise or a cold exam room, can make a big difference in how fast you work.

Monitor your progress. Keep an eye on the time as you work through the exam. There will be 120 questions in each 3-hour exam session, which means 40 questions per hour or 10 questions every 15 minutes. You may deviate some as you work through easier or more difficult questions, but be careful not to let yourself fall too far behind. Note that some test centers will not have clocks, but you will be notified of how much time is remaining in increments of 15 to 30 minutes.

One way to alleviate time pressure is to bank a few minutes by doing an easy topic first. Select a topic you feel comfortable with and start there. If you begin to struggle, move to a different topic. This strategy will help you gain confidence as you progress through the exam, and will also allow you to get a little ahead with your time allocation. Historically, the length and difficulty of ethics questions have made this topic a bad one to start with, even though it will be first during both sessions. Also, the gray areas covered by ethics questions often make you start to second-guess yourself, which is a bad precedent to set early in the exam. Be *very* careful if you jump around between topics to make sure you are marking the correct blanks on the answer sheet.

Have a game plan before you walk into the exam. We like the idea of doing an easy topic first to get going, but we do not recommend skipping around as you work through the exam. Do an easy topic, and then go back and do the remaining questions in order. Skipping back and forth may break your concentration and consume valuable time as you try to figure out what you have and have not done. Skipping around also increases the chance of marking the wrong blank on the answer sheet.

Never panic! Even if you fall behind, panicking will only make things worse. You won't think clearly and you'll miss easy questions. If you need a short break, put your pencil down and take a few deep breaths. The 30 seconds or so that this takes may very well help you think clearly enough to answer several additional questions correctly.

Catch your breath at lunch. As we mentioned before, it is a good idea to have a lunch destination planned beforehand. You may or may not want to join other candidates for lunch. If you do talk to other candidates, do not let their comments influence you. They may say the exam is easier or more difficult than they expected, but they might not be correct about how well they are doing. If you want, you can review a little at lunch. That's fine. But if you need to relax for a few minutes, that may do you just as much good as an additional 30-minute cram session. Do what you are most comfortable with.

## Question Formats at Level I

Here are some guidelines CFA Institute adheres to in constructing questions for the Level I exam:

- Each question draws on one or more Learning Outcome Statements.
- Terminology and symbols will be consistent with those used in the readings (and, therefore, the SchweserNotes).
- Candidates do not need to know the numbers for specific Standards of Practice.
- Empirical results cited in the readings are not tested.
- The exam does not reuse old questions. All questions are new.

- Distractors (the incorrect choices) are written to capture the most common mistakes a candidate is likely to make on a question.
- Each question has three answer choices.
- "None of the above," "all of the above," and "not enough information" are not used.
- The words "true," "false," and "except" do not appear in the question stems. Instead, the questions use phrases like "most accurate," "least likely," or "closest to."
- Every question has its own stem and answer choices. The Level I exam does not have any multiple-part questions.
- Written answer choices are arranged from shortest to longest.
- Numeric answer choices are arranged from lowest to highest.

As to the format of Level I questions, you can expect three varieties.

1.    Sentence completion with three choices, such as the following:

When yields increase:
A.  bond prices fall.
B.  bond prices rise.
C.  bond prices are unaffected.

2.    A complete question with three answer choices:

If the U.S. Federal Reserve decreases its fed funds target rate by 1% and nominal long-term interest rates increase, which of the following is the *most likely* reason?
A.  The Fed also increased its target for long-term rates.
B.  Changes in long-term rates always are opposite to changes in the fed funds target rate.
C.  The expansionary monetary policy action caused an increase in expected future inflation.

3.    Some questions may employ a two-column format. This type often tests two separate questions that each have only two possible answers: true/false or up/down. These may be either in the sentence-completion format or in the question-answer format with yes/no choices:

If a company chooses to capitalize significant advertising costs in the current period, CFO and CFI respectively would:

|     | CFO      | CFI      |
| --- | -------- | -------- |
| A.  | increase | decrease |
| B.  | decrease | decrease |
| C.  | decrease | increase |

With respect to the use of the CFA designation, do the Standards allow the initials CFA to be:

|  | used as a noun? | in larger type than the charterholder's name? |
|---|---|---|
| A. | No | No |
| B. | No | Yes |
| C. | Yes | Yes |

No matter which format you encounter, the advice is the same—read the question carefully, and make sure you answer what is being asked. Two-part questions not only allow the testing of yes/no and up/down types of questions, they can also effectively lengthen the exam and allow more material to be tested.

## Specific Types of Questions You Should Expect

It is very difficult to generalize Level I questions. Some are straightforward, some look straightforward but have a trick to them, and some are just confusing. CFA Institute's objective is to evaluate your grasp of the Level I Candidate Body of Knowledge. They do not set out to confuse or frustrate you, although that *is* a common result.

Following are some general types of questions and answers to expect.

### Cause and Effect Problems

Part of the reason Level I CFA questions seem so difficult is because they ask you to apply your knowledge in ways you may not expect. Many questions combine more than one LOS or ask you to reason out the results and implications of a given series of events. These questions require some thought and will definitely be more difficult if you are not well-rested, or if you are stressed out.

### Long Questions

Look out for these. They are major time-burners. The worst areas are Ethics and Financial Reporting and Analysis. In both areas, you get a lot of irrelevant information, so try to weed out the confusion factors and focus on what's important. It often helps to *read the end of the question first* and then know what information is relevant as you read the body of the question.

## Two-Column Questions

Keep a few things in mind with these types of questions:

- Two concepts are being tested in one question.
- These questions often test a calculation with a qualitative question rather than a quantitative one (but you still need to know the formulas).
- If you can get one column right, you will either be able to choose the correct letter answer or at least eliminate one of the choices.

In questions like these, if you can answer one but not the other, eliminate the wrong choice, make a guess, and go on. Don't let these types of questions take more than a minute and a half.

## Tempting but Unnecessary Calculations

CFA Institute is interested in testing your grasp of the Level I curriculum. They are not particularly interested in whether or not you can use your calculator. CFA Institute has always emphasized the qualitative grasp of a concept over the quantitative "number crunching" type question. You will see questions that appear to call for long, complex calculations. Before you start wearing down your calculator battery, spend a few moments to see if there is a short cut. Here is a question on debt securities to emphasize this point.

1.  Given the spot rates in the table, the 1-year forward rate two years from now is:

| Time (years) | Annual Spot Rate |
|:---:|:---:|
| 1 | 15.0% |
| 2 | 12.5% |
| 3 | 10.0% |
| 4 | 7.5% |

A. −3.21%.
B. 5.17%.
C. 10.00%.

The correct answer is B. This is an example of a calculation question where you can look at the answer choices and reason out a correct answer without doing any calculations. Think about this question for a minute. The spot yield curve is declining. The one-year rate two years from now will have to be a rate such that after earning 12.5% for two years, you will end up with an average return over three years of 10%. The answer *has* to be less than 10%, right? A spot rate can't be negative, and B is the only choice less than 10%. If you want to do the calculation, it is:

$$\frac{(1+S_3)^3}{(1+S_2)^2} - 1 = {}_1F_2; \quad \frac{(1+0.10)^3}{(1+0.125)^2} - 1 = {}_1F_2; {}_1F_2 = 5.17\%$$

This question is an example of how taking a few seconds and applying some big picture understanding can actually save you some time. Also, if you did the calculation, you could use the preceding logic to check yourself.

2.    An annual-pay 3-year note with an 8% coupon has a yield to maturity of 8%. The 1-year spot rate is 5.8% and the 2-year spot rate is 6.5%. Based on this information, the 3-year spot rate is *closest* to:
   A.  7.3%.
   B.  8.0%.
   C.  8.2%.

The correct answer is C. At first glance, this looks like a nasty calculation based on bootstrapping—given a bond's price and the spot rates for the first two interim cash flows, determine the spot rate for the final cash flow. But step back for a moment and look at the answers. This 3-year bond is priced to yield 8%. The yield must equate to a weighted average of the spot rates, due to arbitrage-free pricing. The first two years' cash flows are discounted back at 5.8% and 6.5%. If the weighted average is 8%, the third cash flow *must* have a discount rate greater than 8%. Answer C is the only possibility.

If you prefer, you can do the bootstrap calculation. Since coupon is equal to yield, the bond is priced at par. To get the 3-year spot rate, deduct present values of cash flows for the first two years:

   Year 1 = FV of $80, N = 1, I/Y = 5.8%, PV = 75.61
   Year 2 = FV of $80, N = 2, I/Y = 6.5%, PV = 70.53

The present value of the 1,080 third-year cash flow = 1,000 – 75.61 – 70.53 = 853.86.

So, the 3-year spot rate is $(1{,}080 / 853.86)^{1/3} - 1 = 8.15\%$.

*Indirect or Confusing Wording*

Despite what you might hear from other candidates, we honestly don't think CFA Institute purposely writes confusing questions. It is more likely that a particular question is trying to approach a concept from an unusual perspective. That is a good way to test your grasp of a concept, but sometimes the wording makes it difficult to figure out what is being tested. If you get confused by a question, think it through but don't waste too much time on it. Remember, you are probably not the only one scratching your head.

### Answer Choices That Are Direct Opposites

You will see some questions where there are pairs of answer choices. By pairs we mean answers that are identical except for one word that makes them opposites (e.g., substituting "increase" for "decrease"). There may be similar information in these paired answers, with only slight differences. One of them is likely to be correct, and the difference between the two answers may be the key to answering the question correctly. If you see paired answers, check to see if the difference between them is critical to the question at hand. This can be explained more clearly with an example.

3.  A change in consumer preferences causes a decrease in currency held by the public and an equivalent increase in checkable deposits. Assuming the central bank does not intervene in reaction to this change, the money supply is *most likely* to:
    A.  remain unchanged, because checkable deposits increase by the same amount that currency holdings decrease.
    B.  decrease, because banks' excess reserves will decrease and they must reduce their lending.
    C.  increase, because banks' excess reserves will increase and they can expand their lending.

The correct answer is C. This question is asking how well you understand the fractional reserve system. At first, A seems like a reasonable answer, but answers B and C are a pair of answers that should alert you to the importance of the fractional reserve system in answering this question. With such a system, as people move their cash into banks, the banks will have more funds available to loan.

### "Distractor" Answers That Are True But Not Correct

These are answer choices that seem like good answers for any of several reasons:

*   They might be true, but not appropriate answers (or at least not the best answer).
*   They might be consistent with irrelevant information provided in the question.
*   They might include "buzzwords" or common misconceptions about a concept.

Be very careful with these types of distractors because they may make sense even though they are wrong. They may also make you think you could defend them as an answer choice. You might think, "Well, they want me to answer 'A,' but I think 'B' is okay and I can argue the point with anyone." Think again—you will never get to argue the point. Instead, select the *best* answer that is true all of the time and applies in every case, not the one you think could work.

### *Answer Choices That Can Be Eliminated*

We have stressed the importance of reading every answer choice before making your selection. This strategy will help you avoid missing a better answer. Similarly, when you are struggling with a question, eliminate the worst answer to narrow your choices and improve your odds of earning some points.

# Index

©2011 Kaplan, Inc.

## T

# Notes

# Notes

# Notes

# Notes

# Notes

# Notes

# Notes

# Notes

# Notes

# Notes

# Notes